The IMC Case Book

Cases in Integrated Marketing Communications

EDITORS

J. STEVEN KELLY

DePaul University

SUSAN K. JONES

Ferris State University

@2016 by Midwest Marketing Education Foundation

http://www.mefgroup.org/

Executive Director: Kathleen Stevenson (see web site above for access to Teaching Notes)

Catalog-in-Publication information available from the Library of Congress.

Printed in the United States of America

ISBN-13: **978-0692666692** (Custom)

ISBN-10: **0692666699**

This book is dedicated to:

My friends and loved ones who have supported my staying at the office too long. Most especially thanks to my daughter, Alison, and her lovely family; Peggy Ascherman; Rich Hagle and especially Susan K. Jones
--Steve Kelly

My grandchildren – Sheridan, Ronan, Daphne, Marlowe, and Bowden; and with special thanks to my long-time collaborators and friends, Rich Hagle and Steve Kelly.
--Susan K. Jones

ACKNOWLEDGMENTS

This book would not be possible without the visionary leadership of Ron Jacobs, sponsor of the annual Jacobs & Clevenger Case Writers' Workshop. Thank you, Ron, for your decades of support to direct and interactive marketing education as a teacher, author and philanthropist.

The editors would like to acknowledge the exceptional contributions of the authors of this book's cases and readings. Their names and affiliations are listed at the beginning of each piece. Their willingness to share their research, experience and knowledge with professors and students is very impressive, and much appreciated. Their generosity is exceptional as well; all contributors to this book have agreed that 100% of royalties will go to DePaul University's Interactive Marketing Institute.

The editors would also like to thank the past and present trustees and staff members of the Chicago Association of Direct Marketing Educational Foundation (now the Midwest Marketing Education Foundation) for conceiving and guiding the creation of the original DePaul Case Writers' Workshop, and for continued strong support of the Jacobs & Clevenger Case Writers' Workshop.

Thanks are due as well to Marketing EDGE and its trustees and staff for years of generous support and guidance to the Workshop. We especially appreciate the tireless efforts of Jeff Nesler, our close collaborator from Marketing EDGE.

We would like to acknowledge that great effort and support was given to this and many other projects by Kathleen (Kate) Stevenson, current Executive Director of the Midwest Marketing Education Foundation. Finally, we acknowledge and thank our long-time collaborator, Richard Hagle of RACOM Communications, for his belief in us, and for his unflagging dedication to excellence in marketing education.

THE JACOBS & CLEVENGER CASE WRITERS' WORKSHOP AND THE DEVELOPMENT OF THIS BOOK

Since its origins in the mid-1990s, the DePaul University Case Writers' Workshop (now the Jacobs & Clevenger Case Writers' Workshop) has nurtured the development of more than 50 original cases in Integrated Marketing Communications. The authors of these cases include professors, adjunct instructors and professional writers from all over the world. Case subjects include companies and agencies focused on financial services, product marketing, services marketing, online marketing, the non-profit world, and much more.

Dr. J. Steven Kelly is the Director of DePaul's Interactive Marketing Institute and an Associate Professor of Marketing at DePaul. He spearheaded the development of the Workshop with funding and direction from the Chicago Association of Direct Marketing Educational Foundation (now the Midwest Marketing Education Foundation), the Direct Marketing Educational Foundation (now Marketing EDGE, and Jacobs & Clevenger. These organizations have supported the Workshop because of the strong and demonstrated need among professors and students for timely, authoritative and meaty cases focused on direct marketing, interactive marketing, advertising, sales promotion and public relations.

As a former educator/trustee of the Direct Marketing Educational Foundation (now Marketing EDGE), former chair of the Chicago Association of Direct Marketing Educational Foundation, and current Midwest Marketing Education Foundation trustee, Marketing Professor Susan K. Jones of Ferris State University joined forces with Dr. Kelly in 2002 to help nurture case creation and prepare the cases for publication.

TABLE OF CONTENTS

Acknowledgments

Case Writers' Background

BowTie Cause:

A Signature Way to Rock a Bowtie

By

Stacy Neier Beran – Loyola University Chicago

Step 1: Lift the collar.

Step 2: Place the bowtie around neck.

Step 3: Cross the longer end over the shorter end.

Step 4: Loop the long end under where the two ends cross.

Step 5: Fold the dangling end to make a loop.

Step 6: Drop the longer end over the skinny center of the bow.

Step 7: Pinch the bow together in front of the long end.

Step 8: Feed the middle of the dangling end back through the knot.

Step 9: Pull at the loops.

Step 10: Straighten the bowtie.[1]

Dhani Jones, Founder of BowTie Cause, considered Step 10 to be "*Rock* the bowtie."

Ten simple steps resulted in one crisp bowtie, with a message of support folded into its four corners. According to BowTie Aficionado, as few as 1% of men knew how to tie a bowtie.[2] Yet, through his daily practice of ten simple steps, Dhani showed he knew what most men did not. He not only knew how to tie a bowtie but also how to rock a bowtie built for a cause.

---

[1] http://www.wikihow.com/Tie-a-Bow-Tie
[2] http://www.bowtieaficionado.com/2014/12/02/bow-tie-infographic/#.VZQCTWDvOS0

Dhani's name was publicly known as a linebacker from 2007-2010 for the NFL Cincinnati Bengals. He was an expert with the pigskin, but his role in BowTie Cause demonstrated his expertise with social enterprise. Dhani's ritual to rock a bowtie changed the script about the motivation – and appearance – of social entrepreneurs. As depicted in the business press, contemporary company leaders wore hooded sweatshirts and laid-back sneakers: it appeared the secret to winning market share and shareholder value required entrepreneurs to dress down. Dhani, however, dressed up as an outward expression of his attempt to interrupt the ultra-causal course that underscored trendy enterprises. Dhani's signature bowtie, looped to perfection, instead symbolized the promise for enlightened community dialogue for the sake of common good.

Dhani recognized that bowties were a tricky accessory. The steps to properly tie a bowtie eluded most men, and moreover, men decoded mixed messages about when to wear bowties. When worn casually, bowties challenged cultural norms about what was previously considered a formal accessory. When and why would a man wear a bowtie instead of a traditional necktie? BowTie Cause provided a response to these questions and instigated more questions about how wearing a bowtie supported a cause. Here, the bowtie began conversation through changed attitudes and behaviors. Through BowTie Cause, Dhani celebrated how a bowtie motivated curiosity about the potential to transform a personal style choice to a choice for social responsibility.

Dhani also acknowledged that the bowtie unexpectedly shared common ground with social injustices and philanthropic need observed in communities around the country. As many consumers resisted the sartorial boldness to regularly wear bowties, consumers also faltered through individual efforts to satisfactorily give back to communities. Minor decisions, like bowtie tying, confused people; major decisions, like acting on society's injustices, also eluded people. Conceptually, bowties and social justice were disparate and perhaps unable to be combined, yet Dhani took the risk to interfere with consumer expectations to provide updated solutions to address injustice. Surely, the uncertainty involved in both the minor and major could unite as a tool not yet endeavored by other social enterprises. His approach to discontinuous innovation highlighted how juxtaposing two concepts, previously unrelated, catalyzed the potential to solve problems.

As Dhani has passionately stated, "One day, when you look at me, I want the bowtie to give those answers." To be a somebody – a somebody who understood the importance of giving back to community and support causes – "you gotta rock a BowTie."

Five years into its operations, BowTie Cause remained Dhani's signature contribution to society at large. As an organization, BowTie Cause partnered with 109 causes, manufactured more than 5000 bowties, and donated $300,000 to a range of causes. Within a cluttered environment of fashion accessories and charitable causes, Dhani realized BowTie Cause needed wider acceptance as a signature solution to generate funds and awareness for a myriad of causes. How can bowties be recognized as symbols for causes? He knew there were far more than the ten steps involved in bow-tying to make this signature a reality.

The BowTie Cause Model

History of BowTie Cause

Dhani's path to create social change started with his time on the football field. During the sixth round of the 2000 NFL draft, the New York Giants selected Dhani as a linebacker after his record-setting career at the University of Michigan. Early in his NFL career, Dhani learned that Kunta Littlejohn, a childhood friend, had been diagnosed with lymphoma. For years prior to his diagnosis, Kunta wore bowties. He vocally proclaimed that, "If you want to be anybody in this world, you've got to rock a bowtie." At first, Dhani was skeptical about Kunta's statement but began to wear bowties in silent support of his friend.

Dhani's initial uncertainty about Kunta's adoration of bowties soon turned into a symbolic signature about limitless passion for philanthropy. After retiring from the NFL in 2010, Dhani started BowTie Cause as a conduit to help others rock bowties in support of the causes that deeply impacted their lives. Dhani wanted the bowtie to be more than a fashion statement and sought to make the bowtie a way to become a well-rounded individual, just as Kunta showed Dhani both as a patient and eventually as a survivor. Dhani realized an individual donning a bowtie could be seen as a supporter of a cause or as an advocate for change. As such, the BowTie Cause mission statement conveyed:

Our mission is to generate awareness – and funds – for organizations that make a difference. We accomplish this by telling the story of your organization through the design, creation and promotion of a signature BowTie.

As Dhani built relationships with organizations in Cincinnati (home of his final NFL team), Dhani recruited talent to lead BowTie Cause operations. Dhani served as Chairman of BowTie Cause; Kunta remained involved as the Chief Inspiration Officer. Amanda Williams joined BowTie Cause as CEO nearly three years into operations; her finance and banking background gave BowTie Cause strategic planning expertise. Amanda prioritized repositioning BowTie Cause among her first objectives. She commissioned and guided a website relaunch that emphasized an improved user interface, updated logo, and a relevant tagline (*Get Tied to A Cause*). In conjunction with the website relaunch, Amanda worked to streamline owned social media channels to reflect the improved style and consistently communicate the mission.

As the BowTie Cause Executive Team, Dhani, Kunta, and Amanda delivered the BowTie Cause model to highlight three key competencies. The team executed the BowTie Cause mission statement through consistent (1) organizational representation, (2) collaboration, and (3) process. This combination added value that was unmatched by direct or indirect competitors.

First, to "generate funds," per the mission statement, BowTie Cause donated 25% of profit from online bowtie sales to the organizations specifically represented by customized bowties. Each uniquely designed bowtie captured the essence of the cause it represented through color, pattern, texture, and other fabric embellishments. The suggested retail price for each bowtie was $57. The added value for the cause organization resulted from the difference between the revenue from retail sales and the cost of bowtie production. Additionally, the $57 price point represented Dhani's Cincinnati Bengals number, so "57" was an extra signature nod to Dhani. The BowTie Cause model also accomplished economies of scale. The per unit cost to manufacture the unique design decreased as order amount increased. For example, to order 100 bowties, each bowtie cost $28.50 to manufacture; an order amount of 250 bowties cost $27.50 each. See Appendix A for additional details about the cost structure and financial benefit to organizations.

The BowTie Cause model also required collaboration. The BowTie Cause team shared creative freedom with cause organizations to design the bowtie that best portrayed the causes' missions. Co-creation empowered customization for the cause yet allowed Amanda and her team to share their distinct BowTie Cause expertise. The cause partners understood their historic tactics to generate funds as well as the needs of the populations they served, but they otherwise did not have social enterprise expertise to design a wearable story. BowTie Cause transferred its proven model to supplement generating funds: it guided partners through the manufacturing process and aimed to execute an easy experience for design, creation, and promotion. Inclusive of initiated idea, causes received their bowtie orders in twelve to fourteen weeks. Collaboration and co-creation were emphasized during each phase of interaction. Seemingly minor details, like the size of a cause's symbols woven into the silk textile, made every manipulation of the bowtie prototype stand for the cause's story. Such organizational representation also manifested in bowtie packaging: each bowtie arrived specially packaged to promote the cause's story, logo, website, and social media channels. Objectives to attain exposure, reach, and promotion happened as natural outcomes. Accordingly, a balance between organizational representation and collaboration anchored each partnership with the common mission to generate funds. See Appendix A for an illustration of the process timeline.

Finally, the BowTie Cause mission explicitly aimed to "generate awareness," so BowTie Cause openly partnered with organizations from any sector. No cause was off limits for bowtie design. This flexibility allowed BowTie Cause to work with groups that varied from sport teams' philanthropies to universities and medical societies. Options for BowTie Cause to source prospective partners seemed endless. Increased diversification of partners enabled BowTie Cause to expand its reach and act as an expert contributor to a fragmented cause marketing space.

Cause Marketing

For BowTie Cause to evaluate growth through market expansion, it fundamentally needed an abundance of causes; society's controversies, although largely unsought scenarios, drove opportunity for BowTie Cause to be an authentic problem-solver on behalf of causes that needed funds and awareness. Cause marketing typically involved the cooperative efforts of a for-profit business and a non-profit organization for mutual benefit.[3] Dhani and the BowTie Cause team, as social entrepreneurs, regarded cause marketing as the core of giving back to society. Theoretically, cause marketing had become a minimum expectation for any enterprise's operations; cause marketing no longer acted as a factor of differentiation because consumers looked for companies to represent their values. Per GfK[4], 63% of consumers reported only buying products that appealed to beliefs, values, and ideals. Customers wanted to make the world a better place through their website clicks and in-store purchases, and cause marketing established a convenient way for them to feel their impact. Cause marketing acted to bridge the gap between consumers' attitudes and behaviors. "The number of consumers who say they would switch from one brand to another if the other brand were associated with a good cause has climbed to 87%,"[5] and this dramatic increase came at a time when charitable giving stagnated at 2% of the GDP.[6] BowTie Cause brought cause marketing to the foreground; the branding removed guesswork for consumers that its products held only commercial value. Openly messaging its attachment to "cause" in its brand name promised the cause featured would never be an afterthought for BowTie Cause.

---

[3] http://www.entrepreneur.com/article/197820
[4] http://trendwatching.com/trends/enlightened-brands
[5] http://www.entrepreneur.com/article/197820
[6] http://www.ted.com/talks/dan_pallotta_the_way_we_think_about_charity_is_dead_wrong

BowTie Cause supported a portfolio of 109 cause-related partners represented with one-of-a-
kind bowties. These partners epitomized wide acceptance of philanthropic practice and
embodied social responsibility in their mission statements. Defined to include "the selfless
act of giving back in talent, time, and treasure,"[7] philanthropy united BowTie Cause partners
within a common cause to improve community. BowTie Cause partners included
organizations focused on armed forces, arts, education, foundations, health, and other
specialty interests. Through cultivated partnerships, Bowtie Cause delivered a national
platform to generate funds for diverse causes. It concurrently represented a unique
promotional channel to raise awareness for the partners' causes. Appendix B lists BowTie
Cause Partners by Organization Type and Name.

BowTie Cause's Competitive Niche

Kunta pioneered the bowtie in the midst of a bowtie renaissance, and Dhani articulated this
"resurgence of the gentleman"[8] through his signature combination of dapper dressing and
philanthropic donation. As such, the BowTie Cause team recognized favorable marketplace
conditions to uphold the mission statement through differentiated product strategy that
tapped into this socio-cultural zeitgeist. The strategic objective aimed to capture market share
within a competitive fashion accessories sector. To do so, highlighting attributes of BowTie
Cause signaled how ultimate consumers also understood how and why rocking a Bowtie
Cause bowtie extended beyond a fashion statement and arched into a social statement.

The US market for apparel and accessories surpassed $15 billion, and sales of men's
products continued to outshine women's sales. An anticipated 3% increase in men's apparel
accessories indicated US consumers accepted product development in menswear and desired
more options.[9] Conflicting with overall growth in the menswear category, ties lost their place
as a staple of corporate dress. With continued popularity of causal workplaces and stay-at-

---

[7] Bhagat, V., Loeb, P., & Rovner, M. "The next generation of American giving: A study on
the contrasting charitable habits of Generation Y, Generation X, Baby Boomers and Matures.
Convivo. March 2010. Accessed April 2015.
[8] http://articles.latimes.com/2009/nov/29/image/la-ig-diary29-2009nov29
[9] Euromonitor International. Passport GMID.

home employees, annual tie purchases steadily decreased as retailers responded to consumer preferences for "casual work wear."[10]

Despite slumping necktie sales, the marketplace for other men's accessories experienced resurgence. Decades of casual workplace dressing, including jeans and t-shirts, begged for an upgrade that allowed men to embody personal style through elevated products. Men desired comfortable, unfussy styles that also allowed them to "dress the part" for professional commitments. Unlike infinite consumer choices offered to women – scarves, jewelry, and handbags – men sought straightforward items to serve multiple purposes that merged "business casual and business comfortable."[10] BowTie Cause realized the opportunity to converge this aesthetic while addressing cues that premium products still had a place in men's wardrobes. Recent performance of men's denim signaled that men appreciated premium apparel to be used for multiple occasions. Sales of premium denim had skyrocketed in recent years, yet with its imminent maturity and decline signaled by a near double-digit drop-off in sales[7], men were ready for low- to mid-priced garments to complement their premium-priced denim and keep their look fresh. In other words, men purchased their share of jeans for wear-to-work and wear-to-play occasions, leaving opportunity for confident accessories to supplement emerging dress code expectations. The durability of denim did not require constant replenishment, so while men wore-in their favorite jeans, their closets wore thin of other fashion-forward choices. BowTie Cause's masculine product assortment marked the brand's response to the expected industry uptick with appropriate timing and product utility.

Nascent trends in men's accessories motivated men to respond to a sweeping nostalgia, championed by society's fascination with popular culture influences ranging from Mad Men to Entourage. Products like pocket squares, cufflinks, eyewear, and bowties allowed a mix-and-match wardrobe of choices, thus allowing men to simultaneously embody the well-groomed style of Mad Men's Don Draper and the laid-back look of Justin Timberlake. Men's associations with bowties also began to evolve. The historic image of bowties as "older" or

---

[10] Mintel International Group Ltd. Mintel Reports.

"stiff" succumbed to modern interpretations of how men, representative of a range of lifestyles, "tied one on." The playful, yet sophisticated, nature of bowties elegantly supported BowTie Cause positioning to adequately address changes in the apparel industry. As shown in Appendix C, survey participants expressed descriptions they associate with the word "bowtie."

Although consumers reported a range of perceptions about bowties, positive perceptions like "stylish" and "cultured" matched changing perceptions of luxury. Fifty-five percent of consumers reported that wearing a bowtie implied a sense of luxury.[11] As bowties benefitted from consumers' new willingness to habitually wear bowties for a wider range of occasions, perceptions of luxury benefitted from redefinition prompted by the economic environment. US consumers thirsted for luxury product: the US economy ranked amongst the top five global markets for luxury good sales.[12] With recent recession pressures lifted, luxury products now fit a continuum and satisfied a wider array of consumer desires. Product development freely combined form utility and fanciful appeal. In doing so, accessories responded to consumers' preferences for "masstige"[13] products, designed to blend mass pricing and distribution with prestige quality. Table 1 indicates how brands position luxury product offerings to fit three distinct preferences for luxury. This continuum ultimately points to opportunity for masstige products to encompass traits of each category.

Table 1: Luxury Continuum

	Types of Luxury
Accessible	Lowest, cheapest form of luxury that is accessible to most consumers in the marketplace
Aspirational	Middle tier form of luxury that most consumers aspire to attain

---

[11] proprietary consumer data from BowTie Cause.
[12] Euromonitor International. Passport GMID.
[13] https://hbr.org/2003/04/luxury-for-the-masses

| **Absolute** | Highest, most expensive form of luxury |

Source: Euromonitor International.

Within the luxury spectrum, current positioning of BowTie Cause (see Figure 1) held a position unlike other popular menswear brands. While indirect competitors, like Coach and Ralph Lauren, earned market share through diversification across luxury categories, these brands frequently risked the integrity of the brand and the trust consumers invested to believe a brand evoked absolute luxury. Through penetration of each luxury category with a unique product line, consumers scratched their heads about the true meaning of a luxury product. For example, Coach simultaneously offered $45 leather key rings and $598 duffel bags, leaving consumers skeptical about what the brand meant. Too many masstige product extensions threatened vulnerability and signaled loss of vision by the brand. Consumer confusion prevailed, and brands defaulted on their core competencies. Although the luxury continuum showed opportunity for global brands to recruit consumers to negotiate among luxury options, the aspiration ceiling for luxury diluted as brands strayed from their strengths in favor of opportunities.

Figure 1: BowTie Cause demonstrated positioning of a "masstige" product that represented multiple causes; this differentiated positioning created a niche within a fragmented industry of indirect competitors.

Luxury mixed with cause

What enabled BowTie Cause's differentiated positioning within a competitive luxury continuum was its focus on teaching consumers to connect a bowtie as a signature of a cause. The gaining popularity of bowties presented BowTie Cause with the opportunity to help consumers imagine a masstige bowtie as an evocative, compassionate storyteller. While apparel brands with dominant market share boasted internal foundations as cause-related activity (like The Coach Foundation or the Ralph Lauren Pink Pony Fund), BowTie Cause products disrupted existing practice to invite both organizations and consumers to support *many* causes through *one* product. This contrasted with other brands' support of *one* cause through *many* products.

While BowTie Cause indirectly competed for market share from mainstream fashion brands, it also behaved like Livestrong and (Product)[Red] brands. Both Livestrong and (Product)[Red] experienced admiration from global audiences who sparked dialogue about common good achieved through signature accessories. These brands built industry standards to combine consumers' dress patterns with donation patterns. Like BowTie Cause, each brand achieved fame through heavy endorsements by publicly-known figures. However, controversies intertwined with cause affiliations from Livestrong and (Product)[Red] brands.[14] Consumers again had reason to be confused. Brands associated with causes could be challenged to restore trust in fashionable products with the desire to contribute. BowTie Cause's positioning, therefore, needed to demand a relentless standard of transparency about its organizational representation of hundreds of causes. Appendix D compares BowTie Cause to Livestrong and (Product)[Red].

---

[14] http://www.conecomm.com/productred

The modern bowtie held crossover appeal for philanthropies seeking original ways to tell stories of support. Through philanthropy, consumers contributed selfless acts in three distinct ways. These "3 T's of Philanthropy" involved consumers donating (1) time, (2) treasure, and/or (3) talent.[7] Dynamic 24/7 consumer lifestyles suggested an abundance of time was the real luxury: finding adequate time to volunteer for favorite causes imposed upon a plethora of other commitments, including work. Consumers' tendencies to prioritize workplace commitments resulted in increased disposable income, so luxuries like bowties were attainable with earned disposable "treasure." The $57 retail price for a single BowTie Cause bowtie empowered busy consumers to support causes close to their backgrounds and interests with their treasure instead of their time. Purchases of BowTie Cause bowties satisfied aspiration for luxury accessories and provided the luxury of an accessible way to give treasure without depleting already scarce time to volunteer.

A Product with a Cause and a Brand with Fortitude

By overlapping attitudes about philanthropy with menswear trends, BowTie Cause carved a distinctive niche. In particular, the BowTie Cause brand gained strength through its brand personality. For example, per survey data, consumers associated words like "smart," "intelligent," and "talented" with bowtie wearers. Such descriptions reasonably intersected with dimensions of brand personality,[15] like sophistication and competence. Because bowtie wearers were "intelligent," such characterization suggested the BowTie Cause brand was "competent." When other cause-related brands bred controversy (see Appendix C), BowTie Cause branding was capable to deliver the trusted support it promised.

To strengthen assumptions about the BowTie Cause brand, a more industrious brand strategy drove BowTie Cause to maintain its differentiated niche. Specifically, *brand fortitude* applied to BowTie Cause's heritage to publicly boost well-being. Through brand fortitude, strategic planning involved emphasizing key properties of the bowtie to prevent dilution of

---

[15] Aaker, Jennifer L. (1997). "Dimensions of brand personality." *Journal of marketing research*, 347-356.

the *spirit* of BowTie Cause. In turn, BowTie Cause stood to more readily retain its influence (and share of market) amongst its consumers' encounters with other luxury and cause-related products. In the context of brand fortitude, the bowtie formed a vessel that launched meaning beyond its e-commerce environment: what started out as a commodity – an undecorated swatch of woven silk – *openly* represented and exchanged the values of a cause partner *and* a consumer. When branded to attempt fortitude, BowTie Cause products escaped less mindful associations of a flippant, flavor-of-the-month bowtie fad and instead emboldened consumers to prominently showcase their values. Although causes represented by BowTie Cause partners captured private, sensitive stories – as highly possible given partners like the American Diabetes Association and Armed Forces Foundation – the BowTie Cause brand struck public exposure. The bowtie silently represented BowTie Cause (as the BowTie Cause logo remained separate from the causes' designs) yet availed open, public interaction with each wear and conversation. The exchange of open dialogue between cause and consumer prevailed; the BowTie Cause brand fortified that system.

This exchange of values indicated BowTie Cause embodied openness required by a brand fortitude strategy. This openness, or brands' "permeability and hospitable meanings authored by consumers"[16] encouraged consumers to overtly voice their support stories about causes. By wearing a bowtie linked to a cause, consumers assisted BowTie Cause to articulate its openness as a brand, thus fortifying BowTie Cause in a competitive marketplace. The bowtie extended the meaning of the cause into a culturally meaningful philanthropic tool for ultimate consumers. Dhani's original signature became the recognized signature for anyone who rocked the bowtie.

Signature Segments

As a fortified brand, BowTie Cause placed significant attention on the openness of two distinct market targets. The visual design of each bowtie signified the BowTie Cause

---

[16] Borghini, S., Diamond, N., McGrath, M.A., Sherry, J.F., Kozinets, R.V., & Muniz, A.M. (2014). "Brand fortitude in moments of consumption." *Handbook of Anthropology in Business.*

expertise to merge value systems of those two targets: the ultimate consumers and the cause partners. Therefore, segmentation required BowTie Cause to dually satisfy needs of wearers and philanthropies.

Ultimate Consumers

The ultimate consumers of BowTie Cause prioritized clothing and philanthropy choices as special expressions of their identities. They were motivated to make purchases through which they encountered esteem and confidence. Their choices to wear bowties earned the respect of others, so straightforward demographics became inadequate predictors about the ultimate BowTie Cause consumers. BowTie Cause worked to understand a full portrait of its ultimate consumers. This segment generated 30% of BowTie Cause sales, so outdated conventions on traditional bowtie enthusiasts required an overhaul. Generally, ultimate consumer segments matched three categories designated as "Ringleader," "Happy-Go-Lucky," and "Old Guard."[17]

Ringleaders: The Primary B2C Psychographic

Among ultimate consumers, ringleaders formed the market target that naturally combined existing consumer motivations with the openness of brand fortitude. Ringleaders not only shared their time and treasure through actively choosing causes to support, but they also rallied others to follow their lead. These consumers most closely resembled Dhani and Kunta's initial challenge to be somebody by rocking a bowtie. Ringleaders believed everyone could capably be someone, so as opinion leaders, they seamlessly wore and worked for the brand. By wearing BowTie Cause ties, they mobilized others to build awareness and openly exchange conversations about causes, values, and visions for a better society. Thus, ringleaders supported BowTie Cause branding by enhancing brand fortitude. Ringleaders transcended gender expectations also associated with bowties: because ringleaders were both men and women, women would also openly engage with BowTie Cause without regard for

---

[17] http://www.conecomm.com/beyond-demographics-1

the masculinity of the bowtie. These women understood the cause; for them, the physical bowtie would be secondary to the open connection to the cause.

Happy-Go-Lucky: The Secondary B2C Psychographic

Given consumer perceptions of bowties as "quirky" (see Appendix C), the Happy-Go-Lucky segment promised to be central to BowTie Cause growth. Happy-Go-Lucky consumers primarily valued convenience in their purchase decisions. As such, BowTie Cause satisfied time utility through its "two for one" offering: Happy-Go-Lucky consumers simultaneously gave treasure to a cause while saving time during the e-commerce ordering process. However, to effectively persuade Happy-Go-Lucky consumers, BowTie Cause needed to appeal to the "feel good" factor involved with their investment of treasure. Happy-Go-Lucky consumers wanted to impact society but did so only after being pulled to the cause by the brand itself. Happy-Go-Lucky consumers did not seek social enterprises but instead depended on the brand to interact with them through tools like social media. Such behavior, however, again demonstrated the importance of BowTie Cause's openness to consistent dialogue with consumers about causes and values. Happy-Go-Lucky consumers expected to be inspired to showcase how they felt about the impact manifested in their purchases. BowTie Cause made this head-vs-heart connection for them.

Old Guard: The Tertiary B2C Psychographic

Finally, a tertiary market included consumers who matched traditional bowtie wearers. By combining luxury with cause, these Old Guard consumers stumbled into socially responsible purchases. They conventionally wore bowties – to special occasions instead of an everyday, statement-making piece – and routinely purchased based on price, quality, and convenience expectations. Among old guard consumers, BowTie Cause posed an opportunity for brand switching: one-third of old guard consumers considered adjusting their brand preferences in favor of a brand associated with a cause. Yet, as old guard consumers represented males over the age of 55, BowTie Cause remained a relevant option for these professionals. Consequently, old guard consumers had more professional exposure that sometimes required attendance of high-profile events (like galas and auctions) hosted by the causes represented in the BowTie Cause portfolio. Old guard consumers also had experience with traditional ways of donating and could be persuaded to adjust their donation preferences through an accessory already present in their wardrobes.

Cause Partners

Although segmentation of wearers depicted three diverse psychographics, cause partners received explicit mention in the BowTie Cause mission statement (see page 3). By plainly addressing its partners in the mission statement, BowTie Cause showed its pure focus on relationships with causes. This B2B segmentation followed wholesale practices to satisfy the needs of buying centers formed by the causes to represent countless ultimate consumers affiliated with the causes. To effectively understand the needs of diverse cause sectors, BowTie Cause benefitted from its willingness to articulate the organizations' missions in its design process. Such focus generated 70% of BowTie Cause sales through organizational buying by cause partners.

To properly maintain existing wholesale relationships and cultivate new relationships, the BowTie Cause team included a Cause Curator. As a business development professional, the Cause Curator reported to Amanda the CEO and treated each cause organization as an account. The Cause Curator retained tight records and detailed notes of sales funnel cycles; it was the Cause Curator's responsibility to record all types of contact with organizations. Collected data quickly referenced information like email threads, dates of contact, and website pages. The Cause Curator communicated with causes through email, phone calls, Skype, and in-person meetings; data from these touchpoints delineated between follow-up and in-process status per communication channel. Weekly workload allocation ensured the pipeline for sales funnel leads matched sales goals projected from previous years' sales ledgers. The Cause Curator fulfilled the BowTie Cause mission with each cause interaction and cued a strong, standardized CRM implementation.

The Cause Curator role also responded to the crucial nature of establishing quality contact within cause organizations. Within the business development process, Cause Curators carefully qualified contacts to acknowledge how BowTie Cause generated the connection. Within proprietary CRM documentation, the Cause Curator organized relationships as "current" or "prospect." In both current and prospect relationships, the Cause Curator interacted with multiple stakeholders in organizations' buying centers and procurement groups. Driving compelling communication with influencers, deciders, and buyers required the Cause Curator to acknowledge assumptions about the users represented by buying centers. Users who directly benefited from the missions of the cause partners – cancer patients, veterans, or students, among others – did not typically participate in the wholesale and design process. It became essential for the Cause Curator to be knowledgeable and empathetic about the scope of services that could be represented in a bowtie. See Appendix E for excerpts from documentation generated by the Cause Curator.

For causes with existing relationships, the Cause Curator aimed to renew the relationships through production of existing designs or slighted adjusted designs. For example, the Juvenile Diabetes Research Foundation (JDRF) exemplified the most established relationship within the BowTie Cause portfolio. The JDRF mission was "to find a cure for type 1 diabetes and its complications through the support of research."[18] To support its mission, JDRF collaborated with BowTie Cause to produce three distinct bowtie designs. Generally, health-related organizations accepted the BowTie Cause platform more than any other sector. Existing relationships, like that with JDFR and other health-related organizations, showed the agility of the Cause Curator to customize buying situations to the budget cycle of the cause. Designing three JDFR bowties, for example, demonstrated a "modified rebuy." Making minor adjustments to existing designs extended the relationship by introducing one or two new stakeholders into the design process, yet the relationship between JDFR and BowTie Cause was already entrenched. Modified rebuys like that with JDFR showed the Cause Curator's abilities to penetrate the existing organizational structure. This selling goal, in turn, constructed long-term relationships and avoided ad hoc transactions.

---

[18] jdrf.org

The Cause Curator also generated leads to initiate prospect relationships with cause partners new to BowTie Cause. Although the Cause Curator sourced prospects from organizational websites and non-profit trade associations, personal referrals proved most effective. Internal referrals to new cause stakeholders working for the same mission but different projects proved productive; referrals also came directly from Dhani. To support this "new buy" process and acclimate to unfamiliar buying centers, the Cause Curator shared branded material (Appendix A) with prospects to describe the mission, process, values, and other specifications unique to BowTie Cause. Combined, the branded collateral presented BowTie Cause capabilities as a long-term partner, not a transactional vendor, in the cause's mission.

In particular, local organizations showed the most white space opportunity to produce bowties. Navigating the complex nature of smaller, lesser-known organizational structures made the use of an RFP process essential. Tasked to identify the roles and responsibilities of stakeholders new to BowTie Cause, the Cause Curator was tasked to convert opening communication with prospects into pipeline opportunities. Therefore, acute knowledge of the prospect cause's mission empowered the Cause Curator to show how BowTie Cause provided an imperative platform to generate awareness and funds, each especially important for smaller organizations challenged to compete with budgets of national organizations.

One Signature Communicated through the Promotional Mix

Social Media

Elaborate segmentation addressed B2C and B2B opportunities, so the promotional mix simultaneously required representation of ultimate consumers and cause partners. Social media content constantly illustrated the BowTie Cause mission and partners' missions. Content was scheduled to diversify how BowTie Cause made its online voice relevant for its own brand and the causes it represented. A content calendar recorded major events, such as National Hunger Awareness Day or World Environment Day, and prompted interaction in relevant online channels. Moreover, brand fortitude opened the dialogue to "ringleaders" and "happy-go-lucky" consumers ready to respectively create and view online messages. Metrics, including bounce rates, page views, and likes, tracked month-to-month trends and set goals. With contracted support of Kooda Media, BowTie Cause showed its acumen within a digital environment while focus remained on generating funds and awareness. See Appendix F for excerpts from social media tracking, and see Appendix G for an example timeline of social media content.

With the Internet of Things poised to challenge mass acceptance of interactive Web 2.0 promotional capabilities, BowTie Cause risked what most brands rarely tried. Social media, although used, was purposefully downplayed. Compared to BowTie Cause competitors, social media presence remained intentionally quiet. BowTie Cause maintained presence on Facebook (approximately 6000 fans) and Twitter (approximately 4000 followers). Google Plus, Pinterest, and Tumblr also directed clicks to content via Facebook and Twitter. All social and digital content internally produced by BowTie Cause (in partnership with Kooda Media, also based in Cincinnati) displayed across relevant social networks. For example, promotional video about Dhani's involvement consistently appeared via YouTube and Facebook: the same message showed on both channels. More recently, Instagram emerged as a go-to medium capable of visually highlighting the design of the bowties and wearers' experiences for nearly 500 followers. BowTie Cause understood it could not altogether avoid social media, so it strategically used its owned media to balance presence and sidestep noise. BowTie Cause achieved what so many brands seek: it controlled its presence in social channels and cohesively represented its brand personality with sophisticated messaging and competent dialogue.

BowTie Cause strengthened brand fortitude through an online tool other brands fumbled to effectively use: a hashtag. #TiedToACause specified BowTie Cause social media content and supported the openness BowTie Cause built as a brand. All social content – either about specific products or specific cause partners – mapped to #TiedToACause on all social media channels. The distinct hashtag provided a continuous link that signaled cues about product and mission. Its simple text encoded a message that empowered meaningful online dialogue. Countless brands generated irrelevant hashtags, yet BowTie Cause created a connective thread that openly invited new and existing consumers and causes to engage their values. #TiedToACause performed like a digital signature, extended from the signature bowtie.

User Experience (UX)

Although #TiedToACause stuck to social media interactions, e-commerce and wholesale purchases could not solely depend on social media posts to achieve growth. Judicious social media use suggested BowTie Cause's commitment to the overall user experience (UX) for both ultimate consumers and cause partners. Within interactive online channels, UX generally implied the design efforts brands implemented through digital or technological experiences.[19] The BowTie Cause website represented a crucial touchpoint to unite the experiences of ultimate consumers and cause partners. After nearly four years of operations, BowTie Cause instigated a website redesign to enhance UX: design needed to unite aesthetics and function.[20] The redesign led to marketing research about consumer perceptions of the updated features. Per survey data, the most important visual cue within the website upgrade was the word "shop," thus indicating consumers visited BowTie Cause with potential purchase motivations. Additionally, user experience benefited from visually pleasing design (mean=4.16, on a 5 point Likert scale). Survey respondents reported the website design as "unique and innovative" (mean=3.93) and that website graphics were clear (mean=4.07). Survey data also reported that consumers mostly agreed about ease of use (mean=3.91), ability to find pages within the site (mean=3.69), and changes orders (mean=4.0) See Appendix H for findings from survey data including heat maps and qualitative comments. Also, see Appendix I for integration of the website relaunch via social media.

Brand Ambassadors

---

[19] http://www.fastcodesign.com/3043024/a-brief-history-of-user-experience-design
[20] http://www.marketingprofs.com/articles/2015/27842/10-user-experience-testing-tools-marketers-need-to-know-about

Data about UX pointed to encouraging integration of social and digital interactions. Yet, the BowTie Cause promotional plan aimed to convert purchase behavior and influence signature bowtie wearing. These objectives paralleled the mission to raise funds and generate awareness. With a sound online experience anchored, efforts to involve personalities in the promotional mix publicly showed who advocated for the #TiedToACause community. As a nationally known and popular athlete, Dhani served as the champion for endorsement. Dhani showed how to invest personal treasure with the purpose to "change the world."[21] He acted on making the signature bowtie as a part of his personal mission. In doing so, he always referenced Kunta's story; thus, Kunta too stood as a BowTie Cause Ambassador. Dhani's personal attachment to both philanthropy and style installed an implicit ethos standard to BowTie Cause Ambassadors.

BowTie Ambassadors became a core word-of-mouth medium that richly enhanced BowTie Cause's promotional mix. Ambassadors represented BowTie Cause signature traits and embodied ringleader psychographics. Specifically:

A BowTie Cause Ambassador does not simply make a statement, they are a statement. Their actions, beliefs, and character speak to the things they stand for. A BowTie Ambassador rocks BowTies because of what they represent - not just because they are cool. A BowTie Ambassador is a leader, an influence, a catalyst for conversation and change.[22]

Prominently, Ken Rosenthal, a Senior Major League Baseball (MLB) commentator for Fox Sports, regularly showed how to rock a bowtie. Ken embedded the signature vision of BowTie Cause Ambassadors during each television appearance. Given the national popularity of MLB, Ken exposed BowTie Cause to fans who might have traditional expectations of how bowties are worn. Ken's primary reason to rock a bowtie remained simple: he wanted to "raise awareness for the organizations with which BowTie Cause was partnered."[20] Not only did Ken open conversations during his Fox air time, he further activated the BowTie Cause brand by driving fans to shop online for BowTie Cause. Via

---

[21] http://bowtiecause.com/the-cause/dhanis-words-mobile/
[22] www.bowtiecause.com

bowtiecause.com, a page linked to all bowties Ken wore on air. As an energetic "ringleader", an overall sales increase accompanied each of Ken's Fox appearances. What became significant for the sales boost Ken's exposure influenced was not the sale of the specific tie he wore but that consumers browsed to discover additional bowties that related to their signature style and donation preferences. See Appendix J for additional details about Brand Ambassadors.

However, like social media, BowTie Cause understood celebrity endorsements demanded cautious use. Consumer data collected[11] expressed that consumers did not consider celebrity endorsements as a purchase influence. Thirty percent of survey participants reported "likely" or "very likely" to respond to celebrity influence, and 21% reported they were "undecided" about likelihood to be influenced by celebrity endorsement. Further, 25% of survey participants expressed inclination to wear a bowtie when favorite athletes wear bowties. Dhani and Ken clearly activated the signature message as they rocked bowties in athletic settings. Given that nearly 50% of survey participants avoided celebrity endorsement influence, the Brand Ambassador tactic opened BowTie Cause branding to a wider variety of consumers who personified "celebrity" qualities yet manifested ringleader traits.

Integrated Promotional Mix for Wearers and Causes

The core message of the promotional mix - to change the world by rocking a bowtie - integrated across social media, digital UX, and Brand Ambassadors; the message resonated through business development by the Cause Curator. Yet, due to its twofold segmentation, BowTie Cause diffused across the product life cycle at multiple rates. The purchase decision for ultimate consumers included a shorter journey to point, click, and rock the bowtie. The organizational buying process to reach the bottom of the funnel occurred far more slowly. The messaging potentially fostered the need for two campaigns to represent two BowTie Cause segments. Yet, a split in the cohesive promotional mix signaled a departure from a fortified brand on a path to establish a signature instrument for sharing stories about causes.

The Decision Problem

One signature bowtie could be tied in 10 steps. Yet, BowTie Cause needed one signature strategy to make its signature an accepted common good practice within society. Dhani, Kunta, Amanda, and their team knew that the bowtie pressed bigger questions, and they were ready to rock causes with answers through "the way of a bowtie."

Appendix A: BowTie Cause Model

Thank you for your interest in collaborating with BowTie Cause. Our mission is to provide opportunities for socially-conscious organizations to spark conversation, raise awareness and ultimately generate funds. Today, we primarily accomplish this mission through the co-created design of signature BowTies and the engagement inspired by them.

Organizational Representation

Every BowTie comes specially packaged including bow tying instructions and a custom storycard, which incorporates your organization's narrative, logo, website and Twitter handle. the cost structure is outlined below:

Order Amount	100	250	500	1000 or more
Cost Per BowTie	$28.50	$27.50	$26.00	$23.00
Retail Value	$5,700	$14,250	$28,500	$57,000
Benefit to Organization	$2,850	$7,375	$15,500	$34,000

We suggest that each organization sells each BowTie at $57. The difference in the cost of the BowTie to the organization and revenue from retail sales directly benefits the partnering organization.

Collaboration

BowTie Cause will order additional BowTies to be sold on the BowTie Cause website and will take on the cost to fulfill this inventory. BowTie Cause will then donate 25% of the profit from the online sale of each BowTie to the respective organization.

Process

Narrative Formation	Design	Fabric Sample Reviewed	Production	BowTies Delivered
Week 1	Week 1-2	Week 3-5	Week 6-12	

Added Value

- Each organization's story will be included on the BowTie Cause website with a link to the organization's website.
- Social media will be utilized to promote all partnering organizations.
- Each signature design will be entered into the annual BowTie Challenge. The winning BowTie will be worn by Ken Rosenthal at the World Series.

We look forward to collaborating with you!
Please contact info@bowtiecause.org with any questions.
Go to BowTieCause.com to learn more and see some of our incredible partnerships!

Appendix A: BowTie Cause Model (continued)

BOWTIE CAUSE
SUCCESS PACK

BowTie Cause would like to thank you for your business! We are excited that you have selected the BowTie as an avenue for your organization to raise funds and awareness. Getting your powerful message across to as many individuals as possible is of the upmost importance. We are excited to begin the next phase of this collaboration to help your organization raise awareness for your cause by rockin' a BowTie.

This Organization Success Packet is a guide compiled of best practices from over ninety of our partnering organizations. As you work through the details of your event, we are always happy to answer questions you may have. If you have any suggestions as to how we can make this collaboration better, please feel free to share your feedback with your BowTie Cause contact.

BOWTIE CHAMPION

A BowTie Champion is a person (internal or volunteer) who is in charge of overseeing the project and communicating with BowTie Cause as your event approaches. Through past collaborations we have found that having a designated individual, a BowTie Champion, ensures your BowTie gets to customers and supporters in the most successful way. BowTie Cause will address all decision making with your designated decision makers, but the BowTie Champion will be the contact for BowTie Cause to make certain that your signature BowTie is successfully leveraged before, during, and after your event.

EVENT DETAILS

Event Date?......................☐
Emcee?...........................☐
Where is the event being held?
What is the atmosphere/vibe
of the event?.....................☐
Pre event press event?
Ticket cost?......................☐
Who is attending?
(demographic)...................☐
Likelihood that attendee will
spend? (auction, table sales).......☐
What is the goal for the
BowTie Inventory? (pre-sale,
event sales).....................☐
Location for BowTie Cause at
the event?......................☐
How many volunteers
dedicated to supporting the
BowTie?........................☐

We would like to know as many details about the event as possible. The more information we have, the more help BowTie Cause can offer in order to make certain all aspects of the event are achieved.

BOWTIE MARKETING

Pre-event publicity material?........☐
How will the BowTie be
presented?......................☐
Mention during the event by
the emcee? (when, how often).......☐

Appendix A: BowTie Cause Model (continued)

BOWTIE CAUSE
SUCCESS PACK

BOWTIE CAUSE COMMITMENT

Every collaboration creates its own unique experience; however, we hope to set a standard as to what you can expect from us throughout this process. BowTie Cause will use our available resources to assist in raising awareness for your event.

SOCIAL MEDIA

Two Tweets the week of your event..........................☐
One Facebook post the week of your event.....................☐
One Facebook post the week after your event (Only if images from the event are provided)........☐

If Dhani is scheduled to be at your event, we will need the following information.

INFORMATION FOR DHANI

Does Dhani have a speaking role at your event? If so, length of speaking time?................☐
Topic/talking points?...............☐

BUT WAIT, THERE'S MORE...

After the event we would like to follow-up with your organization to make certain we have captured all pertinent information. This information not only helps us create better collaborations in the future, but it also allows us to fulfill our social engagement responsibilities to your organization.
1 - It is our goal to help your organization achieve it's sales goal for the BowTies; therefore, we are able to help with suggestions on how we can move any remaining inventory if needed.
2 - Please send BowTie Cause a few photos from the event. The photos will be used by BowTie Cause through our social media outlets in order to highlight your event.
3 - If you have any feedback on how we could improve the collaboration we would greatly appreciate it.

WHAT TO DO AFTER

Have we made BowTie Cause aware of the remaining inventory?..........................☐
Have we given the pictures of the event to BowTie Cause?..........☐
Have we given our feedback to BowTie Cause about our experience?.......................☐

THANK YOU

We would like to thank you for your commitment to your cause. We are so happy that you selected BowTie Cause to be a part of your event and that you chose the BowTie to help spread your powerful message. We look forward to hearing your successes and growing our partnership with you in the future.

Appendix B: BowTie Cause Partners

Organization Type	Organization Name	Organization Type	Organization Name	Organization Type	Organization Name	Organization Type	Organization Name
Armed Forces	USO	Foundations	JDRF	Foundations	Cancer Support Community	Foundations	Hunger Network
Armed Forces	Armed Forces Foundation		Leukemia and Lymphoma Society		Autism Speaks		SPCA Cincinnati
Arts	Cincinnati Ballet		Livestrong		Pints for Prostates		Hibiscus Children's Center
	Cincinnati Pops Orchestra		Most Valuable Kids		Lighthouse Youth Services		International Swimming Hall of Fame
	SPIVA Center for the Arts		Cincinnati Zoo		Hope Starts Here		Esophogeal Cancer Awareness Center
	Headlands Center for the Arts		Society of St. Vincent de Paul		Children's Tumor Foundation		American Brain Foundation
	Cincinnati Art Museum		Ronald McDonald House Charities		Chiquita Classic		Detroit Tigers Foundation
	Cora Jean's Old School Café		Alxheimer's Association		The Spirit of Construction Foundation		Envision Children
	May Festival		Boys Hope Girls Hope		James Beard Foundation		Lungevity
	Cincinnati Opera		91.7 WVXU		Cancer Family Care		The Jason Motte Foundation
Education	University of Michigan		Kenzie's Closet		Santonio Holmes III & Long Foundation		Life Center
	Cincinnati Country Day School		Maggie's Hope		Elizabeth Glaser Pediatric AIDS Foundation		Mito
	Breakthrough Cincinnati		Ferdinand's Ball		ALBA		Jewish Family Services
	University of Arkansas		Pablove Foundation		Mission Kids Child Advocacy		Lymphoma Research Foundation
	BTN Live Big		Stand Up To Cancer		Boy Scouts of America		Patrick Dempsey Center
	University of Toledo		Arkansas Commitment		Ulman Cancer Fund		Rock CF Foundation
	ICSJ		ALS Association		Ed Block Courage Award Foundation	Health Related	University of Michigan C.S. Mott Children's Hospital
	Morehouse		Cystic Fibrosis Foundation		Flying Pig Marathon		Arkansas Children's Hospital
	Page Education Foundation		Dress for Success		J. Kyle Braid Leadership Foundation		Scoliosis Research Society
	Syracuse University		Arkansas Prostate Cancer Foundation		National Kidney Foundation		University of Cincinnati Neuroscience Institute
	Nativity School		Village Life Outreach Project		Cooperative for Education		National MS Society
	Mullen		9/11 Memorial		Variety		This Star Won't Go Out
	The Space		Ovarian Cancer Research Fund		Mercantile Library	Specialty	BowTie Foundation
	University of Cincinnati		Easter Seals		The Spirit of Cincinnatus		
	Lupus Foundation of America		American Diabetes Association		SAGA		
	Carnivor		The Charlie Foundation		St. Elizabeth Foundation		
	Wine Down Wednesday		Heroes Foundation		The Salvation Army		
	Marvin Lewis Community Fund		Project Haiti		Transitions		

Appendix C: Survey participants word associations with the word "bowtie"

Appendix D: Comparison of BowTie Cause to Livestrong and (Product)[Red]

	Livestrong	(Red)	BowTie Cause
Non Profit	Yes	Yes	No
Product Offerings	Multiple	Multiple	Few
# of companies partnered with	Multiple	Multiple	Multiple
Online/In Store	Both	Both	Online only
Celebrity Endorser	Formerly- Lance Armstrong	Bono & U2	Dhani Jones
Celebrity's Image	Negative	Positive	Positive
Cause(s) they support	Improving the lives of those with cancer	Funding HIV/AIDS programs in Africa	A wide variety of organizations from health to education to the armed forces

Appendix E: Excerpts from Cause Curator documentation

Week of:

	Actual	Goal	
Emails	64	50	128%
Calls	5	20	25%
Meetings	6	5	120%
Follow-Ups	25	20	125%
Portfolio Contacts	5	2	250%
Networking Events	1	0.5	200%

Appendix F: Excerpts from online tracking records

	Previous Week	Current Week Fans	Increase #	entions / RTS (T\	Total Reach	#of Posts	gh Engagement Post(	Reach / Likes
Facebook	5713	5718	5		1.4K	7	6.17 Lupus BowTie announcement - Ken	10 Total Likes, Comments, Shares
							6.16 Quotes + picture of Ken wearing Pints for Prostate BowTie	16 Likes, comments, shares
Twitter	3357	3379	22	36 RTS | 45 Favs | 62	1.047 Impressions	29	6.17 Lupus BowTie for K Rosenthal	12 RTS | 473.4K impressions
Instagram	145	150	5			6	Picture of Mannequin w/ BTC BowTies covering it	22 Likes | 1 comme
Google+		9		+9	1589 views	2	n/a	n/a
Pinterest		4	4	0				
Blog	Transformations - Kunta Littlejohn							
Promotion?	Review BowTie purchase and receive 10% off	Doggie BowTies on Instagram						
Weekly Highlig	Twitter	Lupus BowTie announcment circulated well						

Sessions	Users
324	289

Pageviews	Pages / Session
1,572	4.85

Avg. Session Duration	Bounce Rate
00:02:41	55.56%

Appendix G: Example of a social media content calendar

Sunday	Monday	Tuesday	Wednesday	Thursday	Friday	Saturday
1 Galloping Pig Promo	2 Quote of the Day (Facebook/Google+)	3 Ken Rosenthal/Bowtie Promo (Facebook/Twitter) **ADA**	4 #BowTie Selfie Submission (Twitter/Instagram)	5 Blog Post	6 Ken Rosenthal/Bowtie Promo (Facebook/Twitter) **ADA**	7 Ken Rosenthal/Bowtie Promo (Facebook/Twitter) **ADA**
8 Galloping Pig Promo	9 Quote of the Day (Facebook/Google+)	10 Ken Rosenthal/Bowtie Promo (Facebook/Twitter) **J Kyle Braid**	11 #BowTie Selfie Submission (Twitter/Instagram)	12 Blog Post	13 Ken Rosenthal/Bowtie Promo (Facebook/Twitter) **J Kyle Braid**	14 Ken Rosenthal/Bowtie Promo (Facebook/Twitter) **J Kyle Braid**
15 Galloping Pig Promo	16 Quote of the Day (Facebook/Google+)	17 Ken Rosenthal/Bowtie Promo (Facebook/Twitter) **Lupus**	18 #BowTie Selfie Submission (Twitter/Instagram)	19 Blog Post	20 Ken Rosenthal/Bowtie Promo (Facebook/Twitter) **Lupus**	21 Ken Rosenthal/Bowtie Promo (Facebook/Twitter) **Lupus**
22 Galloping Pig Promo **Father's Day**	23 Quote of the Day (Facebook/Google+)	24 Ken Rosenthal/Bowtie Promo (Facebook/Twitter) **Alzheimer's**	25 #BowTie Selfie Submission (Twitter/Instagram)	26 Blog Post	27 Ken Rosenthal/Bowtie Promo (Facebook/Twitter) **Alzheimer's**	28 Ken Rosenthal/Bowtie Promo (Facebook/Twitter) **Alzheimer's**
29 Galloping Pig Promo **National HIV Testing Day –EGPAF tie-in**	30 Quote of the Day (Facebook/Google+)					

36

Appendix H: Survey data about BowTie Cause UX website relaunch

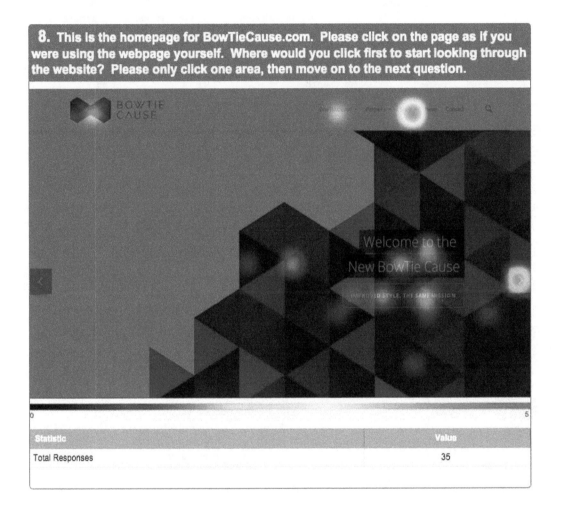

Statistic	Value
Total Responses	35

Appendix H: Survey data about BowTie Cause UX website relaunch (continued)

Statistic	This retailer's advertised items are in stock.	This retailer provides information on how much an item costs with the shipping costs included.	This retailer provides accurate information about when orders will be received.	This retailer's website has a running total of purchases as you add more items to the cart.
Mean	3.96	4.09	3.91	4.07
Variance	0.63	0.45	0.54	0.43
Standard Deviation	0.80	0.67	0.73	0.65
Total Responses	45	45	45	45

Statistic	The retail site is visually pleasing.	The website design is unique and innovative.	The graphics and pictures on the website are clear and crisp.	The text on the website is easy to read.	I do not have to scroll from side to side in order to see the whole page.
Mean	4.16	3.93	4.07	4.14	4.09
Variance	0.93	0.95	0.76	0.63	1.20
Standard Deviation	0.96	0.97	0.87	0.80	1.10
Total Responses	44	44	44	44	44

Statistic	It is easy to get anywhere on this retailer's website.	I don't get lost on this retailer's website.	This website allows you to find a page previously viewed.	This website allows you to go back if you make a mistake or want to change your order.
Mean	3.91	3.84	3.69	4.00
Variance	0.54	0.73	0.63	0.68
Standard Deviation	0.73	0.85	0.79	0.83
Total Responses	45	45	45	45

Statistic	The website does not crash	The website pages load quickly	The retailer provides numerous payment options
Mean	4.20	4.18	4.14
Variance	0.68	0.76	0.49
Standard Deviation	0.82	0.87	0.70
Total Responses	44	44	44

Appendix H: Survey data about BowTie Cause UX website relaunch (continued)

Statistic	Overall, I am very happy with the service experience.	In general, I am very pleased with the quality of the service this retailer provided.	I feel pretty negative about this retailer.
Mean	4.14	4.30	2.34
Variance	0.59	0.49	2.00
Standard Deviation	0.77	0.70	1.41
Total Responses	44	44	44

Qualitative data reported for the survey question,

"What is it that made you happy with your service experience?"

Text Response
Professionalism, simplicity
Well, I purchased a stand up to cancer bow tie last year for my boss. I think that there were a few glitches in your system because I wasn't sure when it was getting shipped. I had to call a couple of times. I really wanted him to get the tie too...he wears a tie everyday but only owns two bow ties. We did have to "youtube" how to tie the bow tie...it was a bit confusing...but, we got it. If you have any coupons, I could use one for a future purchase. Thank you very much, Sincerely, Maureen L. Wright   gmail: littlemo78@gmail.com
How easy it was to navigate throughout the website!
The website is visually pleasing and easy to navigate
Easy to use website
The website navigation and the experience of buying clothing and supporting a cause.
EVERYTHING
Everything
Very easy and straightforward process. Easy to find what you want and easily purchase it.
The website looks clean cut and professional. The presentation is very luring!
I liked the fluidity
I enjoyed the layout of the website and how visually appealing it was. Since I've never owned a bow-tie, it made it easy to figure out which one I wanted, especially the search bar and items related to whatever else I was purchasing. I would recommend this website to my friends and would come back on it to shop for some fancy bow-ties! :)
Everything is quick and responsive. Love the color pallet chosen for the website.
Autism speaks bow ties!
The accessibility and organization of the site
Everything was made very easy, informative, and understandable to the consumer.
the colors on the website were really cool. It kept my attention and caught my interest.
I was tied to the cause of the bow tie i purchased. I just wish it wasnt as expensive or more money went to the cause.
I have purchsed several ties as gits. I have never had any problems and service & delivery are excellent. Also, my son will only wear Dhani's Bowties for a cause.
Well put together website, good products, and supports something worthwhile.
the website looks really colorful and appealing, and is also easy to navigate
The overall format of the page was something different and that something caught my attention
Love the many options of ties offered, and love that I can support so many different philanthropic organizations when purchasing these items.
The items are of high quality and are delivered promptly. Also, they support a cause that I believe to be important.

Appendix I: Social Media presence before and after website relaunch

Logo

Facebook

Appendix I: Social Media presence before and after website relaunch (continued)

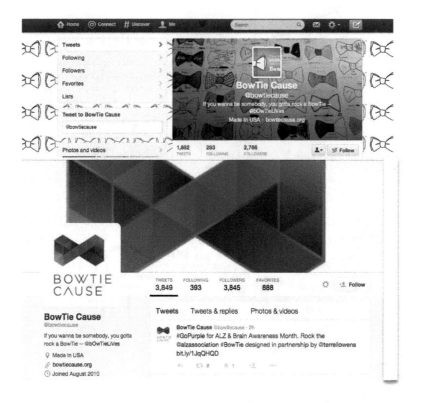

Twitter

Appendix J: BowTie Cause Ambassador Program

BowTies w/ Discount

Fit For:

▶ Local personalities / media
▶ Moderate social media following
▶ Example = News Anchors

BowTies Given @ cost, wholesale $44

Promotional Expectations

▶ Instagram #BowTieSelfie wearing BTC BowTie using Hashtag (#TiedToACause). Tag @BowTieCause.
▶ Twitter #BowTieSelfie wear BTC BowTie using Hashtag (#TiedToACause). Tag @BowTieCause.
▶ Twitter message about the reciept of BTC BowTies using Hashtag (#TiedToACause). Tag @BowTieCause.
▶ Facebook image post of BTC BowTie using Hashtag (#TiedToACause).

BowTies + Capital

Fit For:

▶ Highly visible personalities
▶ Social media following of 500,000+ (Twitter)
▶ Example = Justin Timberlake

BowTies Gratis + Capital

Promotional Expectations

▶ Instagram #BowTieSelfie wearing BTC BowTie using Hashtag (#TiedToACause). Tag @BowTieCause.
▶ Twitter #BowTieSelfie wear BTC BowTie using Hashtag (#TiedToACause). Tag @BowTieCause.
▶ Multiple Twitter messages about the reciept of BTC BowTies using Hashtag (#TiedToACause). Tag @BowTieCause.
▶ Facebook image post of BTC BowTie using Hashtag (#TiedToACause).
▶ Wear BTC BowTie to an event, appearance and provide image to BTC.

BowTies Gratis

Fit For:

▶ Well known, influential personalities
▶ High social media following
▶ Example = Ken Rosenthal

BowTies Gratis

Promotional Expectations

▶ Instagram #BowTieSelfie wearing BTC BowTie using Hashtag (#TiedToACause). Tag @BowTieCause.
▶ Twitter #BowTieSelfie wear BTC BowTie using Hashtag (#TiedToACause). Tag @BowTieCause.
▶ Multiple Twitter messages about the reciept of BTC BowTies using Hashtag (#TiedToACause). Tag @BowTieCause.
▶ Facebook image post of BTC BowTie using Hashtag (#TiedToACause).
▶ Wear BTC BowTie to an event, appearance and provide image to BTC.

*BrandCo: Development and Marketing of a Social Media Index

By

Christopher Polakowski, William Paterson University

Bela Florenthal, William Paterson University

*A fictitious name was used to protect the privacy of the company.

Introduction

BrandCo is a New York City-based branding firm that offers extensive services to major corporations to improve their visual, verbal, and marketplace identity. From logo redesign and brand engagement to verbal strategy and product naming, the company offers a variety of services that help shape its unique business model and identity—underpinned by passion and decades of training and education—in a variety of business sectors (consumer goods, financial services, and technology). As the business seeks to increase its market share and growth in existing and new industries, it seeks to diversify its services by entering into the social media analytics sector.

This case introduces a new service, a social media index that BrandCo has been developing for the grocery industry. It will help supermarket brands utilize their social media platforms more effectively, capture new customers, and establish a social voice that creates a positive online reputation. The new service evokes some serious questions and concerns, such as how to monetize this service, how to name it and develop a marketing campaign to attract leading grocery brands, how to expand this service and market it to other industries, and how to overcome the growing competition in this area.

COMPANY BACKGROUND

Mission and Structure

Located in New York City, BrandCo is a branding and social business intelligence firm that helps businesses solve complex branding and marketing problems through strategy, design, and digital services. The company is managed by TM and GP (the owners' names are not revealed to protect the privacy of the company). TM graduated from the University of Cambridge in England with an MA in Modern Languages and Social Psychology. After working with Interbrand in London and New York, he became Director of Verbal Branding at Landor Associates in New York. There he collaborated with major corporations including Delta Airlines, AT&T, Citibank and Ford Motor Company to implement branding programs. Additionally, he is a former adjunct professor of brand strategy for the MBA program at Georgetown University.

Similar to TM, GP has vast experience in working with small and large corporations. GP graduated from Duncan of Jordanstone College of Art in Dundee, Scotland. Later, he worked as the Creative Director for various companies around the world including Ogilvy and FutureBrand in New York and San Francisco. During his 10 years at FutureBrand, GP created the visual identities for globally recognized companies including MSN, Nissan, and Intel. With over 25 years of design experience, GP's resume extends far beyond these few companies to include numerous design projects for South African Airlines, AMD, GORE-TEX, Microsoft, the San Diego Zoo as well as many others. Currently, GP is the Creative Director of BrandCo, where he ensures that brand strategy is brought to life through compelling, distinctive design executions.

Customers, Products, and Services

From 2000 to present day, BrandCo has helped develop and strengthen numerous brands in the consumer goods, financial services, food & beverage, industrial, media, medical, non-profit, professional services, technology, telecom, and travel & tourism sectors. Clients include Avon, American Express, Starbucks, Caterpillar, Time Inc., Pfizer, NYFA, Dell, and Ensemble Travel. Table 1 summarizes some of the companies BrandCo has worked with, categorized by industry.

Table 1: Selection of Customers Categorized by Industry

Industry	Companies
CONSUMER GOODS	Amway, Avon, Brastilo, Crayola, GORE-TEX, Green Mountain Coffee, HEB, Johnson & Johnson, Procter & Gamble, Smith & Wesson, and Timberland
FINANCIAL SERVICES	American Express, Goldman Sachs, JPMorgan Chase, Legg Mason, Provident Bank, Wachovia, Wilmington Trust
FOOD & BEVERAGE	Bimbo Bakeries, Jelly Belly, Kraft Foods, Pinnacle Foods, Starbucks, and Stirrings
INDUSTRIAL	Caterpillar, Dow Agro, GE Fanuc, Maptek, Monsanto, Rohm & Haas, and Ward Leonard
MEDIA	BrandWeek, Cablevision, Hachette-Filipacchi, McGraw-Hill, Sony, Time, Inc., and Time Warner Cable
MEDICAL/PHARMA	Berlin-Chemie, Cegedim, Elsevier, Pfizer, Eli Lilly, Tapestry Pharmaceuticals, and TideWell Hospice
NON-PROFIT	AASHE, Adirondack Museum, Amnesty, International, Birthright Israel, Doris Duke Charitable Foundation, Human Rights First, JDC, NYFA, Rainforest Alliance, Union for Reform Judaism, and World Education Services

PROFESSIONAL SERVICES	AAA, Attention PR, Epstein Becker Green, and Reputation Institute
TECHNOLOGY	Dell, Dolby, GXS, IEEE, Innocentive, Intel Peer 1, Symbol Technologies, and Tizen
TELECOM	AT&T, Avaya, Nokia, Verizon, and XO Communications
TRAVEL & TOURISM	Ensemble Travel, Grand Bahama Island, Seaway Trail, Verdanza Hotel (Puerto Rico), Streamsong Resort (Florida), Sandpearl Resort (Florida), Remm Hotels (Japan), and National Tour Association

BrandCo's clients turn to the company for expertise in brand strategy, brand architecture and ingredient branding, research, identity and design, naming and messaging, digital strategy and implementation, and social business intelligence.

For instance, Dell, one of the industry's leading computer companies, approached BrandCo to develop a sub-brand name for its new line-up of LCD TVs. At the time, Dell was trying to enter into a new market segment and needed guidance to choose a name that adhered to its overall naming strategy. In response, BrandCo created a naming decision-tree, which helps identify the appropriate time to create a new name, use an existing name, or use general descriptive naming terms. By using this system, Dell saved millions of dollars, since it reduced the number of brand names it tracks regularly.

In addition, after splitting from Lucent as Avaya Telecommunications, Avaya approached BrandCo to create a brand strategy that communicates the new brand to consumers and businesses. BrandCo performed market research and devised a brand position concept that enforced "communications driven results." This facilitated the company in pinpointing its new corporate culture by renaming products and establishing a brand architecture that supports its new "go-to-market" strategy. The success of this implementation has not only improved Avaya performance, but also has aided it in surpassing its competition, Cisco, as the Voice over Internet Protocol (VoIP) leader in the industry.

SWOT ANALYSIS

Businesses operate in an environment that is comprised of many factors including competitors, the availability of resources, and types of consumers. These environmental forces impact how businesses market their products, attract new customers, and seek profits. Therefore, companies need to identify their strengths, weaknesses, opportunities, and threats to better match their internal processes to the external environmental forces.

Strengths

BrandCo offers numerous services that help companies from various industries develop their identity and image in the marketplace. Again, from logo redesign to social media analytics, the company takes an innovative approach to brand and rebrand businesses. The company's talented personnel, reputation, and its history of working with a large number of companies across various industries facilitate business growth. With a lineage of success from its dealings with major corporations including American Express, Sony, and Kraft Foods, the company has an esteemed reputation for delivering quality service to its clients. These services are a product of the company's highly professional personnel, who reap success regardless of the size of business or nature of the project.

Besides its existing services, BrandCo purchased a license of specialized software that provides social media analytics to expand its services to existing customers and attract new segments. While the company has tagged and analyzed social media data on past projects, this acquisition offers clients a sophisticated analysis of their social media usage and another method to redevelop their brand strategy.

Weaknesses

Unlike many younger companies, BrandCo has worked with a variety of notable clients to achieve success in a short time. While its reputation and résumé are impressive, the company is still developing and assimilating into the marketplace. As a small company with only two key players, talent and workload are limited to the availability of its personnel. Thus, new projects may be put on hold or refused due to limited personnel, time restraints, and tight budgets. Additionally, since the company is part of an emerging industry, the brand is still widely unknown. Companies may only become familiar with BrandCo if they are looking for branding services, such as website redesign or social media analytics. Thus, acquiring new projects or clients may be arduous for a company with limited brand awareness in a niche market.

Opportunities

Over the past seven years, Internet users of social media have increased by 65% (PewResearch, 2014). This means that as of September 2013, approximately 73% of Internet users had active social media accounts on various platforms (Bullas, 2014). According to the Pew Internet Research of social media in 2004, Facebook users reached 71% followed by 22% of LinkedIn users, 21% of Pinterest users, and 18% Twitter users (PewResearch, 2014). These social media platforms cater to the wants and needs of all users: men and women of all ages located in various places around the world with different household incomes, races/ethnicities, and educational backgrounds (PewResearch, 2014).

In another study performed by CeBIT, researchers found that "…47% of Americans say Facebook is their #1 influencer in purchasing" goods and services (Bullas, 2014, p. 1). Additionally, "71% of customers that receive a quick brand response on social media are likely to refer that brand to others" (Bennett, 2014, p. 1). This study also found that 81% of consumers are influences by their friends' posts on social media when making purchasing decisions (Bennett, 2014). Due to the rise in social media usage by consumers as well as the reliance on peers for purchase decisions, some companies have created social media accounts to increase their engagement and interaction with existing and potential customers.

In May 2013, Michael A. Stelzner issued his 2013 *Social Media Marketing Industry Report: How Marketers Are Using Social Media to Grow Their Businesses*, which surveyed 3000 marketers from various businesses around the world. According to his findings, approximately 97% of businesses utilize social media to market their business. (Stelzner, 2013). He asserts that by incorporating social media, these businesses have increased their brand exposure and website traffic, developed new business relations and a larger customer base, and improved business operations and sales revenue. Additionally, the author mentions that of the 97% who utilize social media, 86% believe that social media is important to their business.

While these results indicate an overwhelming majority of businesses utilizing various social media platforms, only 26% agree that they understand how to measure their effectiveness (Stelzner, 2013). When these companies were asked, "I am able to measure the return on investment for my social media activities," 36% were uncertain about their effectiveness, 28% disagreed, and another 10% strongly disagreed (Stelzner, 2013). These results demonstrate that while the social media is being employed, its effectiveness, reach, and benefits are not being measured properly.

Thus, businesses need social media training and advice on posting content on various social media platforms to engage customers. Additionally, analytic software is needed to measure the effects of implementing these changes. In turn, businesses require customer engagement, monitoring of interaction and activity, tracking of a large volume of posts, and an understanding of the emotion of these posts. Ultimately, measuring these attributes and then developing a strategy to improve their overall position is a necessity.

These emerging needs offer BrandCo an opportunity to add social media related services to its line-up. With its license acquisition of social media software, there is an opportunity of growth in this emerging market. These services are indispensable to not only established businesses looking to redevelop the social identity of their brands, but also to emerging businesses who want to enter into a new social media market.

Threats

The biggest threat to BrandCo is competition. Since it operates in an emerging industry, competition will only intensify as the need for social media analytics becomes widespread. Besides the threat of increased competition, the cost to develop and purchase newer and more sophisticated analytical tools also poses a threat. For many businesses, the cost of research and development is immense. In 2013, Twitter spent approximately 52% of its revenue on research and development. (Gandel, 2013). Other social media companies and corporations also spend a significant portion of their revenues on research and development including Google and Facebook at 15% and 14%, respectively. For BrandCo, the cost to acquire new analytical software and monitoring tools may impede its growth. While the use of these newer technological advancements may improve the measurement of social media effectiveness, it also comes with a price tag.

Since BrandCo is a third-party branding service, the cost may outweigh the benefit of outsourcing social media analytics and other social media related services for large and even smaller companies. These brands may then develop their own software or hire their own personnel who are trained to perform similar services. This means that BrandCo may lose its competitive advantage, as it could be replaced with in-house services especially as its clients can purchase/license the same or similar software package that the company uses.

SOCIAL MEDIA BACKGROUND

Background

Recently, BrandCo decided to develop a social media index that measures supermarkets' customer engagement, interaction, and social presence. The Company decided to focus on supermarkets to pilot the social media index and develop proof of concept. After analyzing the supermarket industry's social media usage, BrandCo was able to identity how social media was underutilized by each supermarket brand.

While some supermarkets had created accounts on Facebook, Twitter, Instagram, Pinterest, and other social media platforms, other brands had yet to create any social media accounts. In addition, even for those supermarket brands that had an account on different platforms, the company's research revealed that these accounts were being utilized ineffectively. This could have been due to a lack of social media expertise in posting engaging content.

From these findings, the company initiated development of a social media index to satisfy the need for measurement of social media effectiveness for supermarket brands. Monetizing this new service and complementary services (e.g., consulting) to grocery and other industries would help foster the company's continuous growth.

Most importantly, the company's latest and most innovative service, the social media index, would become crucial to improving business's marketing tactics. While the index had many competitors, its features and scoring formula were unique and innovative. By scoring engagement, interaction, activity, net sentiment, emotion, and sponsored presence rather than searchability and connections, it would help supermarkets drastically improve their social media effective usage. Later, the service could potentially be redesigned to fit the needs of other markets, such as financial institutions, real estate agencies, fashion brands, bloggers, authors, and celebrities. Thus, the growth opportunities for this product were endless.

Trends in the Supermarket Industry

Over the past 30 years, the supermarket industry has undergone industry-wide changes due to intense competition and improvements in technology. Today, grocery stores operate in an environment where consumers are more technology literate, environmentally concerned, and educated in regards to food safety, government regulation, and nutrition. Thus, it has become imperative for companies to uphold a business model that allows for swift action and response to consumer demands. As more businesses utilize new technology and combat heightened competition, the need for brand and product differentiation must be satisfied for survival in the marketplace. While some companies have been able to capitalize on these industry changes, others have faltered due to sluggish adaptation.

In a capitalistic economy, competition perpetuates business rivalry, fair trade, quality of goods and services, and reasonable prices. It prevents businesses from monopolizing the market and minimizes profit hoarding from large grocery conglomerates. In turn, this fosters an environment where large and small supermarkets can obtain a portion of the market share. Since capitalism and competition encourage product variety and new entrants into the marketplace, supermarkets are constantly striving to retain old customers and attract new ones. Thus, in an industry with over 65,000 local and national supermarket brands including Whole Foods, Pathmark, and Albertsons, brand awareness, product differentiation, and customer loyalty become essential to financial success.

Moreover, competition has made grocery stores liable for responding to customer demands. With a variety of businesses, consumers have many alternatives if one supermarket does not fulfill their wants and needs. Local and national supermarkets must use customer-buying behaviors to capture that segment of the market and increase their profit share. A failure to respond could be the difference between business growth and bankruptcy.

From the digitalization of inventory control, product scanning, and distribution to new methods of advertising and marketing, technology has also revolutionized industry practices. These internal-technological innovations have been responsible for the growth of many grocery chains and local stores by increasing sales, brand awareness, and profits. Technology has not only improved these internal operations, but has also modernized external communication networks. As a product of technology, social media has created the need for corporations to engage and interact with customers.

Today, 78% of online adults use social media daily (PewResearch, 2013). This means that every day, users are posting, liking, sharing, tweeting, pinning, and commenting on statuses and photos by businesses and their peers. Therefore, these social media platforms give businesses crucial insights into the lives of their customers as well as a cheap and effect way to market, engage, and interact. Facebook, Instagram, Twitter, Pinterest, among other platforms and various blogs are powerful tools that can be utilized by supermarkets to foster brand awareness, discuss company news, and interact with customers. While the benefits of using social media may be obvious, implementation into marketing strategies has been slow due to a variety of factors including a lack of expertise regarding social media usage as well as time and monetary limitations.

In 2014, Ennes conducted a study to measure the effect of social media on companies. After surveying 2,100 companies in various industries, researchers found that of the 79% that utilized or planned to utilize social media, only 12% of them used it effectively. This means that effective companies utilized social media for more than mere brand recognition; they also monitored consumer behavior and developed new products according to Ennes, 2014. The author also uncovered that two-thirds of the 2,100 companies analyzed "had no formalized social media strategy and just 7% had integrated social media into their overall marketing strategy." (Ennes, 2014). Additionally, 61% of companies stated that the reason social media had not been incorporated into their marketing strategy was due to a lack of knowledge regarding effective implementation (Ennes, 2014).

Overall, companies that utilized social media reaped the benefits of engaging consumers across the different social media channels. HBR's survey findings proved that companies that incorporated social media into their marketing strategy increased brand awareness and product recognition by 50%, increased consumer perceptions by 30%, and fostered new business 11% better. (Ennes, 2014).

Development of the Social Media Index

As Ennes (2014) mentions, a large percentage of supermarkets underutilize or do not use social media. While proper education and training may be necessary to increase its usage, a social media index will help supermarket brands understand how it will benefit them. In particular, BrandCo's social media index provides supermarket brands with a breakdown of their current social media usage across specific categories. The company identified 19 categories after analyzing the social media content of five supermarket brands, Whole Foods, Kroger, Pathmark, Albertsons, and Stop & Shop, for one month.

Posts were tagged and categorized into their corresponding social media platform in accordance with a specific dimension. The following 19 categories were found to be the most frequent, reoccurring themes among the five companies:

Community Outreach

Prepared Foods

Recipes

YouTube Links

Product Recalls

Contests/Promotions

Gifts/Entertainment

News Commentaries

Happy_Day

Product Promotion

Kitten/Questions

Private Labels

Health and Wellness

In-Store Experience

Product Buying Guide

Beauty Tips

Coupons

Corporate Brand News

Food Knowledge

To provide a detailed and customized analysis, research was then conducted to determine which social media platforms are most instrumental for the grocery industry. Studies and academic articles involving social media behavior and consumer buying habits were analyzed to determine the top seven most influential social media platforms for supermarkets especially for the identified categories. These articles provided detailed descriptions, statistical evidence, and trends in social media behavior that were used to populate the potential list of platforms to be analyzed.

It was found that Facebook, Twitter, Instagram, Pinterest, blogs, Google+, and YouTube are among the most powerful, useful, insightful, and helpful social media platforms for supermarket brands. Moreover, these platforms could be utilized efficiently for specific grocery categories. The table below provides a summary of why the social media platforms were chosen for the social media index and for which categories they can be employed most effectively:

Table 2: Effective Use of Grocery Categories across Social Media Channels

Social Media Channel	Relevant Grocery Categories
Pinterest (the artist)	
• 3rd largest/ most popular SM network worldwide	Recipes
• 3 of 4 women use Pinterest for new recipes – inspiration for new recipes	Brand Awareness Community Outreach
• Sheds light on community efforts.	Online Promotion
Twitter (the buzz generator)	
• 78% of shoppers expect their brand to have Twitter	Customer service Online Promotion
• Useful for corporate feedback	Community Outreach
• Improvements in local store operations	Shopping Experience
Facebook (the superpower)	
• 1.23 Billion users	All dimensions
• "Like pages" are crucial to brand awareness and interaction	

Instagram (the trendsetter)

- Pictures are the newest and trendiest form of interaction
- Grocery stores can post links to articles, pictures, and websites
- Generates brand awareness and promotes interaction.
- 150 million active monthly users

Prepared Foods

Product Recommendations

Community Outreach

Google+ (the search optimizer)

- Studies suggest it will make a huge impact in the coming years
- Promotes "Social ads"—indicated by the (+1s) in the corner
- Great marketing tactics—engagement

Online Promotion

Shopping Experience

Community Outreach

YouTube (the story teller)

- "How-to" videos
- Community and local commercials and interviews
- Campaigns

Community Outreach

Prepared Foods

Blogs/News Websites (the reporter)

- Social media indexes include blogging websites.
- **Ex:** Buzzfeed, StumbleUpon, Digg
- Gaining popularity and social involvement

Product Recommendations

Community Outreach

The goal of the social media index is to provide users with an overview of their social media accounts' activity including which accounts are active, the amount of likes, shares, and feedback they receive per post per platform, and which categories lack engagement. Most importantly, the index will compare the client's social media usage to the total market's social media usage. This will help clients understand their social impact compared to other brands. The following gives an in-depth, step-by-step overview of the social media index formula used.

Social Media Index Formula

BrandCo has been evaluating several mathematical formulas to devise the most effective social media index. One formula they were considering is illustrated in this case to provide a tangible example of how a social media index can be utilized. This mathematical formula calculates an overall social media score to depict a supermarket brand's influence over the supermarket industry. It accounts for volume, net sentiment, positive sentiments, and sponsored presence. Table 3 explains what each component represents. For each category, the formula below is used:

D_{1-19} = *Sponsored Presence (75% Volume [20% Net Sentiment + 5% Positive Sentiments])*

Table 3: Formula Components

Component	Description
Volume	The number of posts across social medial platforms within each category
Net Sentiment	By adding positive and neutral comments and subtracting negative comments, the amount of net sentiment is derived.
Positive Sentiments	The number of positive posts
Sponsored Presence	This is a coefficient that is calculated by dividing *total volume of brand's social media posts for a single category* by *total volume*

of industry posts for a single category. This indicates the brand's
market share for a single category in a specific industry.

The following steps explain how to derive the social media score (index) for a
specific brand.

1. A selection and analysis of the most popular and relevant social media platforms
   is conducted. As stated in Table 2, the seven social medial platforms that are
   most relevant to the grocery industry are Facebook, Twitter, Instagram, Google+,
   YouTube, blogs, and Pinterest.
2. Key information, such as posts, likes, shares, and comments, are retrieved,
   tagged, and placed into one of 19 grocery-specific categories that were identified
   by the company.
3. These posts are then coded according to the type of sentiment they convey:
   positive, neutral, or negative. Once the posts are coded, they are counted and
   placed in the mathematical formula that is presented above.
4. The final score (index) represents the company's overall social engagement and
   interaction for a specific category.
5. To identify how the brand's category score is compared to its market/industry,
   the brand's category score is divided by the total market's category score. Once
   scores for all 19 categories are calculated, they can be summed and divided by
   the total market score for all categories.

This is the social media index for the brand, which is combined across all relevant social
media platforms and content-driven categories. This index represents not only engagement
and interaction, but also volume in comparison to the market and competitors, consumer
sentiments, and their contribution to the overall market. To clarify the process of deriving the
social media index, an illustration is presented in Appendix A.

Comparison of Social Media Index across Brands

Table 4 represents a real-life example using four major supermarket brands (Pathmark, Whole Foods, Stop & Shop, and Albertsons). The table below shows the score of each brand for each of the 19 categories and the total score for each brand. The table demonstrates how each brand is compared to its competitors. The total percentage (index) has taken each brand's total score across all categories and divided it by the sum of the total score of the industry, which in this case is 20,663.34. The result is a decimal number, which is converted into a percentage to obtain the final social media index. This number signifies a brand's social influence in the marketplace: the higher the score (closer to 100%), the more influence a brand has in terms of social media in its industry.

Table 4: Comparison of Social Media Index across Brands

Categories	Albertson Scores	Pathmark Scores	Whole Foods Scores	Stop & Shop Scores
1. Prepared Foods	582.47	0.01	-	-
2. YouTube Link	340.34	-	-	-
3. Recipes & Crafts	35.74	0.01	3984.59	280.73
4. News	696.20	0.15	2.27	-
5. Product Recalls	586.95	-	-	-
6. Contests/Promotions	3360.49	0.04	87.91	-
7. Happy ___ Day	450.35	8.46	-	52.34
8. Kitten/Questions	579.66	1.97	260.05	98.70
9. Product Promotions	2.09	6.08	58.56	10.316
10. Brand News	73.62	-	5824.80	-
11. Gifts/Entertainment	273.94	-	0.05	-
12. Private Labels	449.87	0.25	-	-
13. Coupons	-	5.45	1497.44	-
14. Beauty	-	18.20	-	-
15. Health/Wellness	-	2.62	54.47	-
16. In-store Experience	-	1.60	-	65.33
17. Buying Guide	-	0.30	312.46	-
18. Food Knowledge	-	-	370.37	-
19. Community Outreach	-	-	207.68	18.42
Total Score	**7431.72**	**45.13**	**12660.66**	**525.84**
Total Percentage (Index)	**35.97%**	**0.22%**	**61.27%**	**2.54%**

Table 4 illustrates how brands can be compared within categories of importance and overall performance across the most crucial social media platforms. When comparing the four brands, it is evident that Pathmark is the weakest among them in terms of engagement and interaction on social media platforms, while Whole Foods is the strongest. Still, Whole Foods can learn from this table that it can improve in YouTube links and holiday related

61

posts/engagements, for instance. Thus, this index gives companies more specific content-related information than more traditional analysis of volume or sentiments on various social medial platforms. With this social media index, brands can tailor their content to issues (categories) that are important to their customers, compare themselves to competitors on these issues, and improve their content-specific performance.

COMPETITORS

Since social media is still developing but has a proven and direct effect on businesses, social media indexing services have become more popular and influential. While there are many free, online websites that offer individuals and companies a "social score," they do not accurately portray social influence. Each online website develops undisclosed and usually patented algorithms to calculate a score based on the social media platforms used and the number of hits from specific keywords in search engines that pertain to a specific brand. While they do measure the volume of posts, they do not measure engagement, interaction, net sentiment, or even specific categories. Thus, it becomes difficult to interpret the score, especially from a business owner's or a marketer's perspective. Besides these online websites, there are three main competitors of BrandCo's social media index: Klout, P2 Digital, and Kred.

Klout

Klout is a free social media index that renders an accumulation score between 1 and 100 to registered users (businesses and individuals) by examining approximately 400 data points. Similar to the free, online websites, Klout also uses different keywords from search engines' populations to determine social influence. While this method measures searchability, it does not measure emotion, interaction, or the ability to connect across all social platforms and dimensions. Additionally, Klout uses a formula that places the most significance on having high-profile connections, friends and followers. Thus, the overall score becomes a measure of personal connection, rather than social influence. However, in response to business demands, Klout has begun developing Klout for Business to help businesses gauge their

social media effectiveness using specific social media platforms. The standard Klout and
Klout for Business both measure the following social media platforms: Facebook, Twitter,
Instagram, LinkedIn, Foursquare, Wikipedia, Google+, and Bing. The following table shows
the Klout scores for the leading supermarket brands:

Table 5: Klout Scores for Supermarket Brands

Supermarket Brand	Klout Score (total)
Whole Foods	87
Trader Joe's	69
Fairway	55
Pathmark	51
Albertsons	29

While Klout has 'clout' in the social index market and even has a positive reputation by its
users, the score caters to individuals, not businesses. Ennes (2014) argues that businesses
need to understand the impact of social media posts on their consumers, how to utilize social
media channels effectively, and which posts will enhance business-to-consumer relations.
Thus, using a score that emphasizes personal connections is not designed to improve
marketability for businesses, but instead is used to measure social influence for individuals.
Klout for Business may be a better competitor, but until product details are released the Klout
score is not the most reliable solution.

L2 Digital

Besides Klout, L2 Digital is another competing social media index that utilizes a standard IQ
scale as a way to gauge social media effectiveness: the higher the IQ, the more socially
effective the organization's social media strategy is. While Klout examines 400 data points
across nine social media platforms, L2 Digital examines over 650 data points across
Facebook, Twitter, Instagram, Google+, YouTube, Pinterest, and Tumblr. Despite analyzing
two fewer social media platforms, L2 Digital chose the seven platforms that are more
prevalent for businesses, especially supermarket brands. Platforms, such as Wikipedia,
Foursquare, and Bing, are not as important for businesses as they are for individuals using

the software. Thus far, social media analytics have been compiled for various industries, but little to no analysis has been performed for the supermarket industries.

Kred

Similar to Klout, Kred is a social media index that utilizes real-time streaming from social media platforms to populate their data engines and render a score. Unlike its competitors, the index renders two scores, one for social influence and one for outreach, from an analysis of Facebook and Twitter usage. According to Kred, both scores reflect trust and generosity, which are two essential components of relationship development. The first score, Influence, is measured on a 1,000-point scale by analyzing the frequency of posts, comments, likes, shares, mentions, tweets, retweets, and replies. The score rendered describes a user's ability to inspire action. The second score, Outreach, is measured on a 10-point scale (currently, but subject to change due to increasing usage of social media) by examining the interactions created by users' posts. This score illustrates a person's engagement with followers and friends on Facebook and Twitter.

Table 6: Key Differences across Three Social Index Competitors

Name	Klout	L2 Digital	Kred
Data	400 data points	650 data points	-
Social Media			
Facebook	+	+	+
Twitter	+	+	+
Instagram	+	+	-
LinkedIn	+	-	-
Foursquare	+	-	-
Wikipedia	+	-	-
Google+	+	-	-
Bing	+	-	-
Klout	+	-	-
YouTube	-	+	-
Pinterest	-	+	-
Tumblr	-	+	-
Measures outreach	-	-	+
Scoring	100-point scale	IQ scale: Genius: 140+ Gifted: 110-139 Average: 90-109 Challenged: 70–89 Feeble <70	Influence: 1000-point scale Outreach: 10-point scale

While competition is fierce amongst these companies, the social media indexes do not actually meet the needs for supermarkets. These indexes render scores that either measure individual connection or are difficult to interpret. Supermarket management needs an index that will help them understand their current social media habits, see where improvements can be made, and build their customer interaction and engagement. Thus, BrandCo's idea to create a social media index for supermarkets was born. Unlike its competitors, BrandCo's social media index responds to the needs of the market, or in this case, the needs of supermarkets.

The biggest advantage of BrandCo's social media index is its versatility. Since the formula considers four main factors that can be quantified and is consistent over each category to obtain the final score, it can be easily manipulated to obtain different statistics if necessary. For instance, if a client wishes to scrutinize all platforms except Twitter posts, the formula allows for this manipulation. Moreover, it is equally feasible for clients to request scores for specific categories, such as recipes, community outreach, food knowledge, brand awareness, and beauty, to compare with competitors. Unlike other social media indexes, the company index is versatile and addresses the issues concerning customer engagement, interaction, volume of posts, customer emotion, and effectiveness. This index is designed to help businesses edge out their competitors in the social media arena.

As BrandCo develops its social media index, it faces two major concerns: (1) how can they monetize this service? Most competitors offer their index information for free; and (2) how to develop and implement an integrated marketing communications strategy to establish itself as reliable and recognized brand in the social media indexing space? Before the product can be offered to supermarket brands, the following questions must be answered and resolved to ensure longevity in the marketplace:

1. What name should the product be given? What are the best methods to market and advertise the index? How do you gain customer attention, interest, and trust through an integrated marketing communications (IMC) plan? Propose an IMC plan and relate it to the attention, interest, desire, and action (AIDA) model.

2. How does the company gain customer trust and enhance brand equity for its new product?

3. What other products/services can be derived, and what other industries and companies
    can be targeted? What pricing strategy and tactics should be employed? How do the
    pricing strategy and tactics relate to the IMC plan you proposed earlier?

References

Bennett, S. (2014, April 25). Social media business statistics, facts, figures & trends 2014
    [Infographic]. Retrieved from http://www.mediabistro.com/alltwitter/social-business-
    trends-2014_b56645

Bullas, J. (n.d.). 22 Social media facts and statistics you should know in 2014 [Jeff Bullas
    Blog RSS]. Retrieved from http://www.jeffbullas.com/2014/01/17/20-social-media-
    facts-and-statistics-you-should-know-in-2014/

Ennes, M. (2014). Social media: What most companies don't know. Harvard Business
    Review, .

Gandel, S. (2013, October 25). Why is Twitter spending so much on R&D? *CNNMoney.*
    Retrieved from http://finance.fortune.cnn.com/2013/10/25/twitter- research-
    development/

PewResearch. (n.d.). Social networking fact sheet. *Pew Research Centers Internet American
    Life Project RSS.* Retrieved from   http://www.pewinternet.org/fact-sheets/social-
    networking-fact-sheet/

Newman, D. (2014, May 5). 6 reasons social media is your secret weapon in customer
    service. *Entrepreneur.* Retrieved from http://www.entrepreneur.com/article/2336

Social networking fact sheet. (2013). *Pew Research Centers Internet American Life Project
    RSS.* PewResearch. Retrieved from

Stelzner, M. (n.d.). Social media marketing industry report 2013. *Social Media Examiner.*
    Retrieved from http://www.socialmediaexaminer.com/Soci

Appendix A

Social Media Score for One Category and One Brand: An Illustration

Category Formula:

D_{1-19} = *Sponsored Presence (75% Volume [20% Net Sentiment + 5% Positive emotions])*

Step 1: Calculating Category Volume (75%)

Table A-1 represents the number of posts that appeared on 7 key social media platforms mentioning information related to recipes (a specific category) for Supermarket A. This information is provided after all social media posts had been analyzed, tagged, and categorized across the seven platforms (Facebook, Twitter, Instagram, Pinterest, Google+, YouTube, and blogs).

Table A-1: Number of Posts per Social Media Platform:

Social Media Platform	Number of Posts for Recipes
Instagram	500
Pinterest	2500
Facebook	10,000
Twitter	2,000
Google+	100
YouTube	5000
Blogs	100
Total	**20,200**

The total number of posts which is 20,200 represents the *total volume*. This number will be used in the "Category Formula," which is the same across all categories.

After finding the *volume* (20,200), the number is multiplied by 75% (see formula above). This number represents the total volume for the recipe category (20,200 x .75 = **15,150**).

Step 2: Calculating Net Sentiment (20%)

In this step, the 75% of the posts' *volume* has been classified into three types of sentiment, positive, negative, and neutral (Table A-2).

Table A-2: Breakdown of 75% of Volume into Sentiment Types

75% of Volume	Type of Sentiment
15,150	Positive: 8,292
	Negative: 4,744
	Neutral: 2,114

The numbers in Table A-2 are used in the category formula [*(Positive + Neutral – Negative = X) x 20%*]:

$$8,292 + 2,114 - 4,744 = 5,662 \text{ x } 20\% = \textbf{1,132}$$

The value 1,132 represents the category's net sentiment.

Step 3: Calculating Positive Sentiment (5%)

The category formula requires multiplying the value positive sentiment by 5%:

$$8,292 \text{ x } 5\% = \textbf{415}$$

This helps balance the error gap between a mischaracterization of a neutral comment.

Thus far, the recipe category formula has the following information:

Table A-3: Values and Percentages of Each Formula Component

Component	Value	% in Formula
Volume	15,150	75
Net Sentiment	1,132	20
Positive Sentiments	415	5
Total	**16,697**	**100**

Step 4: Calculating Sponsored Presence (Coefficient)

In Step 4, sponsored presence is determined, which answers how prevalent the company is in the analyzed recipe category across all seven social media platforms compared to the entire industry.

The following formula is used to come up with this Sponsored Presence Coefficient:

$$\frac{\textit{Total Volume for Single Dimension about Company}}{\textit{Total Volume for Single Dimension made by the entire industry}} = \textit{Percentage}$$

Or

$\frac{20,200 \text{ (see Step 1)}}{38,562 \text{ (fictional number)}}$ = **.5238 or about 52.38%** (This is based on a 100% scale)

This number represents the company's total percentage of the market share in a single category compared to the entire industry. In this case, the company holds 52% of the market share of recipes on seven social media platforms, which means that 48%, the remainder, is held by its competitors within the industry.

Step 5: Calculating Category Score

To find the category score, the category formula is used. The total number from Step 3 in Table A-3 (16,697) is multiplied by its sponsored presence rate of 0.5238 calculated in Step 4. Thus, the category score is

$$16,697 \times 0.5238 = \textbf{8745.88.}$$

The value 8745.88 is the score for the recipes category only.

Step 6: Calculating Total Score

Suppose that this process was repeated another 18 times to render scores for all categories. The following is a chart that depicts these findings:

Table A-4: Scores per Category and Total for All Categories

Category	Score
Recipes	8746
YouTube Link	6835
Prepared Foods	4332
Product Recall	975
Contest/ Promo	122
Gifts/ Entertainment	0
News Commentary	0
Happy _____ Day	0
Product Promo	6343
Kitten/Question	11,003
Private Label	588
Health and Wellness	2,068
In-store Experience	91
Product Buying Guide	1232

Community Outreach	0
Beauty Tips	0
Coupon	0
Corporate brand news	0
Food Knowledge	5,039
Total Score for All Categories	**47,374**

The value 47,374 is the total score of all the categories using the same category formula. A category with a zero value indicates that the company was not active in that category and indicates a new area in which to explore or improve.

To find the total score, the following formula should be used:

$$\frac{\textit{Total of Company's Dimension Scores}}{\textit{Total of all Competitors total dimension scores}} = \textit{Total Score}$$

Or

$$\frac{47,374}{82,093} = \textbf{0.577 or 57.7\% = Total Score.}$$

This signifies that across all 19 categories and seven social media platforms, this company holds 57.7% of the total market share compared to its industry counterparts.

Five Points Housing:
Digital/Direct Marketing Strategies in the Not-For-Profit Sector

By

Kathleen S. Micken, Roger Williams University

Background/History

Five Points Housing had its beginning in the 1960s, when religious institutions united to provide housing for local families who found themselves without a place to live. The grass-roots initiative was successful for a while. By the mid-1980s, however, the parties involved realized that volunteer efforts could not sustain the programs. With a federal Department of Housing and Urban Development grant as seed money, Five Points Housing was born. The name was derived from the five religious organizations that began the work.

Over the years the organization had served the local area through a number of housing initiatives – from providing transitional housing to families to a menu of services designed to help stabilize families so that they could become self-sufficient. In the last year, Five Points helped 150 families avert homelessness through emergency rental assistance funds. An additional 25 families were provided transitional housing (up to two years) and support services. A further 50 families with children with lead poisoning received lead prevention services. Nevertheless, the director and staff jokingly referred to Five Points as the area's "best kept secret."

Other housing organizations had a higher public profile and were better known. Most provided short-term emergency assistance to the homeless. Thus, when a natural disaster occurred, these were the organizations that got the press coverage. Once the maximum time period for providing shelter had passed, it was Five Points that helped families find long-term solutions to their homeless situation. So it was doubly ironic that more people did not know about – and, hence did not support – Five Points Housing.

Five Points is a 501(c)(3) organization, meaning that it is a not-for-profit charitable entity, exempt from federal and state taxes. Initially its budget was comprised almost entirely of federal and state grants. Over the years, however, that funding had decreased, as the federal government cut back on some of its programs. The organization was faced with a $100,000 shortfall. Five Points had made a conscious effort to increase its fundraising efforts in the local community, but had been less successful than it would like.

Reflecting its early ties to religious institutions, Five Points' natural donor constituency was primarily individuals who were fiercely interested in housing justice, but who themselves did not have access to large financial resources. Additionally, the recent decline in the housing market coupled with corporate layoffs had meant that demand for housing services had increased while Five Points' donors had fewer discretionary funds. These economic realities meant that the organization had a minimal budget for marketing and communication.

Five Points was distinguished not only by the housing it provided, but also by the services ("case management") it offered. The organization's mantra was "a hand up and not a hand out." Families in "transitional housing" also received employment and financial counseling to help them get back on their feet, so that the families could become independent contributing members of the community. Another distinguishing feature of the Five Points program was the criterion that at least one person in the family must be employed. This holistic approach to building a foundation for long-term stability has meant that over 85 percent of families that successfully graduated from transitional housing have moved on to stable, independent living.

Five Point's guiding principles were somewhat in contrast to the "Housing First" initiatives that were being promoted both locally and nationally (National Alliance 2015). While the organization's leaders agreed with the emphasis on getting homeless individuals into housing quickly, they believed that the lack of mandated counseling or services was misguided.

Beverly Walker, Five Points Housing's director, explained the difference of opinion this way, "You can't just throw money and a little case management at people and expect success. People don't learn new habits in three-to-six months. Successful outcomes require a longer transition period."

The Marketing Problem

Beverly knew that she needed to address the dual goals of increasing awareness and increasing donations. Her background had prepared her well to help the organization take this next step. She had worked in the not-for-profit sector for more than 20 years, both as a volunteer and in administrative roles. Additionally, her early careers as a legislative research analyst and as a real estate agent had given her insight into the forces driving housing availability and she was able to negotiate well between the private and public sectors. When she was a real estate agent, Beverly had the time to volunteer with Red Cross Disaster Services. In working with families that had lost their homes to fires, floods and hurricanes, she gained a first-hand understanding that the root of homelessness for many people was not under their control. Rather homelessness was something that could happen to anyone.

Beverly knew that the first steps would be to gather data about Five Points Housing's current image and to identify alternative messages that would help the organization tell its story. She contacted a local college for research assistance. Marketing students designed and fielded two surveys and presented the results to Beverly and the Board. Survey data are incorporated in the discussions below.

Competition

It may seem strange to address *competition* in the context of a not-for-profit organization, but competition for donors' attention and funding is very real. While a number of organizations worked with the homeless population in the state, five organizations focused on providing support to the homeless. Three other organizations had a broader advocacy mission and were not direct competitors. A brief summary of each of the four competitor organizations is presented in Exhibit One. To preserve anonymity, the organizations are simply identified by a letter.

Exhibit One

Organizations Focused on Providing Services to the Homeless

Summary Information

Organization	Organizational Focus	Promotional Strengths
Organization A	Short-term shelters; educational and vocational programs; medical and dental care programs	Well established fundraising efforts; website facilitates donations; advertising on TV and billboards. Uses success stories featuring real clients. Visible partnerships with corporations and sponsors.
Organization B	Provides direct services to the homeless and the poor. Conducts a social enterprise as a way to provide job training and experience for clients.	
Organization C	Provides meals and temporary shelter.	A few yearly events to raise funds. Partnership with religious organizations.
Organization D	Services to the homeless are oriented toward mental health and addiction issues. Also offers housing and legal services, as well as education, and job training through partnerships with other organizations.	Primarily public relations with strong news media coverage. Use of success stories featuring real clients.

The research conducted by the students addressed the competition issue. A survey of community members, who had no specific association with Five Points, asked about familiarity with these local organizations. Five Points was in the middle, being less well known than two organizations, but being better known than two others, as illustrated in Exhibit Two. This information offered some reason for hope, but also demonstrated that Five Points had a ways to go in getting the word out to the donor community.

Exhibit Two

Community Awareness of Organizations Serving the Homeless

Survey Results

Organization	I Know Something about this Organization
Organization A	93%
Organization B	74%
Five Points	65%
Organization D	56%
Organization C	24%

Survey respondents who did know something about Five Points were asked to identify what set it apart from other organizations in their minds. A significant number reported, "I am not sure," or "I don't know." When a specific response was provided, these four characteristics were mentioned most often.

- Five Points has a dedicated staff and board.

- Five Points is one of the few organizations to provide longer-term housing support.

- Five Points has a good success rate because it couples the housing with other services.

- Five Points focuses on families, not individuals

In addition to these survey responses, the students provided Beverly with a perceptual map illustrating the differences between Five Points and the other four organizations. Exhibit Three presents that information.

Exhibit Three
Competitive Analysis

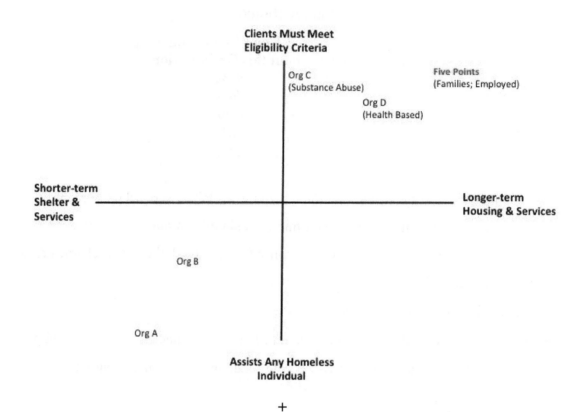

Clients Must Meet Eligibility Criteria

Org C (Substance Abuse)

Five Points (Families; Employed)

Org D (Health Based)

Shorter-term Shelter & Services

Longer-term Housing & Services

Org B

Org A

Assists Any Homeless Individual

+

Donor Relationships and Fundraising Activities

Most fundraising activities centered on activities that involve the community as a way to raise Five Points' public profile while also raising money: bike-a-thons, 5k races, walk-a-thons, and the like. An annual dinner accompanied by a silent auction of items donated by local businesses, however, was the most successful fundraiser. The dinner provided a way to recognize the hard work of the staff, the board, and to recognize donors and supporters. Nevertheless, every organization seemed to organize events such as these, so that over the years the ones sponsored by Five Points had seen declining attendance and a declining return on the investment of energy and time needed to create, promote and implement them.

Five Points also sent a yearly newsletter to its current and former donors as well as to selected community members. The list had been well maintained over the years and provided current postal as well as email addresses for all recipients. With each yearly mailing, those addresses were updated.

Beverly realized, however, that this once-a-year communication was not enough to engage donors and potential donors with Five Points and its mission. Thus, on her own, she developed a basic website for Five Points, but she had not had the time to update it or regularly post information. Working with one of the younger staff members, she also created a Facebook page. It was updated more frequently. While Beverly was happy with this work, she knew that more could be done with these resources. She had seen the websites of the other housing organizations with their slick videos and testimonials; she envied their numbers of "Likes." Exhibit Four presents information about Five Points' social media presence and that of the four competing organizations.

Exhibit Four

Facebook Likes and Twitter Followers

Organizations that Provide Services to the Homeless

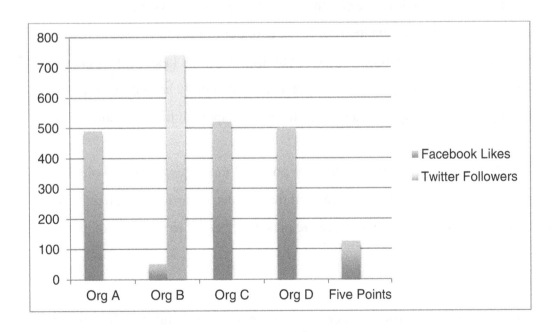

Finally, Beverly realized that she needed to identify different donor segments. Current donors tended to be well-educated individuals, ages 55-to-74, with incomes of $75,000 and up. She wanted to expand the organization's reach to individuals with more discretionary income. She also thought it would be helpful to target younger individuals who believed in Five Points' cause. Such a strategy would allow Five Points to begin to build future major donors and tap into the energy of younger individuals.

Fundraising Obstacles

One of the biggest problems the organization had to overcome was the public perception of homeless individuals. Homeless people were seen either as the victims of a sudden disaster, who will be fine after some short-term assistance, or as chronically homeless – the stereotypical alcoholic bum living under a bridge.[*] As already noted, because Five Points did not work with families needing short-term assistance, it did not get the publicity that other organizations did when a disaster struck. Thus, Beverly knew that Five Points needed to do a better job of getting the word out about the population it did help.

Therein, however, lay part of the problem: homeless families generally did not want others to know that they were homeless; the children in particular did not want their peers to know that they did not have a home. So while other housing organizations were able to feature people they had helped, Five Points was not able to put the names and faces of their clients in the public eye. Developing composite profiles of a "typical" family helped, but it just did not have the ring of authenticity that came with featuring a specific family or individual.

To help with this issue, the survey tested five potential messages that Five Points might use to convey its mission. Respondents identified three as being particularly effective for communicating with donors. These three are presented below, in the order of preference.

---

[*] According to the 2010 census, homeless families make up one-third of the homeless population in the US (Annual Assessment 2010). But in some cities, such as Chicago, 50% of the homeless are people living in families (Chicago Coalition for the Homeless, 2014).

- Homelessness does not discriminate. It does not matter how old you are, if you are well-educated, or have fought for our country. Homelessness can happen to anyone.
- Five Points helps people thrive in society through transitional housing, a work requirement, and skills training.
- Five Points has made a difference in the lives of hundreds of individuals.

As already noted, other area housing organizations had received large donations. As often happens, the high profile donors attracted other high profile donors, and Five Points had found it difficult to tap into that pool. One reason might have been the composition of its board of directors. The board was primarily composed of bank loan officers, real estate agents, college professors, and community members interested in the housing issue. While all the board members were very dedicated to Five Points' mission, they generally were not comfortable with the fundraising function associated with board membership. Additionally, because board members tended to work "in the housing trenches," they did not have higher profile contacts.

Digital/Direct Marketing and Not-for-Profits

In her quest for ideas, Beverly had browsed the websites of other housing organizations, noting how they used video, blogs, and guest posts to enhance their messages. She followed various blogs about digital marketing for not-for-profit organizations, reading that not-for-profits needed to focus on creating conversations around their mission, not just present "about us" information. She also read about the potential for Twitter to engage both clients and donors. One report that caught her eye was a nonprofit benchmark study suggesting that email response rates were declining while social media audiences were growing (M+R Strategic Services & NTEN 2013).

Research about the use of social media by not-for-profits supports Beverly's findings. A 2014 survey by HubSpot (Shattuck) reported that 98 percent of nonprofit organizations have a Facebook page, just over 70 percent have a Twitter account, 55 percent are on LinkedIn, just under 50 percent have a YouTube channel, and just over 20 percent have a Pinterest page. Despite this seeming widespread use of social media, 80 percent of nonprofits participating in the survey said that Facebook was their primary social media focus – though they "would like to focus more time on Twitter and LinkedIn" (Shattuck).

As she reflected on the survey results, Beverly noted some interesting findings about how people learned about charitable organizations and what motivated them to contribute. Both findings lent support to the idea that the proper use of digital media – which tended to have built-in sharing options – would be important to Five Points' future success.

> *Information Sources.* Both donors and community members were asked
> either how they first heard about Five Points (current and former donors) or
> how they learned about the charities they gave to (community members).
> Personal means of contact topped the list. News stories and direct contact
> with an organization were ranked first and second, with information from
> friends and family a close third. Traditional advertising was a distant fourth
> information source, with attending events being the fifth.

> *Motivation for Charitable Gifts.* Survey respondents overwhelmingly
> reported that their belief in the cause is what motivated them to donate to a
> particular charity. Two other factors entered into the final decision, though:
> knowing where one's money goes and being confident that the organization
> spends the money wisely. When asked to identify the charitable
> organizations they supported, respondents identified not only Five Points,
> but also other local organizations that help the homeless, as well as food
> banks, food pantries, and community action agencies.

Once again, national research provides support for these local findings. MDG Advertising (2013) synthesized research about not-for-profits and social media from various sources and reported that 47 percent of Americans learn about causes via social media and online channels. Fifty-six percent who support not-for-profits on social media say that compelling storytelling motivates them to take action. Importantly, that action has a ripple effect: almost 70 percent of people will take the time to learn more about a charitable organization after seeing a friend's post about making a donation; almost 40 percent will themselves donate to the organization.

As a result of her investigation, Beverly became convinced that social media outlets offered considerable potential for enhancing Five Points' engagement with the community – and therefore represented a viable means for achieving the desired marketing objectives.

The Director's Objectives and Tasks

Beverly's overriding objectives were to increase Five Points Housing's visibility in the community and to increase financial support for the organization. To achieve these goals, she needed to implement the following strategies.

- Reposition Five Points Housing to highlight its differences from other organizations that address homelessness so that it will occupy a unique place in people's minds.
- Communicate Five Points' story.
- Keep information about Five Points and its impacts in front of current and potential donors.
- Create opportunities for engagement with Five Points and its mission.
- Attract new donors.

Beverly knew that the budget for marketing efforts was very tight, but she was enthusiastic about what she had learned about how other not-for-profit organizations had successfully employed digital marketing to expand their base of supporters and to engage donors. On the other hand she was cautious about taking on too much too quickly, knowing that her dedicated staff already was stretched thin.

Beverly also knew that she needed to convince her board. Some board members had expressed a reluctance to engage in social media because of the potential for negative comments leading to negative publicity. Other board members urged Beverly to move forward. As she prepared for the board's annual meeting, Beverly had to decide what recommendations she should make.

References

Annual Homeless Assessment Report to Congress (2010), US Department of Housing and Urban Development Office of Community Planning and Development, available on the web (http://www.huduser.org/portal/publications/povsoc/ahar_5.html/).

Chicago Coalition for the Homeless (2014), "FAQ/Studies," n.p., available on the web (http://www.chicagohomeless.org/faq-studies/).

M+R Strategic Services & NTEN (The Nonprofit Technology Network) (2013), "2013 eNonprofit Benchmarks Study," available at www.e-benchmarksstudy.com.

MDG Advertising (2013), "2012: It was a Very Good Year for Social Giving" *MDG Blog*, on the web (http://www.mdgadvertising.com/blog/2012-it-was-a-very-good-year-for-social-giving/).

National Alliance to End Homelessness (2015), "Housing First," on the web (http://www.endhomelessness.org/pages/housing_first).

Shattuck, Steven (2014), "Where Nonprofits Spend Their Time with Social Media Marketing [New Data]," *HubSpot Blogs*, March 20, on the web (http://blog.hubspot.com/marketing/nonprofits-social-media-marketing-data/).

HABLAME Mobile:
Predicting Churn and Customer Retention

By

Blodwen Tarter, Golden Gate University

Debra Zahay-Blatz, St. Edward's University

The Company Background

HABLAME was founded seven years ago by Samantha Jones and Carlos Jimenez, as a telecommunications reseller providing mobile telephone voice service to individuals in California. Samantha and Carlos believed that there was an opportunity for a company that would provide superior customer service, both with real people and online interaction, as well as value-pricing for reliable telecommunications services. They had identified the growing Hispanic market as a then-underserved group that could become quite profitable with the right services, pricing, and marketing.

Carlos' parents were originally from Mexico and Carlos had spent many summers visiting his grandparents and relatives there. He realized that many Spanish-speaking immigrants and migrant workers wanted an affordable, reliable mobile phone service to use to call both within the US and to their home countries. They did not want to be locked into long-term contracts or expensive upfront fees for this service. They wanted a pay-as-you-go service. And, they wanted the choice of customer service in English or Spanish. He thought that providing value-priced phone calls and bilingual customer service while advertising in Spanish and English would make HABLAME stand out and attract a loyal set of customers.

Samantha, who had been a Spanish and Latin American studies major in college, agreed. These two friends from graduate school decided to launch their business first in Northern California. As the business grew, they then rapidly expanded to the rest of California.

The Current Challenge

Early on Wednesday morning, the marketing staff of HABLAME met for their weekly departmental meeting. After the usual updates on financial performance such as revenue, key marketing metrics including new customers, and the status of various projects, the discussion turned to the number of HABLAME customers leaving HABLAME and switching to other mobile service providers. While every company loses some customers, wireless companies have a particular challenge with high rates of switching. Since so many people already have some form of mobile phone service, most new customers now must come from another mobile service provider.

Samantha Jones, company cofounder and the head of marketing, had become quite concerned with HABLAME's customer loss. The most recent estimates were alarming. Could it be true that 40% of HABLAME's customers were leaving annually? Maybe other mobile service companies lost customers at that rate but HABLAME could not afford it.

Samantha needed to better understand which customers were dropping their HABLAME pay-as-you-go mobile phone service. This would help the company develop focused marketing programs to improve customer retention and to attract those prospects most likely to become long-term customers. Samantha knew that HABLAME collected large quantities of data about every customer that used HABLAME's wireless phone service. She was confident that rigorous analysis of this data would yield insights that would help HABLAME target the right customers more efficiently and reduce the number of customers who switched to competitors.

As the discussion began to swirl around her, Samantha reflected briefly on the company's situation.

Overview of the U.S. Telecommunications Industry

In the US, the telecommunications business is a highly competitive industry. Behemoth carriers such as AT&T, Verizon, and T-Mobile compete with a variety of smaller competitors who often resell the capacity provided by the big carriers. The product offerings are often complex combinations of services, making it difficult for people to compare offerings from different companies. In addition, some aspects are highly regulated and many competing companies are simultaneously business partners.

Carriers provide the infrastructure for the transmission of voice and digital data either through landlines or wireless data transmitted from cell towers. Excess carrying capacity from these large operators is often resold to resellers. The profitability of resellers hinges primarily on two factors: negotiating favorable pricing agreements with the big carriers and highly effective marketing. In recent years, resellers focusing only on the benefits of no contracts and low prices have been acquired or gone out of business as the big operators seek to capture greater market share of mobile services. Surviving resellers have been those that focus on differentiated niche markets such as specific ethnic groups. This is the market space in which HABLAME competes.

Technically, HABLAME is a mobile virtual network operator (MVNO) because it does not own a licensed wireless system. Instead, it buys wireless services from the system owners at wholesale prices. HABLAME then resells those services at retail prices under its own name. Because mobile phone users have come to expect low-cost mobile service from all providers, competitive retail pricing is a requirement. Customer service and memorable marketing are the essential competitive differentiators for MVNOs. While the number of MVNOs is decreasing, there are still many small companies targeting niche markets and the arena is highly competitive.

HABLAME competes against other MVNOs and against the big operator-carriers themselves. It has to do everything it can to strengthen its brand and its position in the marketplace. Thus, HABLAME's current focus on the US Hispanic community, a very attractive and growing niche.

The Hispanic Market in the US

According to the most recent US Census[23], people of Hispanic origin (often called Latino) are the largest ethnic minority the United States. In 2012, 53 million people, or 17% of the US population, were Hispanic. Hispanics tend to have larger families than other ethnic groups and immigration from the world's 21[24] Spanish-speaking countries is expected to continue to grow. Consequently, Hispanics are projected to reach 128.8 million by 2060, constituting 31% of the US population. Although Hispanics live all over the United States, California and Texas are two states with the greatest absolute number of Hispanic residents and a higher proportion of Hispanics than the national average. 38% of the California and Texas populations were Hispanic in 2010[25]. By 2060, Hispanics will comprise 48% of the state of California.[26]

While the Hispanic community is an ethnic minority in the US, only Mexico has a larger total Hispanic population (110 million people) than the US.[27] No wonder HABLAME decided that providing mobile phone service to US Hispanics had such great potential! Individuals within ethnic groups are often characterized by their degree of acculturation or adaptation to the dominant culture of the country in which they live. Acculturation characteristics of interest include country of origin (where were they born?), dominant household language (do they speak Spanish or English at home?), English proficiency (are

---

[23]

https://www.census.gov/newsroom/releases/archives/facts_for_features_special_editions/cb1
3-ff19.html

[24] http://www.numberof.net/number-of-spanish-speaking-countries/

[25]

http://factfinder2.census.gov/faces/tableservices/jsf/pages/productview.xhtml?pid=DEC_10_
SF1_QTP10 (California),
http://factfinder2.census.gov/faces/tableservices/jsf/pages/productview.xhtml?pid=DEC_10_
SF1_QTP3 (Texas)

[26] http://www.dof.ca.gov/research/demographic/reports/projections/P-
1/documents/Projections_Press_Release_2010-2060.pdf

[27] https://www.census.gov/population/international/data/idb/informationGateway.php

they fluent in both English and Spanish--truly bi-lingual-- or are they more comfortable in one language?). Marketers are constantly trying to figure out what acculturation characteristics are the most important, and then, how to use this information to design desirable products and effective marketing communications programs. As the immigrant and migrant population changes, acculturation measures are a moving target but helpful to understand.

HABLAME's marketing team was constantly evaluating new information about acculturation among its targets. At the same time, they kept close tabs on other important characteristics of US Hispanics. This included the penetration rate of internet use, the use of social media, the adoption of smartphones, and media preferences. The US is well-served with Spanish-language radio stations, TV networks, magazines and newspapers, and websites.

Acquiring New Customers and Retaining Existing Customers

Historically, HABLAME has relied upon customer word-of-mouth to acquire new customers. Satisfied customers tell their friends about HABLAME, who then investigate the company's offerings and, quite often, decide to switch to HABLAME. Increasingly, social media initiated by satisfied customers has generated inquiries to HABLAME from interested prospects. The social conversation takes place in two languages: English and Spanish, whichever the prospect prefers. Customers can tweet #HABLAMEreferral to friends and family and receive a bonus of free calling time if the person whom they have referred becomes a HABLAME customer.

HABLAME also has an informative bilingual website that helps prospective customers evaluate the different service combinations offered by the company. Prospects can place orders online. Unlike most of its competitors, HABLAME also encourages prospects to call with questions. Live customer service representatives, located in Northern California, answer questions and can guide the caller through the choices available, seeking to match the prospects needs with HABLAME's services.

Recently, HABLAME introduced SMS (text) messaging services for customer service in response to requests. Customer service representatives also encourage customers to use Twitter to request assistance. Most often, the service representative calls the inquirer back via voice to troubleshoot any problems.

Over the past seven years, HABLAME has tried many different media for customer acquisition including radio, print, and paid search. It consistently tests different creative executions of its offers and adjusts its media choices, based on comparative testing. As the Hispanic consumers' preferences change, so does HABLAME's selection of media.

All phone companies lose some of their customers to other telecommunications providers. This is called voluntary churn. It is usually measured as a percentage of the total customer base--how many people leave the company each month (or each year) divided by the total number of customers. Reducing the churn rate or increasing the retention rate is a standard goal for all businesses. Customers who die, move out of a service area, or who fail to pay their bills are involuntary leavers. HABLAME cares about those customers but can do little to impact the involuntary churn rate. Instead, the company concentrates on reducing the voluntary churn rate.

Data and Predictive Analytics

Samantha recognized that HABLAME had lots of information readily available for analysis. The company databases contained behavioral data such as time spent on long distance calls, international calls, and local calls. There was also demographic information that included subscriber age, sex, marital status, number of children, car ownership, and the estimated annual income. The company's data dictionary (Appendix A) listed all of the data available for Samantha's team to use.

Of course, it would be possible for the company to obtain additional information about its customers. HABLAME could survey the customer base, ask callers questions during customer service phone calls, or use a data appending service to enhance the customer database.

So, Samantha knew that there was data available for analysis. How could she use this information to predict which customers would voluntarily leave HABLAME? Fortunately, the newest addition to the marketing department was a recent graduate who had studied statistics and data analytics as part of her business degree. Samantha expected that Maria would have some specific suggestions on how to approach the problem.

And then, what would HABLAME do with this knowledge?

Retaining Customers and Predicting Customer Churn

Samantha returned to the marketing staff's conversation in the conference room.

"OK, people, we need to talk about the specific business issues here. We have a big problem. Our customer churn is too high. Forty percent is huge. We are losing too many customers to the competition. How do we do a better job of getting new customers and keeping our existing ones? If we can predict who will drop our service, maybe we can then figure out why they do so. That will help us design more attractive products, improve our customer service or provide better pricing to keep them. Maybe we need to provide other incentives to keep them.

Or, we can decide how to avoid attracting those people in the first place. If someone is likely to leave do we want to bother signing him or her on as a customer at all? There is a big cost in all the work to attract new customers, process their orders, provide customer service and, then, have them move on to the competition. If I could, I'd avoid that."

Turning to Maria, Samantha put the new hire on the spot by asking, "Maria, I hope that you can help us figure this out. I vaguely remember regression analysis from graduate school and that it can be used to predict things. But it has been a while. We have lots of historical data and we certainly know which customers have left us and which have stayed. What would you suggest we do to predict who will leave HABLAME voluntarily?"

Maria gulped, paused-- and then realized she knew the answer. Since customer attrition is a common business problem across all industries, this is something she had studied in school and, in fact, had practiced in her data analytics class.

Adjusting her glasses, Maria spoke. "There is something called logistic regression that we can probably use. To make sure it's the right approach, I would need to review the data. How about if I set up a meeting to discuss it after I've looked at our data dictionary?"

Samantha nodded in agreement, remarking "Once we can make these predictions, we will need to figure out what we need to do from a marketing perspective. Paul and Enrique, I want you to work with Maria on this."

The next day, Maria convened a brief meeting with Samantha, Paul and Enrique. She started by explaining logistic regression. "It is kind of like ordinary linear multiple regression. For both techniques, we need historical data to create a model that will predict the dependent variable. In ordinary multiple regression, what we are trying to predict (the dependent variable) is a continuous or metric variable – a number such as sales or profits, for example. The dependent variable can assume many values."

Maria could see that Paul and Enrique were listening carefully. She continued. "In contrast, logistic regression is used when the dependent variable is binary—it can be only one of two discrete values. For example, 'yes-no' dependent variables could be whether a customer responded to a marketing campaign or not, whether a person is a homeowner or not, whether a business goes bankrupt or not, or whether a person votes guilty or not guilty. For our purposes of predicting customer churn, the dependent variable is whether a HABLAME customer leaves the company or remains a customer."

Paul interrupted, "Let's call them "leavers" and "stayers." It's not elegant but it is descriptive!"

Maria thought to herself, "Great! This stuff that I learned in school really does get used in business." She then continued her tutorial. "Like ordinary multiple regression, the independent variables we use to help us predict the dependent variable can be metric (e.g., age, income, or number of dropped calls) or categorical (e.g., gender, marital status, or payment method). Indicator or 'dummy' variables are used to include categorical variables as predictors."

As her colleagues nodded thoughtfully, she concluded, "Once a good model is developed, the predictor variables for each new customer can be input into the logistic model and the model will yield a predicted probability that the customer will stay or leave."[28]

Then, Maria shifted her focus to the tools she would need to create the predictive model. "I used SPSS at school for my homework developing logistic regression models." Enrique, who did most of the survey analysis for HABLAME, spoke up. "No problem. We have a company subscription to SPSS." That was a relief—Maria would not have to learn new software. However, she knew that she could also use SAS, another commonly-used statistical package for business and academia. R, an increasingly popular free programming language for statistical analysis, could also be used for logistic regression modeling.

Samantha cut to the chase. "Maria, do you think you can develop a logistic regression model that will predict customer churn for HABLAME? Paul and Enrique know our customer database pretty well and I think it would be useful for them to understand how this logistic regression predictive technique works. They can work with you. You can start with a sample from the customer database. We don't need to look at the entire database to get started with the model.

---

[28] Charlotte Mason, *Note on Applied Logistic Regression*, 2003.

"Once the model is done, I'd like you three to propose a marketing plan that uses this new information. After all, if we can predict who will leave us we should be able to do a better job of keeping them—or avoiding them in the first place."

"But first," said Samantha, "let's start with a quick review. We regularly use descriptive statistics to tell us what our typical customer looks like. Please do that for the total customer database, then look at "leavers" vs. "stayers." That may give you some ideas about the variables that will help predict churn."

Maria smiled, excited by her first big assignment. She reiterated, "So we have three things to do, right? We will start by describing the customer base. Second, develop a logistic regression model that predicts leavers and stayers. Third, develop a marketing plan that uses the new information."

Paul added, "We have a pretty good customer database. However, I suspect we might need even more data to develop a better model. I can imagine different kinds of information that might be useful. What if someone moves to an area where our coverage isn't very good? Should we consider how much texting people do?"

Enrique jumped in, recalling, "We have done some referral promotions in the past where we gave free time to customers who referred a new customer to us. Does that encourage people to stay with us longer or not?"

Paul thought some more. "What if my best friend leaves for a HABLAME competitor? Would that affect the likelihood of me switching away from HABLAME?" Then, he laughed ruefully, "Of course, I would be pretty upset if he did change services but what customers' friends and family do might be relevant. After all, word-of-mouth is our best marketing method!"

Samantha agreed. "OK, let's add a fourth task: identify any additional information that you think might improve the predictive ability of the model. Once you have done your best with the existing data, we can see if we want to spend resources to get additional data. Some of it may be easy to find."

APPENDIX A
Data Dictionary

ID Customer reference number

LONGDIST Time spent on long distance calls per month

International Time spent on international calls per month

LOCAL Time spent on local calls per month

DROPPED Number of dropped calls

PAY_MTHD Payment method of the monthly telephone bill CC (credit card) Auto (auto pay through bank or other method), CH (check).

AGE

SEX Gender, Male, Female

STATUS Marital status Married, Single

CHILDREN Number of Children

Est_Income Estimated income in dollars

Car_Owner Car owner

CHURNED (2 categories) Voluntary, Current

CHURNED2 (2 categories) 0=Leavers, 1=Stayers

Stayers/Current– Still with company

Leavers/Voluntary – Leavers who the company wants to keep

APPENDIX B
Data Set

A sample of data from the HABLAME Mobile customer database is available from your instructor.

Kentucky Speedway:
Getting a Checkered Flag with Customers

By

Deborah Cowles, Virginia Commonwealth University

Jan Owens, Carthage College

Matthew Sauber, Eastern Michigan University

At the end of the most recent professional auto racing season, key marketing decision makers (the marketing team) at the Kentucky Speedway (KYS, the Speedway), in Sparta, Kentucky, wanted to incorporate recent developments influencing the auto racing industry into the Speedway's next 2-year marketing plan. They looked into a number of positive and negative factors affecting NASCAR and stock car racing, as well as the Speedway operation in recent years. Challenges included declining attendance both at the Speedway and at a number of other tracks, a stagnant economy that continued to impact key target markets, declining media revenues, the escalating costs of racecar team ownership and operation in the face of cautious sponsors, and the changing demographics and heightened expectations of current and prospective customers.

The Speedway looked for opportunities in the marketplace as it aimed to put into place a strong and innovative marketing plan for the next two racing seasons, which would provide a solid foundation for growth through the end of the decade. In addition to continuing to serve its traditional markets at the highest possible level, the KYS marketing team wanted also to focus on new customer segments – youth, Millennials, culturally diverse consumers – as a path toward increasing ticket sales, overall revenue, and media ratings. The marketing team considered a number of factors as it contemplated the 2-year marketing plan:

As NASCAR Goes, So Goes Its Partners

Both on and off the track, the National Association for Stock Car Auto Racing (NASCAR) had experienced some exciting times in recent years. The sport's most popular driver, Dale

Earnhardt, Jr., won the 2014 season's opening race – the Daytona 500 – in a green-white-checkered thriller.[29] NASCAR teams were going faster than ever, driving the Gen-6 (Generation-6) model Car of Tomorrow. In the 2014 Sprint Cup Series alone, drivers set 24 track records while qualifying, and 17 of the 23 tracks on the Sprint Cup circuit saw new record speeds.[30] Due to a series of rule changes over a number of years, NASCAR was treating fans to a more exciting level of competition. With increasingly greater emphasis placed on *winning* races, as opposed to just finishing a race well, more story lines developed throughout the year regarding who *could* finish on top at the end of the season. In 2014, the competition went down to the last race, and victory, after 10 months of racing, was decided by a single point.

Despite these positive aspects, NASCAR and its many partners continued to face a number of challenges as the sport looked toward subsequent seasons of racing (Table 1). Team owners struggled with the ever-escalating costs of operating a racing team – particularly in a difficult economic environment. Television ratings (and revenues) were heading downward, and attendance at many tracks continued to decline.[31] "Wide swaths of empty seats have been visible at several tracks."[32] A number of tracks went so far as to remove seats and seating sections. "The Daytona International Speedway – which had entire sections displaying tarpaulins with advertising instead of fans at the Coke Zero 400 over July 4th weekend – will complete a renovation in 2016 that will drop its seating capacity from 147, 000 to 101,000."[33] Talledega Superspeedway and Michigan International race tracks were in

---

[29] http://www.nascar.com/en_us/news-media/articles/2014/2/23/dale-earnhardt-jr-wins-daytona-500-results-standings-wreck.html

[30] http://www.foxsports.com/nascar/story/year-of-speed-nascar-teams-go-faster-than-ever-before-112114

[31] NASCAR reported 4.67 million in attendance during 2005 (an average of 129,722 per event), but just 3.52 million in 2012 (an average of 97,722 per event), a decline of approximately 25 percent in 7 years, or 3.6 percent per year.

[32] *Ibid.*

[33] http://www.news-sentinel.com/apps/pbcs.dll/article?AID=/20140726/SPORTS/140729704/0/SEARCH

the process of downsizing from 143,000 and 137,000 to 80,000 and 72,000, respectively. As part of a 3-year, $400 million renovation, to be completed in 2016, the number of seats at the Indianapolis Motor Speedway would be reduced from 159,000 to 101,000. Within just a few years, 14 of NASCAR's 23 premiere tracks would be settling for permanent reduced seating capacity. According to NASCAR, attendance for Sprint Cup races was 4.67 million in 2005 (an average of 129,722 per race) but only 3.52 million in 2012 (an average 97,722).[34]

Table 1. NASCAR Revenue, Attendance, Expense, and TV Rating Statistics

Statistic Verification	
Source: NASCAR, Columbia Business, Sports Illustrated	
Date Verified: 1.14.2014	
NASCAR Racing Statistics	**Data**
Annual NASCAR revenue	$3.1 Billion
Average NASCAR ticket price	$92.16
Number of NASCAR fans	75 Million
Average NASCAR race attendance	99,853
Total annual NACAR attendance	3.6 Million
Number of households that watch the Daytona 500	12.5 Million
Annual worth of NASCAR television contract	$560 Million
Percent of NASCAR fans who are women	40 %
Annual amount spent by women on NASCAR-licensed products	$250 million
Percent of NASCAR fans who are minorities	21 %
Percent of kids age 7 to 17 that reported being NASCAR fans	50 %
Percent of fans who are willing to pay more to buy a sponsor's product	66 %
Average annual amount a sponsor invest in a racing team	$15 million

---

[34] http://www.usatoday.com/story/sports/nascar/2014/07/26/brickyard-400-indianapolis-motor-speedway-attendance-racing/13213107/

Percent of NASCAR fans who could name every sponsor of the top 30 ranked cars	36 %

NASCAR Team Expense Statistics	Amount
Average NASCAR Drivers' Salary including endorsements	$7.5 Million
Average NASCAR team member salary	$35,000
Average spent annually by a NASCAR team on travel	$1 Million
Average spent per race by a NASCAR team on tires	$20,000
Average spent on in-house engine program by a NASCAR team	$3.5 million
Average spent on a NASCAR racing car	$1.5 Million

Top Television Rated NASCAR Races

	Track	2013	2012
1	Daytona	11.3	10.9
2	California	7.4	7.9
3	Las Vegas	6.2	6.4
4	Atlanta	1.5*	5.5
5	Bristol	6.2	6.3
6	Martinsville	6.2	5.1
7	Texas	5.4	5.7
8	Phoenix	4.8	5.1
9	Talladega	1.7*	7.6
10	Darlington	4.3	4.4
11	Richmond	4.8	5.6
12	Charlotte	5.1	6.1

* Race on Monday because of rain

http://www.statisticbrain.com/nascar-racing-statistics/

The goal for many race track owners and operators was to heighten the demand for tickets and to make race day "look better" on television and "feel better" for fans. With respect to auto racing fans, it was difficult for track owners to determine whether declining attendance should be linked to diminishing interest in the sport, a lack of consumer discretionary income during difficult economic times, or a need to increase the value proposition for current and emerging customer markets. In many ways, race tracks faced challenges similar to those of brick-and-mortar retail stores in terms of declining foot traffic as a result of online shopping and changing demographics.

How could the Speedway enhance its value proposition and the "customer experience" for current and prospective KYS target markets to increase ticket sales, revenue, fan engagement, and television ratings?

This Track, That Track: The Kentucky Speedway

The Kentucky Speedway, a 1.5-mile (intermediate-size) tri-oval track located in Sparta, Kentucky, was one of professional auto racing's newer tracks, having opened to the public on June 16, 2000. Despite Kentucky's rich and colorful history in auto racing, its first NASCAR-eligible track was a late entry into the premiere stock car racing circuit lineup.

Although stock car racing's roots can be traced to a time when drivers ran bootleg whiskey in "souped-up" (modified) stock cars to distribute their illicit products during Prohibition, NASCAR's formal history began in early 1947 with the founding of the "National Championship Stock Car Circuit." The so-called "Cup" series began in 1972, when R.J. Reynolds Tobacco Company – which had been banned from television advertising – "found a popular and demographically suitable consumer base in NASCAR fans and engaged NASCAR as a promotional outlet."[35] Thus was born the "Winston Cup Series," a sponsorship which lasted for more than two decades, later becoming the Nextel Cup and now the Sprint Cup.

---

[35] http://en.wikipedia.org/wiki/NASCAR

In 1948, the newly named NASCAR series featured 52 modified dirt-track races, but since 2001, the premiere Cup series has been comprised of just 36 races at a variety of paved courses in four categories (short-track, intermediate, super speedway, and road course), with the first race beginning in February and the series ending in November. Like other tracks within the NASCAR affiliate ranks, KYS has had to vie for the privilege of hosting popular races and series (see http://galleries.nascar.com/gallery/174/get-to-know-all-23-sprint-cup-series-tracks#/0). From its opening in 2000, the Speedway strived to position itself to become a part of the NASCAR Sprint Cup schedule, along with other speedways in the region: [36]

When the inaugural Brickyard 400 was run in 1994, there were only two other Sprint Cup races within 500 miles of Indianapolis, both at Michigan International Speedway. The expansion that brought NASCAR to Indianapolis and beyond and made the series a national rage had pushed that number to six — the two at Michigan, two at Kansas Speedway and one each at Kentucky Speedway (opened in 2000) and at Chicagoland Speedway (2001).

But that single Sprint Cup race was not easy to come by for KYS; after its grand opening in 2000, too many years had passed with no success in obtaining one or more of the coveted spots on the NASCAR circuit. By 2008, KYS felt it had no other choice but to file a lawsuit, in which it alleged that NASCAR and International Speedway Corp (ISC) violated Sections 1 and 2 of the Sherman Act and conspired to monopolize and restrain trade in auto racing by precluding the Kentucky Speedway from hosting the Sprint Cup series despite its superior amenities. To be able to qualify to host the series, KYS had added amenities and had expanded the seating capacity from 66,000 to its current level of 107,000. The interstate highway near the track was also widened, and a new exit was added to improve traffic flow to accommodate a much bigger crowd.[37] It was clear that KYS was serious about becoming

---

[36] http://www.usatoday.com/story/sports/nascar/2014/07/26/brickyard-400-indianapolis-motor-speedway-attendance-racing/13213107/

[37] http://sports-law.blogspot.com/2008/01/kentucky-speedways-antitrust-suit.html

a part of the NASCAR schedule. Finally, in 2011, the Speedway earned its first spot in stock car racing's preeminent circuit.

Although NASCAR's schedule had been a subject of controversy on an annual basis for many years ("Why a race at *this* track and not at *that* track?"), changing the schedule had been a challenge. Except for adding Iowa Speedway in 2006 and KYS in 2011, the NASCAR schedule had seen few changes since 2001. Factors that complicated scheduling decisions included NASCAR history and folklore, travel and cost considerations for competing teams, the media market, holidays, weather, purse sizes, track category and size, and track ownership.

What could the Kentucky Speedway do to position itself as the premiere intermediate-size auto racing track for NASCAR, as well as for other national and regional racing venues?

Some Bumps in the Road

As mentioned previously, the Speedway hosted its inaugural race in NASCAR's Sprint Cup Series, the Quaker State 400, on July 9, 2011, the marquee and final event of a "tripleheader" that also included Camping World (truck) and Nationwide Series races. Unfortunately, many fans – as well as regional and national media – still remembered the massive traffic and parking problems surrounding that 3-day event, with as many as six hours of gridlock facing KYS ticketholders stuck on Interstate 71, preventing some customers from even being able to attend the Sprint Cup race. This public relations nightmare was particularly disappointing given the extent to which KYS had invested in improving its facilities and fan access to the track to meet NASCAR standards. Although KYS representatives subsequently took steps to solve the problems and apologized publicly to fans, other NASCAR track owners were critical of the Speedway because of the debacle's potential impact on the sport as a whole.[38]

---

[38]

http://sports.espn.go.com/rpm/nascar/cup/columns/story?columnist=blount_terry&id=675925 0

The Speedway also continued to face criticism with respect to the track itself, the surface of which was the fourth-oldest on the Sprint Cup circuit at the close of 2014. Following his win at the track's inaugural NASCAR race in 2011, Joe Gibbs Racing driver Kyle Busch expressed concerns about the adequacy of its SAFER (steel and foam energy reduction) barriers. And, from the beginning, drivers have described the KYS asphalt surface as "bumpy" and "rough," which tended to preclude fan-favorite side-by-side racing.[39] Although KYS officials had attempted to use the bumpiness as a differentiating factor – separating it "from the seven other 1.5-mile venues, which are often lumped together as 'cookie-cutter' tracks,"[40] many drivers were not impressed. In 2014, one Sprint Cup driver told Twitter followers about his bloody nose that was a direct result of the track's condition.[41] According to many experienced drivers, a *worn-out* track was better than a track that was just bumpy or rough, and some drivers had remarked that the Speedway's efforts to smooth out the track had made the problem worse.[42]

Midway through the 2013 season, a regional sports journalist asked readers in a headline: "Is Kentucky Speedway cursed?"[43] He recounted the 2011 Quaker State traffic/parking debacle, the intense summer heat that wilted the 2012 season, and the torrential rain that nearly drowned out the 2013 Sprint Cup race. Even though weather problems can be attributed to "bad luck," many wondered, "What can possibly happen in 2014?"

---

[39] *Ibid.*

[40] http://www.usatoday.com/story/sports/nascar/2014/06/26/kentucky-speedway-bumpy-track-rough-surface/11420895/

[41] http://espn.go.com/racing/nascar/cup/story/_/id/11146237/nascar-bumpy-track-test-kentucky-speedway

[42] *Ibid.*

[43] http://www.kentucky.com/2013/07/01/2700389_mark-story-is-kentucky-speedway.html?rh=1

Unfortunately, just after "The Chase" portion of the 2014 season had begun[44] (when fan attention typically peaks), a tragic event at the Speedway made news in the tri-state area of Kentucky, Indiana, and Ohio – the track's primary geographical markets. A 30-year-old pharmacist from Decatur, Indiana, died as a result of a crash while participating in the Rusty Wallace Racing Experience at Kentucky Speedway. His parents, from Germantown, Ohio, questioned the safety of the fan-experience program, which their son had received as a birthday present – one of a number of similar programs at the Speedway: "It's supposed to be a safe way to drive fast. That's what is so hard to accept." Customers of the Experience could choose to drive from three laps for $249 to a full 50-lap "NASCAR experience" for $1,899. The investigation following the crash was still ongoing and in the news toward the end of 2014.

The Speedway knew that it has its fans' and customers' interests at heart. What could it do to improve its reputation and brand image among current and prospective target markets, as well as other key audiences whose influence can play a significant role in consumer decision making?

Who is the Speedway's Auto Racing Fan-Customer?

For the Kentucky Speedway, a "sold out" venue meant that 107,000 fans were at the track on race day, taking full advantage of all that the "track experience" had to offer. Using ticket sales percentages as a source of information, KYS planners were fairly certain that most Speedway fans came from Cincinnati, Louisville, Lexington, and Dayton, with pockets of loyal fans from Chicago, Atlanta, Florida, and Arizona. Table 2 lists top KYS geographic markets, ranked by ticket sales and camping revenue.

---

[44] http://en.wikipedia.org/wiki/Chase_for_the_Sprint_Cup

Table 2. Kentucky Speedway Geographic Markets by Ticket Sales/Camping Revenue

Market	2014 Ticket/Camping Revenue	% of Individual Ticket Sales
Cincinnati		33.54%
Louisville		18.97%
Lexington		7.70%
Dayton		6.47%
Columbus		5.07%
Indianapolis		2.80%
Evansville		2.75%
Charleston/Huntington		2.30%
Nashville/Bowling Green		1.90%
Cleveland		1.88%
Pittsburgh		0.86%
Detroit		0.75%
Columbus, IN		0.63%
St. Louis		0.61%
Chicago		0.58%
Paducah		0.52%
Toledo		0.51%
Corbin, KY		0.49%
Parkersburg, WV		0.35%
Knoxville, TN		0.32%
Minneapolis, MN		0.31%
Additional Markets		10.70%
Total		

The KYS marketing team felt it needed a better understanding of how members of key target markets planned to attend racing events, including how fans decided where to go and when to go, given other sporting, entertainment, and vacation alternatives. The team felt it would be useful to map target fans' decision journey by representing different touch points to show customer interaction with KYS. They knew that a customer-journey map could provide added insights into each target market's decision-making process. In turn, these insights could be used to generate awareness and visibility via storytelling and showcasing fans' experiences at their KYS destination (e.g., the track, vendor offerings, tailgating, camping).

Fan involvement in auto racing as a whole, and in individual drivers and teams as well, presented both an opportunity and a challenge for the Speedway. In many sports, fans were not always as aware of behind-the-scenes, off-the-track/field intrigue, but for auto racing fans, what happened off the track was almost as important as what went on during a race. And, whatever concerned a fan's favorite race driver and racing team also concerned that fan. Would it be possible for KYS to enhance its collaboration with NASCAR teams and drivers to heighten fan engagement with the Speedway's unique auto racing brand?

As they considered developing the two-year marketing plan, KYS staff members wanted to learn more about what motivated fan involvement and passion for auto racing. They understood that "involvement/passion" varied across sports. For example, "team devotion" had been identified as the major *passion driver* for fans of the National Football League (NFL). For Major League Baseball (MLB) fans, "nostalgia" was the key driver of fans' passion for the sport. "Player affinity" ranked last for NFL and MLB fans but was relatively more important for fans of the National Basketball Association (NBA).[45] To be able to attract loyal fans, KYS knew it would have to develop a better understanding of the "drivers" of fan involvement and loyalty among current and prospective target markets.

---

[45] http://www.sportsbusinessdaily.com/Journal/Issues/2010/04/20100419/SBJ-In-Depth/What-Makes-Fans-Crazy-About-Sports.aspx

Unlike most other professional sporting venues, KYS and other auto racing tracks have enjoyed an opportunity to capture fans' attention for multiple days in a row. For example, the track's premiere auto racing event in July typically featured a major NASCAR race three days in a row (Camping World, Xfinity, Sprint), and the schedule juxtaposed the ARCA race and the season's second Xfinity race in late September.

The KYS marketing team knew that the Speedway was just more than two hours' driving from Indianapolis, Indiana; less than an hour from Cincinnati, Ohio; and about an hour from both Louisville and Lexington, Kentucky. The Speedway itself offered customers six campgrounds with different levels of service and access to the racing venues. There were also other campgrounds in the area. Based on company data, KYS decision-makers knew that about 10,000 fans camped for the entire 3-race NASCAR weekend in July, with most campers driving in on the Wednesday before the first race and leaving on Sunday following the final, Sprint Cup race. The remaining fans tended to be individual-race ticketholders. They arrived several hours prior to the beginning of a race so that they could tailgate and take in – with campers and other race fans – the many activities available at the track: visiting the Fan Zone area, considering the offerings of display vendors, and generally enjoying the pre-race, at-the-track experience.

What steps could the Speedway take to map the customer journey of its target markets? Based on this insight, how could KYS use integrated marketing communication tactics and strategies to target and reach potential visitors – both new and returning – using geo-targeting, interest targeting, remarketing, and demographic and behavioral targeting?

The NASCAR Fan as a Sports Fan

In 2013, nearly 170 million adults (71% of the U.S. adult population) were sports fans,[46] with more than 43 million fans 35-54 and more than 44 million fans 55+. Younger adults aged 18-

---

[46] Global Sports Media. (2013). Global Sports Media Consumption Report 2013. Retrieved from: Sportsmediareport (2013). http://prod.talentleague.com/wp-content/uploads/2013/09/Global_Sports_Media_report_2013.pdf

34 made up nearly 32 million fans, with all adults 45 and older over-indexing as sports fans. There was a healthy youth participation in hockey and soccer, and female fans were growing, particularly for NHL and MLS[47] — with 96% of sports fans watching sports on TV.[48] Auto racing fans were among the most all-round sports fans:

- 84% of NASCAR fans were football fans
- 68% of NASCAR fans were baseball fans
- 48% of NASCAR fans were basketball fans

Taking these statistics into consideration, the Speedway marketing team also considered a study that concluded sports marketers should "evaluate sports fans' motivations, their purchasing and social media behavior, and their lifestyle habits both with and outside sports"[49] as a means to understand better the emotional motivations underlying consumption decision making:

One of the most interesting findings was that fans should no longer be looked at in silos — as an 'NHL fan' or an 'MLB fan,'" said Team Epic principal Mike Reisman. "Segmentation based on avidity misses the point of today's consumers' lifestyle and mind-set. Instead, this study shows empirically that a brand ought to be looking across the lifestyle interests of a consumer. The majority of fans are looking for brands that deliver enrichment across sports, not just for an individual sport."

Results of the study identified five different fan segments based on lifestyle: Couch Curmudgeons, Alumni Association, Super Jocks, Receptive and Limited, and Fitness Edge (see Figure 1).

---

[47] Mintel. (July, 2014). Marketing to sports fans – US. *Mintel.*

[48] http://www.knowthefan.com/infographics/us-overview/#.VHoZHIvF9WE

[49] http://www.sportsbusinessdaily.com/Journal/Issues/2012/07/23/Research-and-Ratings/Team-Epic.aspx

Figure 1: Five Sports Fan Segments

COUCH CURMUDGEONS: Oldest and least active. They prefer watching sports at home. They also are the least optimistic about the future, are the least open to sponsors and are not actively involved in sponsor programs.

ALUMNI ASSOCIATION: Older male sports fans with high disposable income and heavily invested in college sports. Open to sponsorship and influenced by sponsor programs (although not as much as Super Jocks).

SUPER JOCKS: Very young and male-dominated group with the second-highest average household income. Highly social and active, and the most likely to identify themselves as outdoor enthusiasts. They seek live events and are heavily into tailgating and fantasy sports. Very open to sponsorship and exceed all groups in their level of participation in sponsor programs.

RECEPTIVE AND LIMITED: Mix of male and female sports fans. Second-oldest of any segment; below-average income. Much more likely to follow pro sports and like NASCAR. Highly receptive to sponsors (viewing them as important and exhibiting good will toward them) but given their lower levels of disposable income, they are more conscious about spending money.

FITNESS EDGE: Most female of any group and very diverse. Younger and very physically active, with average income levels. More likely to follow pro sports and love the Olympics. Most active on social media. Have a positive view of sponsors but are selective about how they get involved in promotions, sponsor programs, etc.

Source: http://www.sportsbusinessdaily.com/Journal/Issues/2012/07/23/Research-and-Ratings/Team-Epic.aspx

"The study's Receptive and Limited group is the least diverse ethnically of the five groups (91 percent white), has the lowest average household income ($46,100 annually), and its group members are more likely to be fans of NASCAR than any other sport measured in the survey."[50] However, the Speedway was curious if one or more of the remaining four groups – or other lifestyle-oriented fan segments – should be considered when prioritizing marketing efforts. For example, members of the "Alumni Association" segment were thought to be more favorable toward integrated sponsorships. They were also considered to be "more likely than most fans to have children at home and are more likely to have interacted at a live sponsor event."[51]

The Speedway was not alone in attempting to understand its target markets more thoroughly and to broaden its appeal to new and receptive segments. In April 2014, NASCAR's director of Growth Segment Marketing announced the addition of two new positions to its Brand and Consumer Marketing division, as an indication of the association's commitment to "implementing strategic growth plans for several critical segments, including youth, millennial and multicultural."[52] The NASCAR organization also conducted a study that described current NASCAR demographics as:

- Gender neutral: 63% male; 37% female
- Appealing to key demographics: 45% of all NASCAR fans are 18-44
- Above average income: 52% with disposable income over $50,000
- Family-focused: 38% have children at home

Still, Speedway marketing planners felt that for KYS to thrive, their marketing efforts should address U.S. demographic trends to be able to attract audiences that are younger, more urban,

---

[50] *Ibid.*

[51] *Ibid.*

[52] http://www.nascar.com/content/nascar/en_us/news-media/articles/2014/4/21/nascar-release-two-new-hires-growth-segment-marketing-team.html

and multicultural. At the end of 2014, the Speedway had seen some success with commercials in Spanish and digital initiatives like nascar.com, but it wanted to achieve greater success.

What could KYS do to expand its appeal to new, desirable customer segments and enhance the value of its brand proposition by improving the fan/customer experience? What strategies could KYS develop to build upon NASCAR efforts to attract youth, Millennials, and culturally diverse fans to its racing venues?

Millennials: A Special Case

NASCAR and KYS were not the only marketers to believe that Millennials – as a target market – comprised an important segment of consumers whose needs should be addressed in future marketing initiatives. Entertainment industries from movie theaters to music venues to sports arenas had cited one important factor in declining attendance: Millennials' predisposition to finding their entertainment in streaming digital channels, if not other interests entirely. According to NASCAR CMO Steve Phelps, this demographic development was unfortunate since TV ratings and track attendance were most valued by media and brand sponsors when evaluating their promotional ROI. For example, the National Guard announced that it would end its 20-race annual sponsorship of the No. 88 Chevrolet race car because it felt that it was no longer getting enough return on its $32 million investment.[53]

For many marketers, Millennials were thought to comprise one of the most challenging and perplexing target markets. The PEW Research Center defined Millennials as being younger adults between the ages of 18 and 33, or 27% of the adult population in the United States.

---

[53] Ryan, Nate, "Numbers Aren't Adding Up for NASCAR," *USA Today*, August 7, 2014. http://www.usatoday.com/story/sports/nascar/2014/08/07/dale-earnhardt-jr-national-guard-nascar-sponsorships-social-media/13725141/-----

People in the age groups of 23, 24, and 26 were now the largest age groups based on the year they were born. Numerous studies have noted that Millennials:[54]

- Have integrated technology into their everyday lives
- Are linked to their friends and family through social media
- Have a priority of work-life balance
- A concern for authenticity, not just hype
- Are the most ethnically and racially diverse of any adult generation
- Are more likely to approve marriage among different races and same-sex couples than older generations
- Consider themselves politically independent
- Are the best educated of young adult cohort groups

A major factor in spending on entertainment was identified as the economic situation of this age cohort. More than 30% of Millennials lived with at least one parent, largely due to their employment situation.[55] Further, Millennials:

- Have a median income of $33,883 a year on average between 2009 and 2013, lower than previous generations at that age in inflation-adjusted dollars
- Are burdened by more debt than their parents, whether as a function of college loan debt, difficult job prospects in the recession, or stagnant wages in many occupations
- Are in no rush to marry or start a household, largely based on their economic situation
- Are more likely to live in poverty (20%) than their age group in 1980 (13%)

---

[54] *Millennials in Adulthood: Detached from Institutions, Networked with Friends.* PEW Research Center. Study released March 7, 2014. www.pewresearch.org/millennials

[55] Sanburn, Josh, "Four Ways Millennials Have It Worse than Their Parents," *Time*, December 4, 2014. http://time.com/3618322/census-millennials-poverty-unemployment/?xid=newsletter-brief

- Tend to doubt that the Social Security system will be available to them as it
  has been to older generations

Although the KYS team knew that Millennials would most likely pose a significant challenge in terms of the developing the segment into a loyal base of KYS and auto racing fans, the marketing team still felt that it would be important to include a "Millennial strategy" in the 2015-2016 marketing plan.

The Final Pitstop

As KYS marketing decision makers considered these important issues and questions, which would inform their 2-year marketing plan, they knew that they could not move forward until a variety of other factors were brought into the marketing mix, especially as these factors influenced potential new target markets:

Fan Experience

As mentioned previously, an important source of revenue for the Speedway derived from fans' passion for the sport, which created a market for fan experiences. In addition to the Rusty Wallace Driving Experience, fan experiences offered by the Speedway included First Time Fans, NASCAR 101, Driving Schools, Driver Appearances, a Fan Council, and the Ambassadors' Club. Several times per year, "driving experience" opportunities were provided at the track by well-known NASCAR drivers (e.g., Richard Petty Driving Experience, Rusty Wallace Driving Experience). Fans could also visit the track on days that were allocated to NASCAR teams for testing. The KYS marketing team wondered to what extent these fan experiences could lead to increased ticket sales, revenue, and media ratings for the Speedway's premiere racing events.

Also, the Speedway felt there might be other opportunities for fan experiences, given recent examples from college sports teams.[56] The KYS marketing team was also curious about whether it could benefit from the success of a number of online "fantasy auto racing" experiences (e.g., Yahoo Sports Fantasy Auto Racing, FOX Fantasy Auto Racing).

How could "fan experience" offerings (at the track or online) contribute to the Speedway's immediate goal of increasing ticket sales, revenue, and media ratings?

The Speedway's Digital Footprint

KYS Website. Although the Speedway felt that www.kentuckyspeedway.com functioned well, the marketing team knew that it was important to evaluate periodically the extent to which its website not only met the needs and expectations of digital visitors, but also contributed to achieving corporate goals and objectives. As digital marketers, KYS understood that consumers continued to become more sophisticated in their online activities and, perhaps more importantly, technology continues to advance. Was the KYS digital marketing program keeping up with these advances (e.g., increased mobile usage among consumers, responsive design of websites, search engine optimization/search engine marketing developments)?

Social Media. The KYS website homepage featured links to its Facebook, Twitter, YouTube, and Instagram social media platforms. At the end of 2014, the Speedway had earned almost 72,000 Facebook likes and more than 36,300 Facebook visits. Marketing planners felt that Facebook ratings were generally high: 5-star (5,900), 4-star (1,400), 3-star (795), 2-star (173), 1-star (230), for an average of 4.5 stars, but they also felt it would be important to compare KYS numbers and ratings to those of other NASCAR tracks and other indirect competitors. They also believed that Facebook comments, like other digital "buzz" sources, could be a valuable source of fan feedback.

---

[56] Sandomir, Richard, "Want to Run with Tigers or Roll with Tide? Fans Line Up to Bid," *New York Times*, December 13, 2014, A1+

With respect to Twitter, KYS had more than 43,000 followers at the end of 2014, with 1,235 favorites. Twitter was a primary means of keeping fans informed about KYS charities and other humanitarian efforts, informing followers about KYS promotions, keeping fans involved in teams and drivers between races and during the off season, giving "shout outs" to recognize staff members, and generally maintaining top-of-mind awareness for the KYS brand.

The Speedway's YouTube channel highlighted its "Visit Our 2015 NASCAR Tripleheader" video, but also published regular "Track Vision" interviews and reports with hosts Tim Bray and Mike Schmaltz. Videos tended to show low numbers of views, so KYS was looking for ways to drive fans to its YouTube channel to enhance engagement and encourage positive viral communication. Instagram followers totaled just 1,600 at the close of 2014, with only 264 posts.

The KYS marketing team was aware that members of the desirable Millennial target market were most trusting of word-of-mouth communication (both online and offline) when making consumption decisions, and that they were especially interested in the social aspects of sports fandom.

Google Ratings. Although KYS understood that in today's digital age, current and prospective customers, as well as other important audiences, obtained customer-satisfaction and service-quality information from a wide variety of sources – for the purpose of making purchasing decisions – members of the Speedway's marketing team were somewhat concerned about the track's relatively low Google rating (3.5). On average, that was about a full point below most other tracks, based on a 5-point scale.

KYS' digital media footprint was integral to its future success. How could the Speedway use digital marketing communications strategies more effectively to help it achieve its goals and objectives?

Travel Partners

Although KYS was located very near an interstate highway and offered a variety of camping venues in close proximity to the track, it collaborated with a number of "travel partners" for fans either who did not live within driving distance or who might not want to face the challenge of driving to and from the track on a race weekend. At the end of the 2014 season, these partners included:[57]

There and Back Again Adventures – travel packages with first-class hotel accommodations in either Cincinnati or Louisville.

Star Coach Race Tours – bus transportation from a variety of locations in Kentucky, Indiana, Ohio, and Tennessee for four NASCAR races.

Northside RVs – recreational vehicle rentals, sales, parts, and service, located in Lexington, Kentucky.

Galt House – the largest hotel in Kentucky, located in Louisville, with 1,290 guest rooms.

Louisville Marriott – located in downtown Louisville, the hotel is located near a number of well-known tourist destinations.

Information about each of the travel partners was available at the KYS website, along with a link to each partner's website.

A different type of "travel" partnership was the sponsorship of the September Xfinity (previously Nationwide) race at KYS by www.VisitMyrtleBeach.com – the race itself was

---

[57] http://www.kentuckyspeedway.com/tickets/travel_partners/

called the VisitMyrtleBeach.com 300 (a 200-lap race). The partnership began in 2012, and continued through the 2015 season.[58]

"We are excited to be back as the title sponsor for the VisitMyrtleBeach.com 300 at Kentucky Speedway NASCAR XFINITY Series race," said Scott Schult, executive vice president of marketing for the Myrtle Beach Area Chamber of Commerce. "This partnership helps us engage with race fans throughout Kentucky, Ohio and the region to inspire them to visit Myrtle Beach, South Carolina. NASCAR fans and our visitors are very similar – they both love family fun and excitement. This is a great platform for creating future guests."

With the potential for new targeted segments of consumers, should KYS expand its list of travel partners, and what should it do to ensure that all Speedway partners are committed to providing the best experience and highest quality of service for KYS fans?

Driver-Star Power

For almost two decades, the Waltrip brothers (Darrell and Michael) were Kentucky's auto-racing royal family, hailing from Owensboro. Older brother Darrell was more successful on the track throughout his racing career, but some argue that younger brother Michael was equally important to racing fans from Kentucky due to his gregariousness and outgoing personality, in addition to his on-track performances. The younger Waltrip owned 50 percent of Michael Waltrip Racing, which fielded two full-time cars in the Sprint Cup series in 2014. Although Michael was still racing on a very limited basis in 2014, both he and his brother "moved on to the broadcast booth,"[59] leaving Kentuckians hungry for homegrown talent on the NASCAR circuit.

---

[58] http://finance.yahoo.com/news/visitmyrtlebeach-com-renews-sponsorship-kentucky-215200405.html

[59] http://www.courier-journal.com/story/sports/motor/kentuckiana-motorsports/2014/06/24/rhodes-can-enter-nascar-races-kentucky-speedway/11306319/

Enter Ben Rhodes: With the continued racing success of a young driver from Kentucky, sports writers and fans alike began asking the question, "In Louisville teenager Ben Rhodes, has Kentucky found its great NASCAR hope?"[60] They got at least a partial answer to their question in early December 2014, when Dale Earnhardt Jr's race team (JR Motorsports) announced that Rhodes would drive 10 races in the Xfinity Series during the 2015 racing season, and would even get a chance "to pilot the JR Motorsports No. 88 Chevrolet shared with top-level Sprint Cup Series drivers Earnhardt Jr., Kasey Kahne and reigning champion Kevin Harvick."[61] The teen's first Sprint Cup driving opportunity would happen at the Iowa Speedway race, just shortly after Rhodes celebrates his 18th birthday on February 21, 2015.

For a number of years, many observers agonized that KYS had been caught in the middle of a paradox. Although the Waltrip brothers and a number of other drivers had ensured that Kentucky had a steady driving presence at NASCAR's highest levels for nearly two decades, the state did not have a Cup race. "But by the time Kentucky Speedway finally got a Sprint Cup date in 2011, none of those drivers – all of whom were from Owensboro – were [sic] competing regularly."[62]

To what extent can KYS parlay the star power of teen driver Ben Rhodes or other local driving talent into a strategy for motivating Kentuckians to root for the "home team" at the Speedway and to attract young fans?

---

[60] http://www.kentucky.com/2014/09/18/3436303/mark-story-in-louisville-teenager.html?sp=/99/268/305/748/

[61] http://www.usatoday.com/story/sports/nascar/2014/12/05/ben-rhodes-jr-motorsports-xfinity-series-dale-earnhardt-jr/19977011/

[62] http://www.kentucky.com/2014/09/18/3436303/mark-story-in-louisville-teenager.html?sp=/99/268/305/748/

Slide Decks Available?

"The NASCAR Fan: Insights from Consumer Research." Prepared by NASCAR Market and Media Research. Spring 2014
Kentucky Speedway – NASCAR Media and Sponsor Sales Presentation

Conclusion

The marketing team arrived at the point where it needed to develop a two-year marketing plan – it also understood that much of that plan would focus on direct marketing and a comprehensive integrated marketing communications plan. Top management at KYS was expecting a written plan and a 30-minute presentation in two weeks. The proposed promotional budget is $350,000 for two years, split approximate $150,000 in year 1 and $200,000 in year 2. *It was time to get busy.*

NextWave Web: How to Incorporate Social Media and E-commerce into a Company's Strategy

By

Bela Florenthal., William Paterson University

Janine Jansen, William Paterson University

Giuliana Campanelli Andreopoulos, William Paterson University

John Malindretos, William Paterson University

INTRODUCTION

Isa and Alia Suqi are the owners of NextWave Web, which is a New Jersey-based printing company that offers a variety of different printing and binding services to companies and individual consumers. This largely service-centric company aims to offer high-quality performance to its clients. In recent years, the printing industry has confronted many challenges, one of which is the declining demand for printed materials and the increasing preference for digital alternatives. This trend has negatively affected NextWave Web's business. In addition, NextWave Web is struggling to remain profitable in a highly competitive regional and online marketplace. The company's high investment in expensive equipment has added to its challenges in terms of remaining profitable and achieving returns on its investment. To respond to these challenges, Isa and Alia are asking themselves what sustainable strategies they should employ to grow NextWave Web's revenue while remaining competitive in a changing marketplace, and retaining a level of profitability that covers their high investment costs.

THE PRINTING INDUSTRY

Industry Trends

The printing industry had confronted significant challenges in the past five years. The revenue for printed materials declined at an average annual rate of 1.7% between 2010 and 2014. Total revenue was expected to continue to decrease in 2015 to an estimated $78.7 billion at a negative rate of 1.8%. This declining trend was predicted to continue in the future, falling at an average rate of 2.7% per year between 2015 and 2019 and accounting for a total revenue of $69.8 billion in 2019 (McKenna, 2014).

The factors contributing to the declining demand for printed materials included an increase in the demand for digital media, an increase in material costs, and a struggling U.S. economy. The printing industry's primary obstacle had been the rise of digital media, which were growing in popularity and slowly replacing traditional forms of paper media. Digital newspaper audiences rose by 10% between March 2014 and March 2015 (Conaghan, 2014b). Simultaneously, digital advertising revenue also increased by approximately 6% between 2013 and 2014, while print advertising in newspapers and magazines decreased by 9.2% and 4.3%, respectively (Statista, 2015a). This trend caused the printing industry to restructure in continuing its transition to digital media. Newspapers had been investing heavily in digital products and had simultaneously been eliminating traditional newsroom jobs and replacing them with digital media positions to meet the increasing demand. A decline in paper media demand had also forced the printing industry to consolidate significantly in order to manage overcapacity. The number of commercial printing companies fell at an annual rate of 1.3% between 2009 and 2014 (McKenna, 2014) and was expected to continue its decline in the future.

Another factor contributing to the decreasing demand for print media was the increasing consumer prices resulting from rising material and distribution costs. Materials represent the highest costs for the printing industry, accounting for 42.6% of revenue in 2014 (McKenna, 2014). In particular, the price of paper increased at an average annual rate of 1.6% between

2010 and 2014 (Rivera, 2015). The cost of raw materials for ink, such as crude oil, was predicted to increase 3.7% between 2014 and 2019, while the cost of plastic materials and resin was predicted to rise 2.2% during the same time period.

Consumers reacted to price increases by switching to the free digital content available on the Internet. This shift was evidenced by the 20% decline in print-only circulation revenue in 2013 (Conaghan, 2014a) and by the increasing amount of time spent on digital media. Overall, the average time that an adult in the U.S. spent on digital media per day increased from 29.6% in 2010 to 47.1% in 2014, while the time spent on print media decreased from 7.7% in 2010 to 3.5% in 2014 (Figure 1).

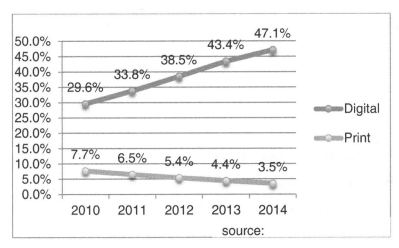

FIGURE 1: Time Spent per Day on Digital and Print Media by Adults in the U.S., 2010-2014 (Percentages)

Continuing improvements in mobile technology contributed to increased access to digital content online. Mobile devices such as smartphones, tablets, and e-readers allowed individuals to consume digital content anywhere and anytime via Wi-Fi or mobile broadband. Research indicated that 56% of all online content was consumed via mobile devices such as smartphones (44%) and tablets (12%; Gunelius, 2014). A survey showed that only 28% of people read news and 51% read magazines in print; by contrast, 43% read news and 29% read magazines on mobile devices (ComScore, 2011). Furthermore, the use of mobile devices for digital content was expected to increase as more people chose to replace desktop computers with mobile devices to access digital content (Gunelius, 2014).

Finally, the economic conditions in recent years (e.g., the recession and slow recovery) had negatively affected the printing industry. During the recession in 2009, the printing industry experienced a major decline in revenue. Figure 2 demonstrates how printing revenue decreased from $105.1 billion in 2008 to $87.5 billion in 2009, representing a 16.8% decline. Despite a period of recovery between 2009 and 2010, the industry continued to decline slowly from 2010 through 2014, and the industry was expected to undergo a very slow recovery through 2019.

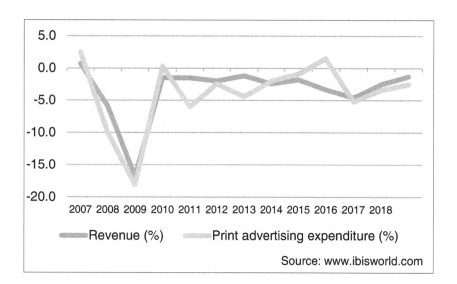

FIGURE 2: Annual Changes in Revenue and Print Advertising Expenditures, 2007 – 2019

This decline resulted from businesses' reduced spending on print advertising and the decline in magazine and newspaper distribution to consumers. Subscriptions to newspapers and magazines had declined significantly from 2008 to 2013. According to the Pew Research Center, news magazines lost 43% of their average single copy sales between 2008 and 2013 (Pew Research Center, 2014).

Despite the decline in the printing industry and its predicted continued contraction in the future, it still generated approximately $80 billion in revenue annually. This figure suggests that the demand for print and printing products remained high and that it was still worthwhile for businesses to operate in this industry. Most of the demand came from business segments such as advertising, retail (e.g., clothing, packaging) and publishing (e.g., catalogs, books).

Segments That Use Printing Services

In 2014, three segments—advertising, publishing, and retail—accounted for nearly two-thirds of the demand for printing (Figure 3). Three other segments—consumer goods manufacturers, stationary and textile manufacturers, and financial and legal firms— accounted for approximately 20% of the printing demand. Advertising demands products such as direct mail, inserts, catalogs, directories and screen-printed signs. Publishers primarily commission books, magazines and periodicals to be printed. Retail requires printing for grocery bags, catalogs, and direct mail advertising. Consumer goods manufacturing uses printing services for product packaging, labels and wrapping. The demand from retail and consumer goods manufacturers was expected to increase in 2015. The demand from stationary and textile manufacturers had also exhibited growth in recovering consumer sentiments (McKenna, 2014).

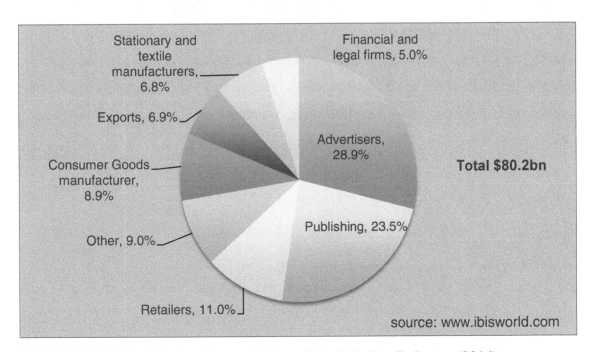

FIGURE 3: Major Market Segmentation of the Printing Industry (2014)

To adequately serve different market segments, the printing industry offered a variety of products and services, including commercial lithographic printing for advertising, magazines and periodicals, flexographic printing primarily used by manufacturers for product packaging, and book printing and binding for publishers.

Products and Services

Commercial lithographic printing, which has low operating costs, accounted for the largest share (54.7%) of total revenue in 2014 (Figure 4). Commercial screen printing, which is primarily used for textile surfaces, accounted for approximately 9% of revenue in 2014. Commercial flexographic printing is another important method that is primarily used for consumer goods manufacturers to print labels and wrappers and that accounted for 7.6% of total revenue in 2014. Digital printing generated 6.6% of total revenue. This type of printing is cost-effective for small print runs; however, its quality is lower than that of lithographic printing. Finally, book printing accounted for 5.3% of total revenue.

In addition to these five major processes, various plate-less printing processes that are comparatively new technologies include digital electronic printing processes (e.g., xerography, ink jet printing, and the Mead Cycolor Photo capsule process). Plate-less printing was gradually becoming a major process in the printing industry because of its relative ease of use and the growing application of computer-controlled printing operations.

FIGURE 4: Product and Services of the Printing Industry (2014)

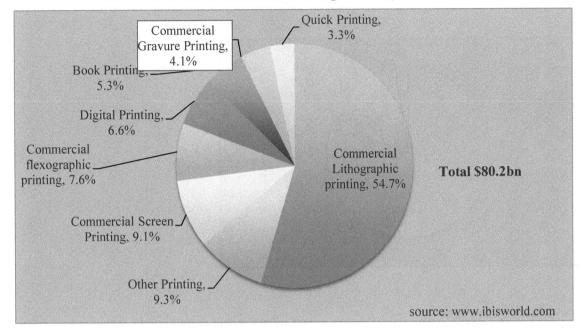

Cost Structure of the Printing Industry

Company size, the types of clients served, and the products offered are all factors influencing the cost structure of firms in the printing industry and affecting profit. Additionally, purchases of raw materials, wages, rent, utilities and depreciation are major cost factors (Figure 3). Profit margins can vary between 2.6% and 5% depending on the product segment (McKenna, 2014). Profit margins are also influenced by intense competition and restructuring in the industry. The purchase of raw materials such as paper, ink, and chemicals typically represents the highest costs in a printing business (42.6% in 2014). Furthermore, because printing is a labor-intensive industry, wages account for nearly a quarter of total costs. Finally, rent, utilities, depreciation, and administration account for the remainder of costs and nearly one-third of total industry costs. (See Figure 5:)

FIGURE 5: Cost Breakdown of the Printing Industry in 2014

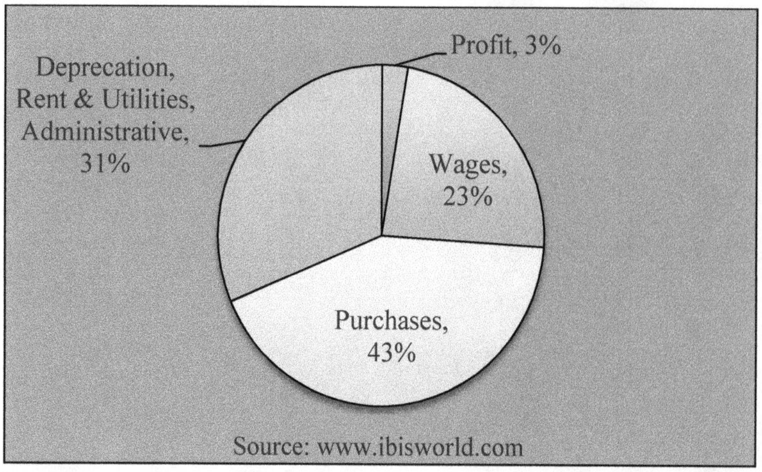

Source: www.ibisworld.com

Competition Landscape

As of 2014, four companies (RR Donnelley & Sons Co., Quad/Graphics Inc., Cenveo Inc., and Valassis Corp.) accounted for slightly more than 21% of the revenue in the printing industry, and the remaining 80% of revenue was distributed among approximately 49,000 smaller firms (McKenna, 2014). These figures suggest that the entry barriers were not very high, although they varied by industry segment. Offset printing requires a high investment in capital. To reduce costs, companies in this segment are inclined to consolidate to be able to offer cost-effective economies of scale through large print capacities and long-term contracts. By contrast, quick digital printing is primarily used by small businesses, as it requires less capital investment and has lower barriers to entry. These companies offer short print runs with the efficient use of proprietary software programs and processes; their productivity is augmented through high printing volumes that reduce the cost per unit.

The printing industry competes based on five key factors: price, quality, geographical location, technological capacity, and add-on services offered. Price is a major factor for competition and is affected by the cost of raw materials, excess industry capacity and the introduction of alternative technologies that reduce demand in some segments. As most printers provide comparable quality, companies must differentiate themselves through other factors, such as flexibility and response times. With the increasing use of online printing services, the location of printers becomes less important. Variety in the technological capacities of printers can serve as a competitive advantage for a company, as it can fulfill more specific customer requirements. For example, a company's ability to print highly sensitive documents in a high-security facility may serve as a competitive advantage. Using newer digital printing processes and more sophisticated printing software, the company can provide secure file transfers to its customers.

Finally, printing companies can be competitive based on the add-on services that they provide as they deepen their relationships with customers. Such services can include stock holding and warehousing, logistic services, databases and personalization (e.g., for direct mail), marketing lists, creative services (e.g., content creation), and digital content management. In some product segments (e.g., directories, catalogs, and magazines), printing companies can have long-term contracts spanning a period of many years, which can create a temporary barrier for competitors. Customers consider these factors when choosing a printing company. Thus, the ability to fulfill as many customer demands as possible increases a company's competitiveness.

Company Background

NextWave Web was a family-based printing company located in Paterson, New Jersey. Isa and Alia Suqi, who also acted as CEOs of the company, founded NextWave Web in 2003. The company had a 60:40 ratio of majority female ownership because female business owners have access to more resources and assistance. Alia managed tasks such as marketing, sales, human resource management, and accounting, whereas Isa's primary tasks included managing the production process and providing customer service. The company attempted to target larger customers, and it had recently provided services to Clinique and Horizon Blue Cross Blue Shield. The company employed seven full-time and part-time employees and occasionally employed additional staff when needed for large projects. The company also hired two graphic designers, as Isa and Alia intend to expand their business into web design. NextWave Web was dedicated to providing high-quality products and excellent customer service, and the company was known for its quick turnaround of printing jobs.

To ensure high quality and flexibility in servicing its customers, the company had acquired printing machines with sophisticated technology. The company was heavily invested in such machines, which had a high rate of depreciation and large overhead costs. NextWave Web currently owned approximately 20 machines, which included three digital imaging printers, five large format printers, four pre-press machines, eight bindery machines and two machines for mailing services such as envelope printing. With this large quantity of machines, NextWave could offer a wide variety of products and services, which might serve as a competitive advantage. However, the machines had been significantly depreciated since they were purchased, and they were currently underused (they were used for 18-20 days a month). Therefore, the owners realize that it was important to increase orders from customers to prevent the machines from sitting idle and to use the machines efficiently.

The Company's Competitiveness

NextWave Web had four direct competitors based on the following three criteria: location, product and service offerings, and social media presence. All four companies were located within eight miles of NextWave Web. Alpha Graphics was a global leader in marketing and print communications and a one-stop shop for the marketing and printing needs of its customers. Alchemy Digital Imaging was a full-service large format digital printing company that supplied printing services to retail and wholesale companies. JC Printing and Advertising provided a wide variety of products to target a large customer base, and its products ranged from banners, brochures, T-shirts, and wedding invitations to mailing services and binding. Trinity Press was similar to NextWave Web in its production capabilities, which range from pre-press to pressroom and include finishing and binding processes.

Table 1 summarizes the product mix of each competitor compared with that of NextWave Web, demonstrating that NextWave Web was the least competitive of these companies. Similar to NextWave Web, all four competitors offered quick and digital printing. Quick printing included rush jobs with quicker turnaround times. Digital printing refers to a method through which digital-based images are printed directly on a variety of media. Alchemy Digital differentiated itself by offering UV printing, which allowed for direct printing of high-resolution (720dpi) images on rigid materials such as coroplast, foamcore, wood, and glass. The other three competitors offered business supply printing (e.g., business cards, letterheads, color copying, stationary, and business forms) and wedding invitations, which NextWave Web and Alchemy Digital did not offer.

TABLE 1: Printing Services Offered by NextWave Web and Its Competitors

Company	Quick Printing	Digital Printing	UV Printing	Wedding Invitations & Announcements	Business Supplies
NextWave Web	Yes	Yes	No	No	No
JC Printing	Yes	Yes	No	Yes	Yes
Trinity Press	Yes	Yes	No	Yes	Yes
Alchemy Digital	Yes	Yes	Yes	No	No
Alpha Graphics	Yes	Yes	No	Yes	Yes

To differentiate themselves, printing companies can offer additional services such as marketing and direct mail, "outside the press" promotional items, website development and mobile application development. Marketing and direct mail include managing advertising campaigns, from idea generation and the design of advertising pieces to their implementation through mailing list acquisition and the fulfillment of mailing services. "Outside the press" promotional items can include t-shirts, political campaign signs, coffee mugs, and pens. With the increasing importance of digital media, a growing number of printing companies were offering web design services and mobile application development. Table 2 provides additional support for the claim that NextWave Web is not competitive in terms of its service and product offerings. Alpha Graphics offers all additional services and has a clear advantage over its competitors. Trinity Press and Alchemy Digital offer only "outside the press" services. JC Printing is slightly more competitive than Trinity Press and Alchemy Digital, as it offers marketing and direct mail services in addition to "outside the press" services. NextWave Web is the least competitive, as it offers only marketing and direct mail services.

TABLE 2: Additional Services Offered by NextWave Web and Its Competitors

Company	Marketing and Direct Mail	"Outside the Press" (Shirts, pens, etc.)	Web Site Development	Mobile Application Development
NextWave Web	Yes	No	No	No
JC Printing	Yes	Yes	No	No
Trinity Press	No	Yes	No	No
Alchemy Digital	No	Yes	No	No
Alpha Graphics	Yes	Yes	Yes	Yes

Website Analysis

In today's business world, a well-designed company website and a substantial social media presence are vital to ensure success. Company websites are frequently assessed based on the following criteria: visibility, visual design, content, navigation, and promotions. NextWave Web's website was evaluated and compared with the websites of its direct competitors based on these criteria. Three rating levels were used: poor, good, and excellent. The results in Table 3 indicate that NextWave Web did not compete well in its website assessment, scoring only "good" in the first four categories and "poor" in the last category. Visibility refers to how easily the company can be found using search engines and direct URL searches. Both NextWave Web and JC Printing scored "good" on website visibility; both were in the top search results when specifying the geographic location "Paterson" in the search terms, but neither appeared in the results of generic searches with "printing" as the search term. By contrast, Alpha Graphics had excellent visibility, as it is always appeared in the top search results with generic or location-specific search terms. Trinity Press and Alchemy Digital had poor visibility, as neither business appeared in the search results when any of the search terms are used.

TABLE 3: Website Comparison of NextWave Web and Its Competitors

Website	Visibility	Visual Design	Content	Navigation	Promotions
NextWave Web	Good	Good	Good	Good	Poor
JC Printing	Good	Good	Good	Good	Poor
Trinity Press	Poor	Poor	Good	Poor	Poor
Alchemy Digital	Poor	Excellent	Excellent	Excellent	Poor
Alpha Graphics	Excellent	Good	Good	Good	Poor

Visual design focuses on the aesthetics of a site and its related materials through the strategic use of images, colors, fonts and other elements. Alchemy Digital had an excellent clean visual design that uses pictures to present its products, materials, and services. NextWave Web, JC Printing and Alpha Graphics lacked visual images to present their products and services and thus received only a "good" score. Trinity Press' visual design was poor, as it did not use any visual images to present its products and services; its website used dark colors and had a busy background, which resulted in an unappealing visual design.

Content refers to the structure and functionality of the website. NextWave Web had "good" content, as it used tabs to organize its content, but it did not use drop-down menus similar to those on Alchemy Digital's website to enable visitors to easily find information on products and services. Navigation focused on how easily a user could maneuver through the site content. Navigation on Alchemy Digital's website was "excellent," as individuals could easily find product information and scroll through its services. By contrast, NextWave Web's website received only a "good" score because its left sidebar needed improvement. The sidebar currently only listed NextWave Web's products and services and did not include active links to the product list. Trinity Press had a "poor" navigation bar; instead of being placed at the top of the website, the bar appeared at the bottom. Depending on the web browser used, the website might not be scaled correctly, and the footer might be hidden. Finally, in terms of promotional postings, such as special offers, all companies performed poorly. None of the companies displayed any promotional deals.

Social Media Presence

In addition to having a well-designed company website, successful businesses must develop and maintain an engaging social media presence. Studies have shown that the use of social media platforms by businesses can increase referrals, company website traffic, and overall revenue (DeMers, 2015). Social media refer to online communities in which people can share and publicize information, ideas, personal messages, and other rich content, such as video.

Over the past 10 years, social media marketing has been integrated into most companies' strategies, as it is cost-effective and much more efficient than traditional promotional efforts. Establishing an account on online social media platforms is typically free, and the associated promotional costs are a fraction of those for TV, radio, or magazine ads. According to *Adweek*, the cost of a 30-second TV ad in 2011 ranged from $25,000 to $127,000, depending on the broadcaster, program, and time of day (Crupi, 2012). By contrast, advertising on social media typically incurs a cost per click (CPC) or a cost per thousand impressions (CPM). In 2013, U.S. advertisers paid an average of $0.24 for CPC and $0.66 for CPM on Facebook (Prosser, 2013).

Furthermore, the cost of designing an ad for a social media site is significantly less expensive than creating an ad for TV or radio. The former can simply be designed with a computer program, whereas the latter may require expensive video equipment, voiceovers or professional actors. Social media campaigns also have the advantage of greater flexibility, as changing or deleting information in a social media ad is much easier and faster than doing so in traditional print, TV or radio ads. Finally, social media promotions can be tailored to different target audiences, whereas traditional media promotions tend to be mass distributed; hence, social media promotions are more efficient than traditional promotions.

Most Facebook, Twitter, Instagram, and Pinterest users were between 18 and 29 years old and accounted for 87%, 37%, 53% and 34%, respectively, of the total user base (Duggan et al., 2015). LinkedIn was the only social media site whose users are predominantly between 30 and 49 years old; however, the 18-29 age group of LinkedIn users had grown 8% between 2013 and 2014, which was double the growth in the number of users between 30 and 49 years (Duggan et al., 2015.). Instagram experienced the highest increase of Internet users from 17% in 2013 to 26% in 2014, representing a 9% increase. Therefore, a growing number of businesses were using social media sites for customized advertising and brand management.

Currently, the five most popular social media sites were Facebook, Twitter, LinkedIn, Pinterest, and Instagram. With a total of 1.39 billion active users as of the fourth quarter of 2014, Facebook was considered the most popular social networking site (Statista, 2015a). Twitter, which had a total of 288 million active users as of December 2014 (Statista, 2015b), was often described as a microblogging service because messages were limited to 140 characters.

LinkedIn is a social media service that is geared toward college students, business professionals and businesses worldwide. As of the fourth quarter in 2014, it had a total of 347 active users (Statista, 2015c). LinkedIn could serve businesses beyond personal or professional networking. Businesses could improve business-to-business relationships by finding vendors, suppliers, and manufacturers and by connecting with companies with similar interests. By staying active on LinkedIn, companies could build their brand image and increase their customer base.

Pinterest is a social networking site that allows users to share visual content such as images and videos. Users can organize "pinned" pictures and videos by interests or themes on their own or another's "pinboard." Items that have been pinned can also be liked, repinned, or commented on by users. Pinterest has been demonstrated to be more effective in driving traffic to a company's website than other social media sites are (Georgieva, n.d.). A photo of a company's product that is "pinned" may receive positive reviews and lead potential customers to a company's website (Georgieva, n.d.). According to Forbes.com, social media drive approximately 31% of all referral traffic (2015), with Pinterest being the only social media site experiencing an increase from 2014. As of January 2015, Pinterest had 50.5 million unique visitors (Statista, 2015d). Women currently dominated the Pinterest website, representing 42% of all users (Duggan et al., 2015).

Similar to Pinterest, Instagram is a social media site that primarily uses photos and videos to create visual content and share content primarily across mobile devices. In December 2014, Instagram had reached 300 million active users (Statista, 2015e). The site significantly increased in popularity between 2013 and 2014 and even surpassed Twitter, with a total of 26% of Internet-connected adults using the service compared with 23% of those using Twitter (Duggan et al., 2015).

To use these social media sites effectively, companies can create profiles, upload photos and videos, share information and send messages to remain in contact with their customers. Visuals such as photos and videos are particularly important, as users are more likely to engage with visual content rather than with textual content. For example, photos on Facebook generate 53% more "likes" than regular status updates (Corliss, 2012), and "tweets" with image links on Twitter obtain two times the engagement rates of those without such links (Cooper, 2013). As social media sites attract different demographic groups, businesses should tailor their communication to each audience. Companies should remain in continuous communication with their followers to increase engagement in sharing company content and attracting new customers.

When NextWave Web was compared with its competitors in their use of social media marketing, the results clearly indicated that none of these companies, except Alpha Graphics, were using social media platforms effectively (Table 4). NextWave Web currently had Facebook and LinkedIn accounts that were not very active. NextWave Web's Facebook page had 118 "likes," and its LinkedIn profile had only 14 followers; the company did not have Twitter, Pinterest or Instagram accounts. Furthermore, its direct competitors were not very

active on social media. For example, JC Printing, which is similar to NextWave Web, had
Facebook and LinkedIn accounts that were not very active. JC Printing's Facebook page had
102 "likes," and its LinkedIn profile had 12 followers. One advantage that the company had
over NextWave Web was that it had several favorable public reviews on Facebook. Although
JC Printing had opened a Pinterest account, it had no "followers," "likes," or "pins," and the
account was not active.

TABLE 4: Social Media Comparison of NextWave Web and Its Competitors

Company	Facebook	LinkedIn	Twitter	Pinterest	Instagram
NextWave Web	118 likes	14 followers	-	-	-
JC Printing	102 likes	12 followers		• Has an Account • No followers, likes, or pins	
Trinity Press	-	-	-	-	-
Alchemy Digital	-	12 followers	-	-	-
Alpha Graphics	• Wayne/Totowa – 73 likes • Corporate headquarters – 1,500 likes	5,000 followers	• Corporate headquarters – 1,654 followers and 3,000 tweets	-	• Several accounts • 6-36 employees

Both Trinity Press and Alchemy Digital had no social media presence, as they did not have
any active accounts. Only Alchemy Digital had a LinkedIn profile, with a total of 12
followers, but the profile did not link employees and did not show any effort toward building
a network of connections with other businesses or suppliers in the industry. The company did
not create any content in the form of publications or other shared information that might
interest potential customers or create visibility, and it did not use LinkedIn to hire new
employees.

Alpha Graphics was the most active competitor on social media. Its Facebook page for the Wayne/Totowa location had only 73 likes, but the corporate headquarters' official Facebook page had nearly 1,500 likes. The page regularly published useful and relevant content such as visuals (e.g., photos, videos) of their employees, completed projects, and work events. It had a high public review rating, with a 4.4 average out of 5 stars. Although the company did not have a Totowa-specific Twitter account, the Twitter account for its corporate headquarters was highly active, with a total of 1,654 followers and nearly 3,000 "tweets." The company's Twitter account also included pictures of company events and links to other posts that showcased its products and work. Its LinkedIn profile had nearly 5,000 followers and 1,361 connected employees; it frequently provided informative updates and leveraged "tweets" by sharing them on LinkedIn. Moreover, Alpha Graphics was the only printing business that had several Instagram accounts for different business locations, ranging from six to 36 followers. All of these accounts shared visuals that showcased the company's work, employees, and important business events.

To increase its competitiveness in the printing industry and to remain profitable, NextWave Web recognized the need to reevaluate its current marketing strategy and to identify new growth opportunities. In particular, Isa and Alia wanted to harness emerging opportunities in e-commerce and social media marketing. Therefore, they were seeking operative answers to the following questions:

1. What are their strengths and weakness, and how can they approach the opportunities and threats that they face in the shifting marketplace of the printing industry?
2. How can they expand their product and service offerings to attract new customers, boost revenue, and increase the profitability of their equipment?
3. As e-commerce and social media marketing are critical to any company's success, how can they develop their e-commerce operations and increase their social media presence?

4. What additional promotional tools can NextWave Web use to complement its social media and e-commerce operations and to leverage other online advertising services?

References

ComScore. (2011). Digital Omnivores: How Tablets, Smartphones and Connected Devices are Changing U.S. Digital Media Consumption Habits. [Retrieved May 6, 2015] Available: http://www.iab.net/media/file/Digital%2BOmnivores.pdf

Conaghan, J. (2014a). Business Model Evolving, Circulation Revenue Rising. *Newspaper Association of America*. [Retrieved February 19, 2015] Available: http://www.naa.org/Trends-and-Numbers/Newspaper-Revenue/Newspaper-MediaIndustry-Revenue-Profile-2013.aspx

Conaghan, J. (2014b). Newspaper Digital Audience. *Newspaper Association of America*. [Retrieved February 19, 2015] Available: http://www.naa.org/Trends-and-Numbers/Newspaper-Websites/Newspaper-Web-Audience.aspx.

Cooper, B. B. (2013). 10 Surprising New Twitter Stats to help you Reach More Followers. [Retrieved March 26, 2015] Available: https://blog.bufferapp.com/10-new-twitter-stats-twitter-statistics-to-help-you-reach-your-followers

Corliss, R. (2012). Photos on Facebook Generate 53% More Likes Than the Average Post. [Retrieved March 26, 2015] Available: http://blog.hubspot.com/blog/tabid/6307/bid/33800/Photos-on-Facebook-Generate-53-More-Likes-Than-the-Average-Post-NEW-DATA.aspx

Crupi, A. (2012). Broadcast Spot Pricing Continues to Creep Up Average: 30 Network Prime Time Increased 3 Percent in 2011. *Adweek*. [Retrieved March 26, 2015] Available: http://www.adweek.com/news/advertising-branding/broadcast-spot-pricing-continues-creep-138106

DeMers, J. (2015). Social Media Now Drives 31% Of All Referral traffic. *Forbes.com*. [Retrieved March 26, 2015] Available: http://www.forbes.com/sites/jaysondemers/2015/02/03/social-media-now-drives-31-of-all-referral-traffic/

Duggan, M., Ellison, N. B., Lampe, C., Lenhart A., Madden, M. (2015). Demographics of
    Key Social Networking Platforms. *Pew Research Center.* [Retrieved March 26, 2015]
    Available: http://www.pewinternet.org/2015/01/09/demographics-of-key-social-
    networking-platforms-2/

Georgieva, M. (n.d.). How to Use Pinterest for Business: Drive Traffic & Lead to Your
Website
    with Pinterest. [Retrieved March 25, 2015] Available:
    http://cdn2.hubspot.net/hub/53/blog/docs/ebooks/howtousepinterestforbusiness.pdf

Gunelius, S. (2014). More than Half of Digital Content Now Consumed on Mobile Devices.
    ACI Blog. [Retrieved May 12, 2015] Available: http://aci.info/2014/05/14/more-than-
    half-of-digital-content-now-consumed-on-mobile-devices/

McKenna, F. (2014, December). IBISWorld Industry Report 32311. Printing in the US. *IBIS
    World database.* [Retrieved January 29, 2015] Available:
    http://www.ibisworld.com/industry/default.aspx?indid=433

Pew Research Center. (2014). State of the news media 2014: Key Indicators in Media &
    News. [Retrieved February 2, 2015] Available:
    http://www.journalism.org/2014/03/26/state-of-the-news-media-2014-key-indicators-
    in-media-and-news/

Prosser, M. (2013). How much does Facebook Advertising Cost? [Retrieved March 26,
    2015] Available: http://fitsmallbusiness.com/how-much-does-facebook-advertising-
    cost/

Rivera, E. (2015). IBISWorld Industry Report 42411. Paper Wholesaling in the U.S. *IBIS
    World database.* [Retrieved February 4, 2015] Available:
    http://www.ibisworld.com/industry/default.aspx?indid=960

Statista - The Statistics Portal. (2015). Change in advertising spending in the United States
    from January to September 2013 and 2014, by medium. [Retrieved March 26, 2015]
    Available: http://www.statista.com/statistics/233742/change-in-advertising-spending-
    in-the-us-by-media-type/

Statista - The Statistics Portal. (2015a). Facebook. Number of monthly active Facebook users worldwide as of 4th quarter 2014 (in millions). [Retrieved March 11, 2015] Available: http://www.statista.com/statistics/264810/number-of-monthly-active-facebook-users-worldwide/

Statista - The Statistics Portal (2015b). Twitter. Number of monthly active Twitter users worldwide from 1st quarter 2010 to 4th quarter 2014 (in millions). [Retrieved March 26, 2015] Available: http://www.statista.com/statistics/282087/number-of-monthly-active-twitter-users/

Statista - The Statistics Portal (2015c). LinkedIn. Numbers of LinkedIn members from 1st quarter 2009 to 4th quarter 2014 (in millions). [Retrieved March 26, 2015] Available: http://www.statista.com/statistics/274050/quarterly-numbers-of-linkedin-members/

Statista - The Statistics Portal (2015d). Unique U.S. visitors to Pinterest.com 2011-2015. [Retrieved March 26, 2015] Available: http://www.statista.com/statistics/277694/number-of-unique-us-visitors-to-pinterestcom/

Statista - The Statistics Portal (2015e). Number of Monthly Active Instagram Users from January 2013 to December 2014 (in millions). [Retrieved March 26, 2015] Available: http://www.statista.com/statistics/253577/number-of-monthly-active-instagram-users/

PasseportSanté

A Large Consumer Health Information Web Site Turns 2.0

By

Sandrine Prom Tep – University of Quebec in Montreal

Annie Couture – HEC Montreal

Sylvain Senecal – HEC Montreal

Abstract

This case study describes the various decisional steps undertaken by one of Canada's largest consumer health information Web sites and its managers in order to determine which 2.0 functionalities should be implemented so that visitors could efficiently appropriate site content, thereby stimulating both visitor interest and the growth of the website. This study presents the site development process and critical turning points, as well as the current status of the website. This is followed by an examination of benchmark websites with similar health-related content, in both English and French, with particular emphasis on Web 2.0 features and their level of use. The report concludes with strategic recommendations derived from this exercise, targeted at providing data-driven managerial decisions based on actual site utilization.

Introduction

Charmian Harvey, the CEO of the PasseportSanté.net website, was convinced that the future of the site would depend on implementation of Web 2.0 features. In her opinion, such interactive features should allow visitors to find appropriate site content, stimulating their interest and participation and thus stimulating the growth of the website.

However, with the multitude of available options and the limits of each, Charmian wondered: What type of functionalities should be included? What does each imply in terms of site management? And especially, what needs to be done to satisfy visitors to the site, to encourage them to participate and, ultimately, to ensure the success of the site?

The stated mission of the PasseportSanté.net web portal was to "offer the public practical, reliable and accessible information and solutions concerning health promotion, disease prevention and the judicious use of alternative and complementary medicine in conjunction with traditional medicine" [1].

The website was created in 1998 by Christian Lamontagne under the name *Réseau Proteus*. Originally, it came into being to fill the need for a source of neutral, scientific information in French about complementary approaches to health and healthcare. During its first year online, Réseau Proteus received approximately 30,000 visitors. Forums were introduced during those early years, but blogs first appeared on the site only in 2007. Réseau Proteus was acquired by the *Fondation Lucie et André Chagnon* in 2001, which is devoted to promoting and improving health through prevention [2]. Among the first actions taken by the new owners was to remove all publicity from the site in order to ensure its independence from potential pressure from advertisers. Réseau Proteus was also provided with access to the new funding resources required for the growth of the site [3].

In 2004, a nutrition section was added, presenting an encyclopedia of foods, in addition to an on-line cookbook, a ranking of nutrients and an index of weight-loss and other specialized diets. In 2005, the name was changed to *PasseportSanté.net* [4]. Having grown to more than 3000 pages, the website contained information on some 200 diseases, 200 natural health products, some 100 therapies and approximately 160 foods [5], as well as health news items. In 2007, the time had come to review the interface, its user-friendliness and web ergonomics.

Currently, PasseportSanté.net was an essential web resource. The information on the site was rigorously and scientifically validated; all content was closely examined by a scientific review team composed of more than 45 collaborators. The portal received two million visits per month, including 620,000 from Canada alone. More than 130,000 individuals had subscribed to the weekly newsletter and 4000 members were active participants in the forums. There was also a new section called *Vivre en santé* (Living Healthy). All content was written by an editorial team with eight writers, assisted by a broad network of collaborators.

PasseportSanté.net had already implemented some interactive features (see webshot of site, Figure 1). First, the forum mentioned above, which received 100,000 page-views per month. The site also had four regular blogs, in addition to a blog for invited columnists which appeared occasionally. Articles were changed every week or two. The blogs were quite popular: in a recent 31-day period, 86,000 page-views had been recorded for the blogs alone. In addition, a quiz entitled *La question Santé* (The Health Question) posed questions about health habits and knowledge. Finally, the portal allowed visitors to make comments and write testimonials if they so desired.

Figure 1. Webshot of the PasseportSanté.net gateway

Health Websites

The website CEO, Charmian Harvey, also knew that many Internet sites that dealt with health issues offered Web 2.0 features, some of which are presented here, grouped into four categories which well represented the range of functionalities available on health websites. Table1 presents the language, date of creation and monthly traffic information for each site.

The first category is Parenting websites, which includes sites covering subjects related mainly to pregnancy and pediatrics. The examples in this category are BabyCenter, Parents.com, Babyworld, Magicmaman, Tiboo.com and Maman pour la vie.

The second category is Traditional Medicine, which is limited to sites covering traditional medical approaches and issues concerning medications. This category is represented by the MedHelp website.

The third category is Overall Health, which includes websites that deal with a wide variety of health-related issues, such as medications; nutrition and diets; pregnancy; psychology and mental health; sexuality; alternative medicine; and healthy lifestyles in general. This category includes WebMD, Revolution Health, Doctissimo and, the subject of this case study, PasseportSanté.net.

Finally, certain websites are limited to questions of Nutrition and Fitness. Spark People was selected to represent this category.

Table 1. A sampling of health-related websites.

Categories and websites	Language	Date created	Canada*	Quebec*	U.S.*
Parenting Websites					
- Babycenter	English and others	1997	500	33	3,212
- Parents.com	(N.A. in French)	1997	141	10	1,906
- Babyworld	English	1999			
- Magicmaman	English	2000	74	56	--
- Tiboo.com	French	1999	--	--	--
- Maman pour la vie	French	2004	106	97	--
	French				
Traditional Medicine	English, Spanish	1996	379	37	2,140
- MedHelp					
Overall Health					
- WebMD	English	1996	579	37	10,357
- Revolution Health	English	2000	165	24	4,366
- Doctissimo	French	2000	1,078	943	55
- PasseportSanté.net	**French**	**1998**	239	225	--
Nutrition and Fitness	English		137	6	1740
- SparkPeople					

(*total visits per month. Source: Comscore; www.comscore.com)

Use of Web 2.0 by the Competition

All of the competing websites listed in Table 1 use interactive interfaces in various ways and with varied degrees of success. Charmian Harvey wanted to know more about the types of interactive interfaces used elsewhere and about how they were used. Above all, she wanted to know more about the factors influencing the success of implementing these features. She wanted to undertake a major shift toward 2.0 functionality, but she wanted to make sure that no interactive features were implemented, only to be removed later due to lack of interest. To clarify the decision-making process, she decided to consult the RBC Financial Group Electronic Commerce Chair at the *École des Hautes Études Commerciales* of Montréal for a comparative analysis.

Benchmarking was chosen as the preferred method for comparative analysis. It consists of comparing many entities (in this case, websites) with respect to certain key elements (in this case, interactive features). The goal of the study was to shed light on the factors contributing to the success of each feature and to identify the best practices for management of such interactive features. Each of the websites listed in Table 1 was examined with respect the following interactive features: *forums, blogs, chat, newsletters, personalized pages* and *groups.*

Among the aspects of each feature that was examined were moderation, hosting and rating. *Moderation* consists of accepting or rejecting, in whole or in part, the posting of information submitted by a website user. Moderation may be distinguished from hosting, however the two functions are not contradictory and a moderator may serve in both capacities. Many types of moderation exist, including *pre-moderation*, in which messages are edited before being placed online, and *post-moderation*, in which messages are placed online directly and edited if there is a problem. In *peer moderation*, members of the group take on part of the moderation duties by giving ratings to each user and reporting misconduct to the moderator.

147

Hosting consists of all of the actions that are aimed at helping a group interact, resolving problems, orienting discussions, finding pertinent information and even suggestion discussion topics. Hosting helps ensure the quality of interactive features and thus contributes to the growth of the web site.

Rating systems allow participants in social media to evaluate the comments and contributions of their fellow site users. Ratings may be overall evaluations of a given user, or more specific, for each comment or posting. Ratings may be designed to function as a type of peer moderation, insofar as they motivate users to post quality content on the site.

Forums

A **forum** is a discussion group concerned with a given topic. Each user can read the comments of other users at any time and contribute to the discussion with articles, comments or responses to previous postings. Hosting and moderation are essential to ensure that the forum remains on topic and pleasant for the participants. Forums require a critical mass of participation to remain interesting. Table 2 presents the data collected for forums on health-related websites.

Table 2. Summary of data collected for forums on health-related websites

FORUMS Evaluated elements	Babycenter	Parents.com	Babyworld	Magicmaman	Tiboo.com	Maman pour la vie	MedHelp	WebMD	Revolution Health	Doctissimo	PasseportSanté.net	SparkPeople
- One or more forums on the site		X	X	X	X	X	X	X	X	X	**X**	X
- Visitor traffic (H: high; M: medium; L: low)		M	L	M	L	M	?	H	H	H	**M**	H
Classification												
- Discussions classified by category		X	X	X	X	X	X	X	X	X	**X**	X
- Discussions classified by date		X	X	X	X	X			X	X	**X**	X
- Choice of classification method				X	X	X	X	X	X			X
Features												
- Search engine		X	X	X	X			X	X	X	**X**	X
- Quizzes, surveys and other topic-related interactive tools			X	X	X			X		X	**X**	X
- Help section		X		X			X	X	X	X		X
- Personal profile; possibility to add discussions to a list of favorites												
Moderation												
- Moderated forums		X	X	X	X	X	X	X	X	X	**X**	X
- Pre-moderated forums		X	X	X	X	X	X	X		X		X
- Post-moderated forums									X		**X**	
- Hosted forums								X	X	X		
- Forum rating possible								X	X			

Blogs

A **blog** is a collection of postings or articles, often enriched with hyperlinks and multimedia elements. Blogs are maintained by bloggers, who write articles and supply the blog content.

Other web users can react to the articles by writing comments which follow each blog entry. The success of a blog depends largely on the knowledge and competence of the blogger. Table 3 presents the data collected for blogs featured on health-related websites.

Table 3. Summary of data collected for blogs on health-related websites

BLOGS Evaluated elements	Babycenter	Parents.com	Babyworld	Magicmaman	Tiboo.com	Maman pour la vie	MedHelp	WebMD	Revolution Health	Doctissimo	PasseportSanté.net	SparkPeople
- One or more blogs on the site - Visitor traffic (H: high; M: medium; L: low)	X L	X M		X ?	X ?		X ?	X ?	X H	X H	**X** **M**	
Expertise - Blogs created by site users - Blogs created by experts	X	X		X	X		X X	X	X X	X	**X** **X**	
Features - Obligatory registration to create and edit a blog - Search engine - Help section - Blogs available by RSS feed - Personal profile; possible to add discussions to a list of favorites	X	X		X X X X	X X		X X	 X X X	X X X	X X X X	 X	
Moderation - Moderated blogs - Post-moderated blogs - Peer-moderated blogs - Blog rating possible	X X X	X X X		X X X	X X X			X X X	X X X	X X X X	**X** **X** **X**	

Chat Rooms

A **chat room** is a forum for real-time dialog. User comments are recorded only for the duration of the discussion, after which they are deleted. Chat should be closely monitored, and hosted if possible, to ensure that the comments made by users do not damage the overall image of the website. Table 4 presents the data collected for chat rooms available on health-related websites.

Table 4. Summary of data collected for chat rooms on health-related websites

CHAT Evaluated elements	Babycenter	Parents.com	Babyworld	Magicmaman	Tiboo.com	Maman pour la vie	MedHelp	WebMD	Revolution Health	Doctissimo	PasseportSanté.net	SparkPeople
- Site accommodates chat - Visitor traffic (H: high; M: medium; L: low)	X L		X L		X L					X M		
Classification - Chat rooms classified by date of last message	X											
Features - Search engine - Possibility of adding a chat room to a list of favorites	X X											
Moderation - Moderated chat rooms - Post-moderated chat rooms - Hosted chat rooms	X X X											

Newsletters

A **newsletter** is a news or information bulletin which is periodically sent by email to the subscribers. Newsletters may be interactive or not, depending on the content, which may or may not be supplied by site users. The quality of the content and its pertinence for users are critical to the success of newsletters. Table 5 presents the data collected for newsletters offered on health-related websites.

Table 5. Summary of data collected for newsletters on health-related websites

NEWSLETTERS Evaluated elements	Babycenter	Parents.com	Babyworld	Magicmaman	Tiboo.com	Maman pour la vie	MedHelp	WebMD	Revolution Health	Doctissimo	PasseportSanté.net	SparkPeople
- Site offers a newsletter	X	X	X	X		X		X	X	X	X	
Access and distribution	X	X	X	X		X		X	X	X	X	
- Registration required	X	X	X	X				X	X	X	X	
- Possible to see an example before		X						X		X		
subscribing	X	X	X	X		X		X	X	X	X	
- Daily bulletin								X				
- Weekly bulletin	X	X	X	X		X		X		X	X	
- Bi-weekly bulletin												
- Link provided for cancellation												
Features - Presents applications related to bulletin		X							X	X	X	
topics - Offers surveys	X		X							X	X	

Personal Pages

Some websites allows users to have their own **personal pages**, which may be viewed by other members of the community. Such pages allow users to present themselves in a relatively in-depth manner, with text, photos or any other feature of interest to the community. Probably the best-known site for this type of page is Facebook. The content posted on personal pages should be monitored to ensure that it does not damage the image of the site. Personal pages also require a certain critical mass to retain the interest of the community. Table 6 presents the data collected on the options for posting personal pages on health-related websites.

Table 6. Summary of data collected for personal pages on health-related websites

PERSONAL PAGES Evaluated elements	Babycenter	Parents.com	Babyworld	Magicmaman	Tiboo.com	Maman pour la vie	MedHelp	WebMD	Revolution Health	Doctissimo	PasseportSanté.net	SparkPeople
- Website allows posting a personal page		X	X									X
Access and creation												
- Private access to pages		X	X									X
- Public access to pages		X	X									X
- Page easily edited once created		X	X									X
- Allows posting personal information related to the site's goals		X										X
- Allows posting of favorite content												
Features												
- Search engine			X									X
- Help section		X	X									X
Classification												
- Pages classified by popularity, date or subject		X										
Moderation												
- Moderated pages			X									
- Pre-moderated pages			X									

154

Groups

A **group** is a collection of individuals centered on a given topic of interest (e.g., breast cancer survivors' group). Interested web users may register with the group and are generally members for a relatively long period. Group members use tools such as forums to communicate with each other. Hosting/moderation are important to ensure that the discussion remains on-topic and the atmosphere is pleasant for the participants. Like forums and personal pages, groups require a certain critical mass to be of ongoing interest to participants. **Table 7 presents data collected for special-interest groups on health-related websites.**

GROUPS Evaluated elements	Babycenter	Parents.com	Babyworld	Magicmaman	Tiboo.com	Maman pour la vie	MedHelp	WebMD	Revolution Health	Doctissimo	PassportSanté.net	SparkPeople
- Site accommodates groups	X						X		X			X
Classification - Groups listed by category or in alphabetical order	X						X		X			X
- Groups listed by popularity	X								X			
Expertise - Support groups	X								X			X
- Information groups	X						X					
- Open to site users	X						X		X			X
- Open to experts									X			
Features - Search engine	X						X		X			X
- Help section												X
- RSS feed or other applications to follow groups	X						X					X
- Personal profile; possible to add discussions to a list of favorites												
Moderation - Moderated groups	X						X		X			X
- Post-moderated groups	X						X		X			X
- Hosted groups							X		X			

Additional Observations

The benchmark analysis also revealed a few general trends and additional observations for each type of interactive feature, including the following:

Forums

- Most common content: pre-conception; pregnancy and maternity; illnesses and diseases
- Least common content: cooking and recipes; rare physical conditions
- The more serious the image of the forum, the more the participants tend to use language with care

Blogs

- Most common content: general health subjects, newborns, new mothers, new families
- Least common content: very specialized health subjects

Chat rooms

- Most common content: general discussion forums, sex, psychology, pregnancy
- Least common content: all other health-related subjects (no activity)

- In general, language usage on chat sites is relatively careless, compared to the forums and the blogs.

Newsletters

- The amount of information included in bulletins does not appear to make them less accessible or readable. However very dense, non-intuitive organization of the sections can make reading difficult, as can poor page-design in general.

Acceleration of the Shift to Web 2.0

Now that Charmian Harvey and her team have examined the report — and have armed themselves with additional reinforcement from their own prior experience with the interactive features already on their website — they are in a good position to establish a Web 2.0 strategy for the PasseportSanté.net gateway over the short, medium and long term.

Acknowledgements

The authors would like to thank the CEO of PasseportSanté.net, Ms. Charmian Harvey, for agreeing to collaborate in this case study.

References

[1] Mission statement from the website of PasseportSanté.net.

[2] Mission statement from the website of the Fondation Lucie et André Chagnon.

[3] Lamontagne Christian, "10 ans de PasseportSanté.net et un vœu…" [Ten years of PasseportSanté.net and a wish...], PasseportSanté.net, Blog of Christian Lamontagne, 2008, on-line.

[4] "Nouveau portail Internet sur la médecine alternative" [New Internet gateway for alternative medicine] Le Soleil (Actualités), Friday, September 30, 2005, p. A4.

[5] "Nouveau site Web axé sur la santé et la prévention de la maladie" [New website focused on health and disease prevention]. Les Affaires (Entreprendre), Saturday, October 8, 2005, p. 44

Redskins: What's In a Name?
Powerful Forces Are on the Warpath
Against a Professional Sports Team Brand

By

Deborah Cowles -- Virginia Commonwealth University

Jan Owens – Carthage College

Matthew Sauber – Eastern Michigan University

Juliet: *"What's in a name? That which we call a rose*
by any other name would smell as sweet."
William Shakespeare: ***Romeo and Juliet (II, ii, 1-2)***

Introduction

Even before its National Football League (NFL) season began, the Washington Redskins professional football team faced a number of difficult scrimmages – powerful forces attacking from different angles – all part of a broader effort to force the team to change its brand name, logo, and mascot. Supporters believed that the team's name – Redskins – and its logo "represent the very best of the noble qualities exemplified by Native Americans."[63] But for detractors, the name was thought to be "a stubborn disregard for the feelings of Native Americans who find it demeaning and offensive and an irrational fear of losing your NFL identity."[64]

---

[63] http://www.redskinsfacts.com/about-us

[64] http://www.bostonglobe.com/sports/football/2014/08/04/washington-redskins-name-needs-changed/xookx46DbYsW4xUNz8ANII/story.html

All entities involved knew that the Washington Redskins' name controversy was decades old – dating to the early 1970s when several prominent Native Americans led a movement to help those living on Indian reservations in the United States to gain greater control over issues concerning their communities – such as education and economic affairs. Jack Kent Cooke, who owned the Redskins team and the franchise from 1974 (about the time the controversy began publicly) until 1997, had always been adamant about keeping the name. The subsequent Redskins team owner, Dan Snyder, appeared to be equally insistent that the name should not be changed.

Although there had been some signals in earlier years, the issue seemed to be reaching a critical point, and Dan Snyder found himself at the center of the controversy. He once had instructed reporters to use capital letters when quoting him, saying that he would "NEVER change the [team] name." He felt strongly about his pledge to keep the team's current brand name, logo, and mascot, but he also felt that it was his duty – as team owner– to evaluate *both sides* of the issue at hand. He was, after all, also the primary investor in Red Zebra Broadcasting – home to the Redskins Radio ESPN. In 1996, he had become the youngest-ever CEO of a New York Stock Exchange listed company (Snyder Communications), at the age of 32. He felt it was incumbent upon him to learn more about whether a brand such as the Washington Redskins should continue to take a stand.[65]

Origin of the Term "Redskins"

Some scholars believed that the term "redskins" was coined to differentiate Native Americans by the tone of their skin color. Others maintained that the name referred to the color of body paint used by certain Indian tribes for ceremonial and other purposes. European settlers used the term to identify all Native American parties while negotiating treaties. The name was also used to identify people's origins by skin color such as white men, black men, and red men.

---

[65] http://www.forbes.com/sites/datafreaks/2015/03/12/brands-take-a-stand-when-speaking-up-about-controversial-issues-hurts-or-helps-business/

Ives Goddard, a senior linguist and curator *emeritus* at the **Smithsonian Institution**, asserted that the term "redskins" was originally benign in meaning, and indicated early positive relations between Native Americans and "whites" (European settlers). Goddard cited historical instances where Native Americans identified themselves as red men, or RED-SKIN, and redskins.[66] Johnathan Buffalo, historic preservation director of the **Meskwaki** Nation, an Indian tribe, maintained that tribal members in the 1800s used the term "redskins" simply to identify themselves — just as they identified others as "whiteskins" or ."blackskins" — without any derogatory connotation.[67]

A linguistic analysis of 42 books published between 1875 and 1930 indicated that negative contexts in the use of "redskin" were significantly more frequent than positive contexts; whereas the use of the word "Indian" to refer to Native Americans in similar contexts was more balanced.[68] American dictionaries classified the term "redskin" as offensive and disparaging.[69] [70] Nevertheless, NFL Commissioner, Roger Goodell, defended the team's name by affirming:[71]

The Washington Redskins name has from its origin represented a positive meaning distinct from any disparagement that could be viewed in some other context. For the

---

[66] http://anthropology.si.edu/goddard/redskin.pdf

[67] http://thegazette.com/subject/news/redskins-name-has-complicated-history-for-meskwaki-other-tribes-20140810

[5] Bruce Stapleton (March 6, 2001). *Redskins: Racial Slur or Symbol of Success?*. iUniverse. ISBN 0595171672.

[69] "Definition of REDSKIN". Merriam-Webster.

[70] *The American Heritage® Dictionary of the English Language, Fifth Edition*. Houghton Mifflin Harcourt Publishing Company. 2011.

[71] http://www.forbes.com/sites/tomvanriper/2013/06/14/why-the-washington-redskins-will-never-change-their-name/

*team's millions of fans and customers, who represent one of America's most
ethnically and geographically diverse fan bases, the name is a unifying force that
stands for strength, courage, pride and respect.*

The argument for an independent, non-derogatory meaning of the term in the context of the
team's name was rebutted by the U.S. Patent and Trademark Office's Trademark Trial and
Appeal Board (USPTO TTAB), which rejected the Washington Redskins' legal argument in
2014 by stating that dictionary definitions and general usage of "redskin" place the term in a
negative context.[72]

Public Opinion

Roughly two-thirds of the U.S. public did not think the name was disrespectful, but that
percentage had been falling – albeit slowly – for a number of years.[73]   One poll found that
eight out of 10 Redskins fans felt that the team name should remain the same, and there was
some evidence that a name change could undermine support from the team's most avid
fans.[74] Other polls found that percentage to be somewhat lower. Among other factors
complicating the thorny issue: The media reported that "Red Mesa Navajo High School in
Arizona [located on the largest Indian reservation in the United States] is proud of its football
team's moniker: the Redskins."[75] In contrast, California's State Assembly "approved

---

[72] http://www.washingtonpost.com/local/judges-rule-for-dictionary-over-redskins-feeble-attempts-to-defend-team-name/2014/06/18/9b29765e-f72f-11e3-a606-946fd632f9f1_story.html

[73] http://www.washingtonpost.com/sports/redskins/new-poll-says-large-majority-of-americans-believe-redskins-should-not-change-name/2014/09/02/496e3dd0-32e0-11e4-9e92-0899b306bbea_story.html

[74] http://www.washingtonpost.com/sports/redskins/washington-redskins-name-washington-post-poll-finds-most-dc-area-fans-support-it/2013/06/24/84bc2d0e-dd03-11e2-a484-7b7f79cd66a1_story.html

[75] http://www.newsmax.com/TheWire/red-mesa-navajo-high-school-moniker-redskins/2014/10/29/id/603902/

legislation barring California public schools from using the Redskins name for teams and mascots."[76]

Controversy aside, Redskins team and staff members continued to show up every summer on schedule at their state-of-the-art Bon Secours Virginia Health System training camp facility in Richmond, Virginia, to prepare for each season. Despite the success of training camp events – both from the perspective of fans and from the perspective of the City of Richmond and Bon Secours – team owner Dan Snyder faced a number of lingering concerns as the next season was about to begin, including 1) potential legal and regulatory actions emanating – somewhat ironically – from the team's historical home town of Washington, D.C., 2) policy changes on the part of publishers and broadcasters regarding use of the team's name, 3) a growing number of negative editorials in major U.S. newspapers and media outlets, and 4) the changing tide of public opinion.

Even President Barack Obama had taken sides, saying publicly that "the Redskins should change their name."[77]

Despite his apparently immutable position, Dan Snyder couldn't help but consider the marketing and public relations challenges that were facing the historic and valuable Redskins brand.

- Dan Snyder purchased the team in 1999 for $750 million. In recent years, *Forbes* magazine had estimated the value of the Redskins *team* to be as much as $2.4 billion (Figure 1 – at end of case). The Redskins *brand* itself was estimated to comprise $214 million of that valuation.[78] The Redskins team was thought to be the third most

[76] http://www.visaliatimesdelta.com/story/news/local/2015/05/04/assembly-approves-ban-redskins-school-team-name/26897793/

[77] http://www.bostonglobe.com/sports/football/2014/08/04/washington-redskins-name-needs-changed/xookx46DbYsW4xUNz8ANII/story.html

[78] http://www.forbes.com/teams/washington-redskins/

valuable NFL franchise (out of 32 teams), behind the Cowboys (#1) and the Patriots (#2). How would this controversy affect the brand's value in the marketplace?

- A relatively steady stream of distracting publicity was a problem. All one had to do was to conduct the Internet search "Washington Redskins name controversy" to get a plethora of search results from news and opinion sources describing one complaint or another from entities representing **both** sides of the controversy. Was this unwanted distraction a temporary phenomenon, or would it persist?

- Although most Redskins' sponsors appeared to be willing to sit out the controversy over the team's name,[79] a number of them periodically stirred up some fiscal uncertainty for the franchise/brand. Could the team count on the continued support of key corporate sponsors?

Should Brands Take a Stand?

With the growth of the Internet and social media, it had become more and more difficult for brands to avoid controversy by "taking a stand" on almost any issue. The list of brands that – either intentionally or unintentionally – had attracted the wrath of disapproving consumers continued to grow:[80]

- Chick-fil-A, a privately owned fast food company, was closed on Sundays and made no apologies for letting it be known that Christian values guided how it conducted business.

- In-N-Out Burger, whose chain's founder was a born-again Christian, had been taking a pro-Christian stance for years, including imprinting references to Bible verses on

---

[79] http://www.usatoday.com/story/sports/nfl/redskins/2014/06/19/washington-redskins-trademarks-native-americans-sponsors-fedex/10974081/

[80] http://www.imediaconnection.com/content/31106.asp#multiview

drink cups and celebrating Christmas with an iconic radio jingle with an overtly Christian message.

- Lowe's never anticipated that when it bought advertising time on the reality series "All-American Muslim," the retail giant would get caught between consumers who were angry that the company pulled its advertising support and others who disapproved of the series altogether.

- The Pepsi Refresh project was intended to fund community non-profit organizations without political ties, but project managers inadvertently approved a number of applications "from groups with loose ties to political parties," so some very vocal consumers were upset.

Starbucks CEO Howard Schultz was not one to shy away from controversy, having stated publicly and forcefully on a number of occasions his company's unwavering support for same-sex marriage, and serving as the face of the Starbucks' campaign to encourage customers to talk about race relations by asking baristas to put the slogan "Race Together" on coffee cups. But negative publicity forced Mr. Schultz to backtrack. Starbucks stopped the in-store, cup-labeling aspect of its "Race Together" campaign fairly quickly, based on social media backlash; however, it did not abandon its support for the controversial cause. Mr. Schultz vowed to continue Starbucks' support for improving race relations.[81]

It had become apparent to business leaders that the digital/social media had likely forever changed the dynamics of cause marketing. In the past, cause marketing was a fairly safe "bet" in terms of motivating employees, solidifying a place in the community, mobilizing consumer interest, and boosting the bottom line. However, consumers had become quick to take to social media to point out when either unforeseen circumstances or changing public opinion rendered a company's cause-marketing strategies counterproductive. No longer

---

[81] http://www.wsj.com/articles/starbucks-ends-key-phase-in-race-together-campaign-1427076211

could CEOs and CMOs assume that "everybody loves a good cause." Rather, they would have to:[82]

- Be realistic – Understand that selling a cause and a product are two different things and, in many cases, cannot be perfectly aligned.

- Ask hard questions – What will the brand or company do if the good cause becomes tarnished? What happens if profits decline? The leadership team should be able to debate the overall value of the effort in the larger corporate context.

- Gather perspectives – Don't be myopic, get out of the corporate silo. Consult with customers, front line employees, and other relevant publics to get their opinions about the risks and benefits of the plan.

- Be flexible – Make sure that the cause marketing campaign is adaptable enough to counter whatever pressures the competition and other external forces exert.

- Have courage – Understand that most cause marketing campaigns – either well-conceived or imperfect – eventually will come to an end.

Although the team-name controversy was not a "cause" in the traditional sense, Mr. Snyder and his executive team felt that they were engaged in a cause on behalf of Redskins' fans, supporters, and sponsors. Also, they thought it might be possible to learn something about dealing with controversy from cause marketers like Starbucks.

After all, most brands tended to shy away from controversy, but some brands found ways to benefit from it. Co-authors Melissa Dodd and Dustin Supa observed: "When companies engage in controversial social-political issues they ultimately risk the loss of profits and

---

[82] http://www.forbes.com/sites/forbesleadershipforum/2011/10/20/beware-the-hidden-traps-in-cause-marketing/

attention of activist groups that may result in the expenditure of additional resources—but depending on the issue, and the age demographic of their target customer, vocalizing support or opposition could benefit a company." [83] Was it possible for the Redskins to benefit from the controversy surrounding its name, logo, and mascot?

Even when brands were not taking a stand or supporting a cause, it was possible for them to get into "reputation hell" quite by accident – by making a mistake or an error in judgment. There seemed to be no limit to the ways consumers could create public relations challenges for otherwise well-intentioned brands. For example, Anheuser-Busch had to backpedal, change its Bud Light can label, and apologize to consumers for printing the tagline "The perfect beer for removing 'no' from your vocabulary for the night."[84]

Most firms understood that social media could make or break customer perceptions of their brands, and many of them struggled with these challenges on a daily basis. Although consumer involvement with social media made it increasingly difficult for brands to engage in any cause or controversy without some type of backlash, or to get back into the good graces of consumers after hitting a public relations speed bump, Mr. Snyder and his executive team hoped that social media and other direct-to-consumer media platforms might offer the team a way out of its lingering predicament.

Powerful Forces on the Attack

The Government's Quiver of Arrows

Even without the controversy over the Redskins' name, Washington D.C. seemed never to be without plenty of skirmishes that played out in the halls of Congress, in the press, and via

---

[83] http://www.forbes.com/sites/datafreaks/2015/03/12/brands-take-a-stand-when-speaking-up-about-controversial-issues-hurts-or-helps-business/

[84] http://www.nytimes.com/2015/04/29/business/bud-light-withdraws-slogan-after-it-draws-ire-online.html?_r=0

social media. There was hardly an issue that was free from political overtones. When Senate Majority Leader Harry Reid penned a letter (on behalf of himself and 49 other Democrat Senators) to NFL Commissioner Roger Goodell to call on him to urge the Washington Redskins to change its team name,[85] Redskins' fans went on the offensive with a Twitter campaign directed to @SenatorReid and @RedskinsPride.[86]

The U.S. Patent and Trademark Office (USPTO) -- who some observers said was responding to pressure from politicians – canceled the Washington Redskins' trademark registration in a 99-page decision by the Trademark Trial and Appeal Board. The USPTO argued that federal trademark law prevents the registration of trademarks that "may disparage" groups or individuals or bring them into contempt or disrepute. "But its [the cancellation's] effect is largely symbolic. The ruling cannot stop the team from selling T-shirts, beer glasses and license-plate holders with the moniker or keep the team from trying to defend itself against others who try to profit from the logo. And the trademark registrations will remain effective during any appeal process."[87]

According to one expert, commenting on the USPTO action: "Brand equity is influenced by customer perceptions about the brand, specifically, consumer attitudes about positive brand attributes and favorable consequences of brand use. When there are too many negative associations with a brand, people stop 'buying' the brand."[88]

---

[85] http://multicultclassics.blogspot.com/2014/05/11872-washington-senators-vs-redskins.html

[86] http://www.sportingnews.com/nfl/story/2014-05-29/redskins-name-change-twitter-campaign-nickname-washington-dan-snyder-rg3-senators-fans-nfl-franchise

[87] http://www.washingtonpost.com/local/us-patent-office-cancels-redskins-trademark-registration-says-name-is-disparaging/2014/06/18/e7737bb8-f6ee-11e3-8aa9-dad2ec039789_story.html

[88] http://www.uh.edu/news-events/stories/2014/June/061814KacenExpertRedskins.php

Shortly thereafter, Department of Justice (DOJ) Attorney General Eric Holder "made it clear he was opposed to the [Redskins] name during an appearance on ABC's *This Week*"[89] news program. Although politicians generally tried to steer clear of such issues, the attorney general became one more prominent voice against the Washington franchise.

A few months after the USPTO action and DOJ comments, the Federal Communications Commission (FCC) began deliberations to consider whether the agency should "punish broadcasters for using the moniker of the Washington NFL team."[90] Specifically: "The FCC, which enforces broadcast indecency violations, has received a petition from legal activist John Banzhaf III, asking that regulators strip local radio station WWXX-FM of its broadcasting license when it comes up for renewal for using the name 'Redskins.'"[91]

The FCC continued to consider the petition, but First Amendment supporters were quick to comment on the futility of any regulatory action in the matter – not only on the basis of Constitutionally protected speech, but also because previous FCC rulings explicitly declined to bar speech that some individuals and groups found offensive.[92] Nonetheless, Redskins fans began to wonder if their team had simply become a convenient target for politically motivated attacks.

The "Washington Team"

Whether it was concern for potential FCC regulatory action or a principled statement, a number of publications and broadcasters decided not to use the Redskins moniker -- notably,

---

[89] http://profootballtalk.nbcsports.com/2014/07/14/u-s-attorney-general-redskins-name-offensive/

[90] http://www.huffingtonpost.com/2014/09/30/fcc-redskins-nickname_n_5909796.html

[91] http://www.huffingtonpost.com/2014/09/30/fcc-redskins-nickname_n_5909796.html

[92] http://www.washingtonpost.com/news/volokh-conspiracy/wp/2014/10/01/no-the-fcc-may-not-ban-the-use-of-redskins-on-radio-and-tv-broadcasting/

Lisa Salters from ESPN, Phil Simms and James Brown from CBS, and Tony Dungy from NBC.[93] Subsequently, the list grew longer and included outlets like *The Washington Post* and the *New York Daily News*.[94] As opposed to the "Redskins," the team would be referred to as the "Washington team."

As well, the number of sports writers and commentators who took the position that the team name should be changed continued to grow.[95] Moreover, a "coalition of more than 100 Native American and social justice groups" urged television and radio broadcasters to stop using "the R-word" when reporting on the team.[96] In contrast, a columnist at Philadelphia's *The Inquirer* newspaper argued that journalists had an obligation to use the Redskins name in their reporting:[97]

*This idea might come off as old-fashioned, especially in our diverse and ever-expanding media world, but if you're a reporter or a columnist or a newspaper or a magazine or a news website or maybe even an independent blogger or pretty much anyone who practices what can be called **journalism**, your primary responsibility ought to be the same: Report the facts as accurately and completely as possible, present them as accurately and completely as possible, and don't let any agenda - political, social, personal - get in the way of those goals.*

---

[93] http://profootballtalk.nbcsports.com/2014/09/04/native-american-group-urges-broadcasters-not-to-say-redskins/

[94] http://www.washingtonpost.com/local/native-american-coalition-urging-broadcasters-not-to-use-redskins-name/2014/09/03/1a33cce4-337e-11e4-9e92-0899b306bbea_story.html

[95] http://en.wikipedia.org/wiki/Washington_Redskins_name_controversy (also: http://www.poynter.org/news/mediawire/256258/heres-a-list-of-outlets-and-journalists-who-wont-use-the-name-redskins/

[96] http://www.washingtonpost.com/local/native-american-coalition-urging-broadcasters-not-to-use-redskins-name/2014/09/03/1a33cce4-337e-11e4-9e92-0899b306bbea_story.html

[97] http://www.philly.com/philly/blogs/sports/eagles/The-Obligation-to-Use-Redskins.html

This commentary was especially noteworthy given that the Philadelphia Eagles were considered to be an archenemy of the Redskins on the gridiron by fans and supporters.

To some extent, the controversy spotlight began to come off the Redskins, when the NFL faced scrutiny over domestic violence accusations of a number of prominent players. By this time, both the Redskins' and the NFL's public relations problems were becoming part of the pop culture scene, as evidenced by the opening episode of the 18th season of the animated comedy show "South Park." "Along the way, 'South Park' managed to take shots at the NFL, its beleaguered commissioner Roger Goodell and Dallas Cowboys owner Jerry Jones," in addition to the Redskins.[98]

To Mr. Snyder and his executive team, it seemed as though all six of the uncontrollable forces of marketing's external environment[99] (competition, government policies, natural forces, social and cultural forces, demographic factors, technological changes) were taking turns attacking his beloved Redskins franchise.

The Redskins & Supporters Fight Back

In response to the growing tide of concern about the team's brand name, logo, and mascot, fan advocates of the Redskins, known as the Redskins Alumni (an online community of team alumni, including players and cheerleaders, and fans) sponsored a website – Redskins Facts.[100] The site provided visitors the history of the team name and logo, written and video testimonials from Native Americans, a live Twitter feed, and an opportunity to show support for the franchise.

---

[98] http://www.huffingtonpost.com/2014/09/25/south-park-washington-redskins_n_5881468.html

[99] http://mymarketingnotebook.blogspot.com/2012/11/the-six-6-external-environmental-forces.html

[100] http://www.redskinsfacts.com/

The website also included a link to an academic article, which appeared in the scholarly journal *Native American Studies* in 2005, " 'I AM A RED-SKIN': The Adoption of a Native American Expression (1769-1826)." At the time of the publication, the author, Ives Goddard, was the senior linguist and curator at the Smithsonian Institution, and he concluded that the term "redskins" was created by Native Americans to serve as "an inclusive expression of solidarity by multi-tribal delegations who traveled to Washington, D.C. to negotiate national policy toward Native Americans."[101]

Philanthropy

Separate and apart from the Washington Redskins Charitable Foundation,[102] Dan Snyder launched the "Original Americans Foundation" on behalf of the Redskins brand and the NFL. In a letter to "Everyone in our Washington Redskins Nation," the team owner described that he had "traveled to 26 Tribal reservations across 20 states to listen and learn first-hand about the views, attitudes, and the experiences of the Tribes," which in turn led to the creation of the foundation:[103]

The mission of the Original Americans Foundation is to provide meaningful and measurable resources that provide genuine opportunities for Tribal communities. With open arms and determined minds, we will work as partners to begin to tackle the troubling realities facing so many tribes across our country. Our efforts will address the urgent challenges plaguing Indian country based on what Tribal leaders tell us

---

[101] http://www.redskinsfacts.com/facts

[102] The mission of the foundation is "to utilize the assets of the Washington Redskins and its corporate and community partners to make a positive and measurable impact on youth development in the greater Washington, D.C. region in the areas of education, community outreach, and health and wellness." http://www.redskins.com/community/charitable-foundation.html

[103] http://www.nfl.com/news/story/0ap2000000336553/article/redskins-dan-snyder-launches-original-americans-foundation

they need most. We may have created this new organization, but the direction of the Foundation is truly theirs.

Celebrities on the Redskins' Side

In addition to fans, the Redskins also had a number of celebrities who were supportive of the current team name. Iconic NFL football-coach-turned-NASCAR-team-owner Joe Gibbs, who coached the Redskins for 16 seasons and led them to three Super Bowl wins in four appearances, said that he had "never heard anybody say anything negative about the Redskins' name; it was always prideful, courageous. We have a song; we sing, 'Hail to the Redskins.'"[104]

Even Academy Award winner Matthew McConaughey got into the act by telling *GQ* magazine:[105]

What interests me is how quickly it got pushed into the social consciousness. We were all fine with it since the 1930s, and all of a sudden we go, "No, gotta change it"? It seems like when the first levee breaks, everybody gets on board...I love the emblem. I dig it. It gives me a little fire and some "oomph." But now it's in the court of public opinion, it's going to change. I wish it wouldn't, but it will.

Former Redskins quarterbacks Billy Kilmer and Jay Schroeder chimed in about the controversy, with Kilmer saying: *"I think they should keep it [the name]. It's been there for so long. Everybody's got to be so politically correct today. ... I think it's all politically connected and I think it's festered by liberals against [Redskins owner] Dan Snyder, who's a*

---

[104] http://espn.go.com/blog/washington-redskins/post/_/id/8607/gibbs-redskins-name-prideful-courageous

[105] http://ftw.usatoday.com/2014/10/matthew-mcconaughey-washington-redskins-gq-name-change

conservative.[106] *Schroeder echoed Kilmer's sentiments: "I think it's been blown way out of proportion. I think that the Washington Redskins have represented the Redskins name very well through the years and bringing glory to it. If you look around the country, if you want to change the Redskins, you've got to change a lot of names. I'm wondering why everybody is going after the Redskins and not everybody else."*[107]

Well-known television personality and game-show host Alex Trebek – a longtime Redskins fan – publicly stated his support for the team's controversial name in a radio interview:[108] "I'm not a fair-weather friend. If things turn bad, I am not going to abandon you. I am still a Washington Redskins fan, since the days of Sam Huff and Sonny Jurgensen, and I still cheer for them. They weren't called the Redskins because we thought Redskins were terrible; it's because we admire their strength, their abilities."

Dan Snyder and his executive team felt that Mr. Trebek echoed the sentiments of Redskins fans and supporters across the country and around the world.

Mr. Snyder also appreciated the fact that Virginia Governor Terry McAuliffe (Virginia was where the team had its headquarters and training facility) stated during his campaign for the governorship that *the name of the team is a business decision.*[109] Mr. Snyder agreed with that observation – it's a business decision. *What should the decision be?*

The Decision

---

[106] http://washington.cbslocal.com/2014/10/31/jay-schroeder-likens-redskins-name-controversy-to-black-panthers-movement/

[107] *Ibid.*

[108] http://www.washingtonpost.com/blogs/dc-sports-bog/wp/2014/05/16/jeopardy-host-alex-trebek-thinks-redskins-shouldnt-change-name/

[109] http://www.nbcwashington.com/blogs/capital-games/Terry-McAuliffe-Ken-Cuccinelli-Asked-About-Redskins-Name-During-Gubernatorial-Debate-225349302.html

Mr. Snyder has hired you to advise him and his executive team on the correct course of action for the Redskins (brand, logo, mascot) and for the team's fans, supporters, and sponsors. The pivotal question is:

Should the Washington Redskins football team abandon or keep its current brand name (Redskins), logo, and mascot? Be sure to take a stand and defend your answer.

You should begin with a SWOT analysis. Mr. Snyder and his executive team want your objective and thoughtful assessment of the brand's internal (strengths and weaknesses) and external (opportunities and threats) marketing environment.

In addition to his personal investment in – and commitment to – the Redskins, Mr. Snyder is aware that many sectors of local and regional economies in the United States have relied on the Redskins' success as an NFL franchise. For example, the Redskins' three-week-long training camp yielded more than $10 million in economic impact to the Richmond (Virginia) metropolitan area during its first year.[110] Mr. Snyder and his executive team want you to understand that making the wrong decision would influence the lives of many people.[111]

Beyond the SWOT analysis, your professor/instructor will likely provide you with other, specific requirements for completing this case assignment successfully. Elements of your response might focus on marketing research, public relations guidance, digital and social media analysis, and/or the development of an integrated marketing communications plan for the Redskins brand. For example, depending on your answer to the pivotal case question:

If you recommend that the Redskins abandon the current team name:

---

[110] http://redskinsrva.bonsecours.com/redskins-training-camp-yields-10-5-million-economic-impact-richmond-metro-area

[111] http://www.washingtontimes.com/news/2013/oct/17/renaming-the-redskins-could-have-a-major-financial/?page=all

- What are the specific digital- and direct-marketing strategies and tactics that Dan Snyder should pursue to bring about the best brand outcome for the renamed team? What segments should the team target with digital- and direct-marketing strategies? What communications objectives should be established? How will the Redskins measure the success of the strategies and tactics recommended?

    o The campaign should formulate and pursue clear communication objectives using specific communication mix on the intended target audience(s) in a set period of time. It should also include an implementation plan to specify message, media, creative, time length, and metrics to measure the campaign's intended impact.

- Develop one or more online data collection instruments that would serve as the basis for determining the best name for "the Washington team" (other than the Redskins). What segments should be targeted for completion of the data collection instrument?

- Using the online data collection instrument you develop, conduct an online survey to determine the three best name alternatives. Prioritize and defend each of the three alternatives for Mr. Snyder and his executive team, based on your research results.

- How should the Redskins address relationships with current and future corporate sponsors when the team name changes?

If you recommend that the Redskins keep the current team name:

- What are the specific digital- and direct-marketing strategies and tactics that the Redskins marketing team should pursue to bring about the best brand outcome for the team that continues to call itself the Redskins? What segments should the team target with digital- and direct-marketing strategies? What communications objectives should be established? How will the Redskins measure the success of the strategies and tactics recommended?

- The campaign should formulate and pursue clear communication objectives using specific communication mix on the intended target audience(s) in a set period of time. It should also include an implementation plan to specify message, media, creative, time length, and metrics to measure the campaign's intended impact.

- Develop a research plan that will enable the Redskins to monitor public opinion, legal and regulatory threats, and other relevant factors that would cause Mr. Snyder and his executive team to rethink the issue in the future.

- In addition to steps already taken by the franchise to respond to critics, how can the team embrace digital- and direct-marketing tools and tactics to continue to build brand equity with its current name?

- How should the Redskins address relationships with current and future corporate sponsors in the event the team's name remains the same?

In either case:

- Conduct qualitative and quantitative research to determine if the value of the Redskins' *brand* has increased or decreased in the past three years, and whether the *team* valuation would be harmed or helped with a name change (or without a name change).

- What can the Redskins learn from other brands that have "taken a stand" and/or brands that have cultivated controversy to their benefit? What can the Redskins learn from other brands that have dug their way out of "reputation hell" for honest mistakes, poor judgment, or changing circumstances? Be sure to identify brands other than those named in the case description, as well as the specific lessons that can inform Mr. Snyder and his executive team as they move forward.

Thinking Critically

Your response to this case assignment should be rooted in (and should demonstrate) your critical thinking skills. According to the Foundation for Critical Thinking:[112]

Critical thinking is that mode of thinking — about any subject, content, or problem — in which the thinker improves the quality of his or her thinking by skillfully analyzing, assessing, and reconstructing it. Critical thinking is self-directed, self-disciplined, self-monitored, and self-corrective thinking. It presupposes assent to rigorous standards of excellence and mindful command of their use. It entails effective communication and problem-solving abilities, as well as a commitment to overcome our native egocentrism and sociocentrism.

Further, the Foundation concludes that a "well-cultivated" critical thinker:

- Raises vital questions and problems, formulating them clearly and precisely

- Gathers and assesses relevant information, using abstract ideas to interpret it effectively

- Comes to well-reasoned conclusions and solutions, testing them against relevant criteria and standards

- Thinks open-mindedly within alternative systems of thought, recognizing and assessing, as needs be, their assumptions, implications, and practical consequences

---

[112] http://www.criticalthinking.org/pages/our-concept-and-definition-of-critical-thinking/411

- Communicates effectively with others in figuring out solutions to complex problems

You may already have a favorite professional football team. You may also have preconceived notions about the main case question – *i.e.*, should the Redskins team change its name, logo, and mascot? Thinking critically, can you set aside your "native egocentrism" to produce an objective analysis and evaluation of the case, as well as a compelling strategic marketing solution to this complex marketing problem?

Critical thinking is not only used for analysis, it is also used for synthesis. In the context of present case, your SWOT analysis should provide a roadmap toward action-oriented strategies. **For example, can you:**

Identify and describe the key constituencies of the Redskins? What is the priority of each constituency in its relationship with the Redskins?

Recommend marketing communication strategies that Dan Snyder and his management team should use to keep the team's current brand name?

Recommend marketing communication strategies that Dan Snyder and his management team should use to facilitate a name change?

Figure 1 –Washington Redskins Team Value

Washington Redskins

Team Value [1] **$2,400 M**

Team Value calculated August 2014

+ Follow (24)

At a Glance

Owner: **Daniel Snyder**

Championships: **5**

Price Paid: **$750 M**

Year Purchased: **1999**

Revenue [2] : **$395 M**

Operating Income [3] : **$143.4 M**

Debt/Value [4] : **10%**

Player Expenses [5] : **$118 M**

Gate Receipts [6] : **$82 M**

Wins-to-player cost ratio [7] : **44**

Revenue per Fan [8] : **$38**

Metro Area Population: **5.9 M**

Forbes Lists

#3 NFL Team Valuations

Numbers

Valuation Breakdown

■ Sport [9]
$1150 M

■ Market [10]
$550 M

■ Stadium [11]
$511 M

■ Brand [12]
$214 M

Source: http://www.forbes.com/teams/washington-redskins/

Scleroderma: Gaining Support For (What?)

By

Jan P. Owens, Carthage College

Anjala S. Krishen, University of Nevada, Las Vegas

Scleroderma: What Is It?

Scleroderma is a chronic connective tissue disorder that is generally classified as an autoimmune rheumatic disease. Scleroderma literally means "hard skin," and it occurs when otherwise soft tissue overproduces collagen, which hardens and becomes less elastic, often causing pain and discomfort. While it is not contagious, infectious, cancerous, or malignant, it can be potentially life-threatening. For example, scleroderma in the lungs may inhibit effective breathing, eventually leading to death. Even in mild cases, the condition affects the quality of life of the patient. It affects approximately 300,000 men, women, and children in the United States, and about 80% of its patients are women.

There is no known cure for this disease, and there are few proven treatment options. Patients are often misdiagnosed or the diagnosis is delayed. Because scleroderma afflicts a smaller number of people than some better-known diseases, it lacks widespread recognition. Without a well implemented, popular advocacy campaign, Government attention and funding for research for a cure or treatments will continue to be low, and researchers will face scant research opportunities. Therefore, the philanthropic need to support research to cure this disease is not top-of-mind among the general population.

The Scleroderma Foundation

The Scleroderma Foundation is the national organization for people with scleroderma, and their families and friends. The national organization was formed in 1998, which joined existing West Coast and East Coast scleroderma federations. Briefly, its three-fold mission, summarized from the Scleroderma website at www.scleroderma.org.

includes:

> Support for patients and their families who suffer from the disease;
>
> Education to create greater awareness of the disease in the general public and medical practitioners;
>
> Research programs that seek to find better treatments and a cure for the disease.

The national foundation and its 24 chapters coordinate such activities as family and peer counseling, physician referrals, publicity campaigns, professional seminars, advocacy, and research support. Information is available through brochures, booklets, online newsletters, a quarterly magazine called, "Scleroderma Voice," the central website, and various social media channels. The Foundation hosts a National Patient Education Conference to provide educational and networking opportunities for patients living with scleroderma, their caregivers, family, and friends.

The SF has already raised more than $1 million to support research in the field. A peer advisory board carefully reviews all medical research proposals.

Current Marketing Communications and Fundraising Activities

The Scleroderma Foundation has a professional-looking website that serves many purposes (www.scleroderma.org). It clearly describes the affliction and the situation of the many people who suffer from the disease. The web content provides valuable and extensive information in terms of medical knowledge, resources, and support groups. Family members, friends, and care-givers are also given information and resources to help patients cope. The celebrity Queen Latifah has been featured on the website, describing the challenges of a family member with scleroderma.

There are numerous web features that encourage visitors to donate, support an ongoing event, and facilitate a fund-raising event. In three steps, people can choose a fund-raising event type, create a web page to promote the event, and use their social media connections to spread both awareness and the opportunity to support the cause. However, an important issue remains, which is that citizens are not aware of the disease, and often have a difficult time spelling the word, "scleroderma." To address this problem, the foundation might require some defensive search engine optimization.

The website also displays links to Facebook, Twitter, and Youtube for its national information and announcements, and has links to its 24 chapters for their own communication platforms. The chapters have extensive information about resources and upcoming events. Unfortunately, not every chapter has an up-to-date newsletter posted or newslink.

The national organization also coordinates many direct marketing programs, such as quarterly appeals through direct mail; the "Scleroderma Voice" quarterly magazine; a national database of past donors; and a national email list.

Target Constituencies for Donations to Non-Profits

An important characteristic of non-profits is that the key beneficiaries are often not the constituencies that help accomplish the organization's goals. These groups usually include individuals and organizations that can be tapped for a variety of resources, including financial support, in-kind goods, services, advocacy, and volunteer time. General humanitarian concern is normally a strong motivator among donor segments, but each can often be appealed to for other reasons. The following are target constituencies:

1. **Individuals**. Individuals often donate or support campaign activities when they have a friend or family member who suffers from the affliction. They may also invite friends to join a fund-raising activity as a social event, or an appeal based on friendship. Individuals can be tapped for volunteer activities, such as advocacy (letter-writing or giving speeches at fund-raising events), time in organizing and implementing fundraising activities, and promoting the

organization by generating buzz marketing about events and increasing awareness.

2. **For-profit Businesses**. For-profit businesses increasingly want to be seen as giving back to the community or other worthy causes, in the form of corporate social responsibility. Some corporations match financial contributions for approved charities. Others might encourage direct employee involvement, whether through direct release time, pro bono work (e.g. website development, legal advice, marketing advice, etc.), or awarding employees' activities with various forms of recognition. For example, S. C. Johnson & Sons gives annual awards for selected employees' volunteer service, which includes a trophy and a financial stipend for the employee's favored charity.

For-profit businesses also help organize work groups for one-time community and charitable causes. This may be the result of a charity approaching the company, or an employee who has been motivated to suggest an activity.

For-profit businesses have also been valuable sources of in-kind goods and services which support fundraising activities. Many benefits rely on donated food and refreshments, entertainment, give-away premiums (e.g. water bottles and T-shirts) and prizes that may be incorporated into the event.

3. Formal Service Organizations. Many communities offer various forms of service organizations whose mission is to support worthy causes. These can range from long-standing formal organizations (e.g., Rotary and Kiwanis) to those that also have a social component (college clubs, service fraternities, and sororities).

While these organizations often do not have the financial resources of for-profit businesses, they can be rich in providing volunteer help for service efforts, activities, and communication mechanisms with membership.

4. Other non-professional organizations and associations. These groups have missions and objectives that may not be directly focused on service, but can provide effective communication networks and support for the right cause. These can include book clubs, scouts, hobby circles, religious groups, and so on. The motivation for these groups might be working for a common cause or supporting members of the group.

5. Professionals who can help or hinder the cause with their influence and support. For charities focused on medical research, some of these important groups include medical researchers themselves, and sources of their funding.

The Chicago Chapter of the Scleroderma Foundation

Paula Winters*, the Executive Director of the Greater Chicago Chapter of the Scleroderma Foundation, reviewed the fundraising results of the past year. National programs and events had been as busy as ever. The results from the usual fundraising activities that are coordinated at the local level, such as walk-a-thons and direct mail campaigns, were good.

The local appeals were also going well. The walk-a-thons were documented in the chapter's social media sites, and a list of upcoming events was also posted, with alerts distributed throughout the chapter's Facebook, Twitter, and email. Paula was glad to see that the number of participants in the walk-a-thon grew, which resulted in more and more people wearing the SF T-shirts in the community. She noted that her efforts at recruiting social and professional groups, such as friends who were nurses and sororities from neighboring colleges, had helped to grow the walk-a-thon exponentially.

The Food Fight

Paula was looking forward to a fairly unique event in the fundraising world of Chicago: the SF celebrity chef "Food Fight." Chicago's restaurant scene had grown more varied and sophisticated over the years, and earned a reputation as a center for culinary exploration and innovative ideas. The local population had responded well to both new recipes and updates on traditional foods.

Through cold calling and personal contacts, the Chicago SF chapter had organized an event that brought together the "foodie" world of Chicago for a good cause. The interactive format had the chefs engaged in a cook-off challenge, while patrons/donors sampled the results. The guests then acted as the judges. During the evening, hors d'oeuvres, beer and wine were provided by sponsoring companies. Other companies donated prizes in the raffle, and all guests received goodie bags with coupons and products to take home. For those who wanted even more opportunities to mingle with the chefs, a VIP ticket bought an hour-long reception before the event with the chefs and mixologists, where patrons could snack on additional food samples and specialty drinks.

The event had been a success for a number of years running, and consequently had built a repeat business of patrons. What especially pleased Ms. Winters was that it not only created awareness in a group who were otherwise unaffiliated with the disease, but it also provided an additional fundraising venue that did not cannibalize their other events. Because of the support of the sponsoring companies, costs were lowered, which helped increase the net profit. Since the competing chefs owned renowned restaurants in Chicago, they posted flyers promoting the event, and promoting awareness of the Scleroderma Foundation, at their restaurants and on their websites. Paula Winters hoped that the severe winter would not persist and negatively impact attendance at the April event.

Given the success of this event in previous years, Paula tried to think of other lifestyle groups that could be approached to sponsor events or donations in some form, who might find the SF cause to be consistent with their ongoing interests. If it was difficult to break through the clutter of charitable appeals that people often face, something in their own interest might first gather their attention, and then build awareness for the cause.

As Paula thought about SF's recent fundraising accomplishments, she came back to the main objectives in planning for the future:

1. How can she create awareness of a relatively unknown disease?

2. Given the relatively small number of people afflicted by the disease, how should SF create interest in supporting the cause, even if individuals and organizations are not directly affected by the disease? Essentially, how can SF increase community awareness?

3. How should SF raise funds for ongoing research, events, and fundraising programs?

REFERENCES

Cheung, C.M.K and Lee, M.K.O (2009). User Satisfaction with an Internet-based Portal: An Asymmetric and Non-linear Approach. *Journal of the American Society for Information Science and Technology*, 60 (1), 111-122.

Kinci, Tomas (2012). "Measuring Website Quality: Asymmetric Effect of User Satisfaction." *Behavior & Information Technology*, 31, 7, 647-657.

The Scleroderma Foundation. www.scleroderma.org.

Song.com

Digital Music, Distribution, and Debatable Revenue: To App or Not to App?

By

Lilliana Stelmach, California State University, Northridge

Kristen Walker, California State University, Northridge

Mary Curren, California State University, Northridge

A Partnership (Trio) Develops

Don Velson had always loved music and computers. In 1994, when the World Wide Web was emerging as a means for providing information to consumers, Don saw the strength of owning web page domain names. He searched a variety of domains and eventually his love of songs led him to buy the domain name www.song.com for $150. A decade would go by before he took any action on using the domain. In 2004, Don teamed up with Thomas Hanneman, a self-made millionaire in web hosting services. Although investment was discussed, again almost a decade went by with no progress. Feeling defeated but still knowing the valuable nature of a good web site with a viable domain name, Don met Justin Hendrick. Justin's experience and success in digital advertising meant that Velson's interest in music and computers and Hanneman's financial backing could mesh with the digital and interactive landscape in the music industry. In 2014, the three of them entered into a verbal contract to give music fans the ability to get the music they want, when they want, where they want – for free (see Figure 1 for a timeline). They felt their vision was different and viewed the music industry more as a "music universe." How could they accomplish their vision to create and sustain competitive advantage in an industry that has experienced revolutionary changes in distribution? There's an app for that…

The music app industry has experienced explosive growth (Hotch, Localytics, 2014). Nielsen notes that demand for music streaming closed in on 164 billion songs in 2014 (Nielsen, D, 2015). Music is now primarily obtained through *digital* means (Nielsen 2014) and Song.com had formulated a plan to enter this already congested market. As of May 2015, Song.com was nearing completion of its prototype app and fine-tuning proof of concepts for the app. The target date for release of the app's beta launch was planned before year end.

Around this time Tango, Spotify, Pinterest and Uber were being valued in the vicinity of 1 billion dollars each (Dickey, 2014). Justin considered mobile to be the future and recommended that Velson build an app. He suggested the best approach for the company would be to build a music app featured around the domain name, Song.com.

In September 2014, Velson, Hendrick and Hanneman had entered into a verbal contract where Velson would own 55% of the company, Hendrick 40% and Hanneman 5%. Velson brought experience in programming; Hendrick brought experience in marketing as well as the seed money to hire app developers and begin creating a prototype; and Hanneman would help with hosting connections and launch money.

Figure 1. Song.com Timeline

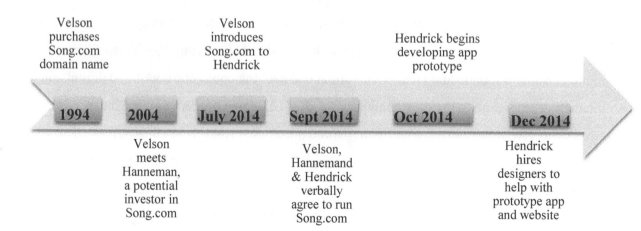

Velson and Hendrick's Vision

Velson and Hendrick wanted to make Song.com the center of the music universe with the best features of iTunes and Spotify in one app. Their vision was to give users every song imaginable for free with endless sharing capabilities.

Financial Resources

Hendrick and Hanneman were prepared to invest up to $300k each to launch the initial Song.com app. The going rate to hire one app company, two full-time developers and two part-time designers, working a total of 120 hours on an app was $150,000 (Hurd, 2013). To date Hendrick had spent less than $30,000 on the prototype app, logo design, website design and other technical aspects. Hendrick had done a lot of the work himself in addition to using Athena, connections, and some outsourcing.

PLANNED STRATEGIES

Target Market

Velson and Hendrick planned to focus solely on mobile users aged 18-35, otherwise known as millennials. Their belief was that this age category grew up on technology and so were the most receptive to it.

Beta App Features

Song.com intended to offer an unlimited free music streaming service, available as an app and website, first for iPhone and then Android. The free music streaming service would offer no ads, no premium add-ons, no subscription fees, unlimited skipping, on-demand song tracks, playlist features, search features and much more.

By December 2014, the app already had several features built in. The standout feature was the aggregate playlist. Song.com utilized different music services' Application Program Interface (API), retrieved the data from those services (songs and playlists), and aggregated all the data into one organized format to allow for the creation of "hybrid" playlists. This feature was unique to Song.com.

Once a user downloaded the Song.com app, Song.com would find all the user's songs and playlists across all the platforms and services used, and merge them into one easily accessible place. As with Spotify, the program would find music on a user's local hard drive and allow a user to import music. Song.com would also search a user's other music streaming services.[113] Users could see each service used (RDIO, YouTube) and every song/playlist added under that service. Song.com then gave users the capability to make new playlists by combining songs from different services, called hybrid playlists.

Users would also have the capacity to share playlists with friends who had different music streaming services. Once a user shared a playlist with a friend, Song.com's intuitive programming would find the playlist songs from the services people had available.

The app would include features found in other apps (e.g., search, import, organization and sharing) though some would have added benefits. For example, users would be able to search multiple categories/topics at once and have the results delivered in an organized fashion. Additionally, users will be able to add several songs to a playlist from the search results, as opposed to adding songs one at a time.

Services Song.com would offer customers:

- Music streaming app
- Music Discovery
- Internet Radio
- On-Demand plays

---

[113] Spotify is capable of finding music on a user's local hard drive as well as importing whole music collections in different formats such as mp3 and iTunes files. It does not have the feature of using songs from other services/apps (Chandler, 2011).

- Playlist features
- Search features
- Large catalogue
- Mobile/desktop integration

- Sharing features
- Download features
- 3rd party app integration
- App customization features

Beta App Distribution

Currently, the company operated out of El Segundo, California using loaned workspaces at Athena Interactive headquarters. Hendrick planned to beta test the app locally in Los Angeles at various college campuses, where he could easily find Millennials at the numerous universities, including multiple Cal States, Loyola Marymount, Pepperdine, UCLA and USC. The 2014 White House Council of Economic Advisors' report indicated "more millennials have a college degree than any other generation of young adults" (p. 12). The report went on to state that more millennials are enrolling, attending and finishing college right after high school. With a college beta test, Song.com expected to garner a lot of valuable information to use in developing the final product and features.

Product Pricing

Song.com would not be able to advertise on its app due to its usage of other music streaming services APIs. Nonetheless, Hendrick and Velson had no plans to monetize the app or charge users a fee. Instead, they believed the money was in the users themselves. They said that after the app was released and the company attracted enough users, they would find the investors, the money, and a way to monetize the app.

Forbes' article, "How do Investors value pre-revenue companies," notes that investors look at the founding team, traction and revenues, growth and engagement, market size, competition, market forces, quality of other investors, and other comparable companies (Polovets, 2014). A comparable start-up company, Bop.fm, that "builds a home for every song" regardless of the services used managed to raise $2 million in its series A funding (Kolodny, 2014).

Promotion

Hendrick planned to use his connections and start with a campaign utilizing musical venues, such as concerts, festivals, clubs, and electronic dance music festivals, at which to promote and distribute the app to Millennial users. Possibilities included using promotional booths to hold contests, giveaways and prizes, using club promoters with massive social media followings to promote the app, and/or using talent for endorsements.

Website

Song.com would also offer the same features on its website, but in a distinctive way. Unlike most music streaming services, such as iTunes or Spotify, Song.com would not require users to download any sort of player, plug-in or program in order to search for or play music.[114] As long as a user has Internet access, s/he would be able to login at the Song.com webpage and start playing music, searching music, or sharing playlists.

COMPETITIVE ENVIRONMENT

According to Flurry Insights' Khalaf, "2014 was the year apps got down to serious business" (2015, para. 1). Each month brought more new music apps. As more competitors entered, it became harder to break through the clutter and make an impression on consumers. At this time, the best known most direct competition included iTunes, Spotify, Google Play Music Key, Sony Music Unlimited, Beats, Deezer and Bop.fm (Smith, 2014). Pandora was a radio streaming service that did not offer users a playlist creation or songs on demand, but its basic offering was music entertainment on the go and it had a significant share of the music streaming app market. Other indirect competitors included RDIO, Soundcloud, Songza, Mixcloud, Slacker Radio, TuneIn Radio, Amazon, IheartRadio, Rhapsody and others.

---

[114] In order to use Spotify users must first "download and install the Spotify program to [their] hard drives." (Chandler, 2011, para. 6)

As of September 2014, the industry leaders in the music listening app category by downloads and revenues, were Pandora and Spotify. Third and fourth in revenue were Beats and RDIO. iHeartRadio and Soundcloud were in the top 5 by downloads (AppAnnie, 2014). Figure 2 presents brand awareness figures as reported by Edison Research and Triton Digital.

Figure 2. Brand Awareness of Top Music Listening Apps in the U.S.

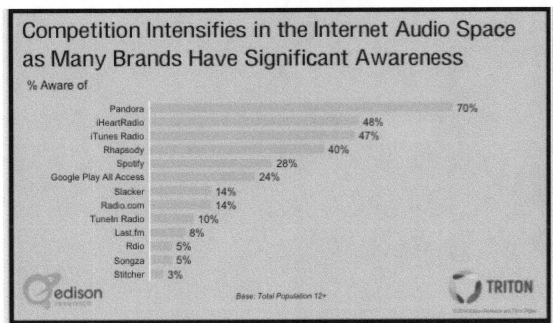

Brand Awareness of top music listening apps in the US. Adapted from "The Infinite Dial 2014" by Edison Research and Triton Digital, 2014. Copyright 2014 by Edison Research and Triton Digital.

For an overview of how PwC envisions the short-term future of the music industry, see Figure 3.

Figure 3. PwC's Short-Term Projections for the Music Industry

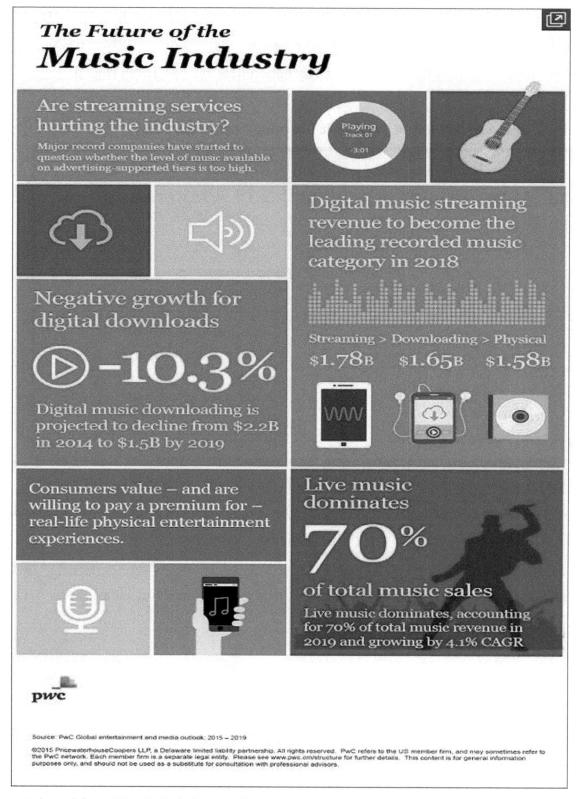

Adapted from "PwC Global entertainment and media outlook: 2015-2019" by PwC 2015.

Copyright 2015 by PricewaterhouseCoopers LLP.

Pandora. Pandora was by far the biggest competitor and led music streaming. Pandora utilized its Music Genome Project to personalize Internet radio for each user. Pandora held 9.2% of the entire broadcast satellite and Internet radio market and 77.6% of the total market share of Internet radio in the U.S. as of Sept. 2014 (GuruFocus, 2014). "Pandora—which is available only in the U.S., Australia and New Zealand—said it had more than 79 million active users in March; it lost $30 million on about $921 million revenue last year" (Smith & Wakabayashi, 2015, para. 14).

At the end of 2014, Pandora's strategies included delving further into "digital enriched media…with a number of key initiatives such as user engagement, rising listener hours and constant focus on the local advertising and mobile monetization." In 2012 Pandora also began expanding advertising efforts to reach the Spanish and Spanglish markets by releasing Spanish-only music artist campaigns. Research showed Hispanics as being more mobile and according to Pandora's VP of ad sales, Priscilla Valls, "eighty percent of Pandora's Hispanic users listen via mobile devices," (Heine, 2012, para. 3). Also in 2014, Pandora initiated its "Discover Den" into Miami to further drive growth among the Latin music listener segments.

Pandora's technology investments included creating advanced databases for advertisers, launching new Promoted Stations/brand stations for advertisers, integrating native advertisements to further drive monetization, and also, providing big data analytics to their artists. Some examples of Pandora's Promoted Brand stations included partnership with Peet's Coffee (where Pandora would be featured exclusively), and more recently, brand stations for Kleenex, Sketchers, Stub Hub, Taco Bell and Toyota (GuruFocus, 2014).

Pandora was also heavily investing in music communities by helping them with self-promotion and holding various events dedicated to them. Some of these events included Pandora Presents, Pandora Discovery Den and Pandora Premiers (GuruFocus, 2014). In July 2014, Pandora hired Lars Murray from Columbia Records to help artists increase their digital fan base (Pandora, July 2014). In October of 2014, Pandora launched a free service for artists and managers, the Artist Marketing Platform (AMP), which provided large-scale analytics updated daily regarding the artist's audience on Pandora (Pandora, October 2014).

Spotify. "Spotify reported more than $1 billion in revenue last year and said it ended the year with 15 million paying subscribers, plus around 45 million free users. In the U.S., according to data shared with music publishers, Spotify accounts for 86% of the on-demand music-streaming market. Its share of the international market is believed to be similar" (Smith & Wakabayashi, 2015, para. 13).

Spotify currently had partnerships with Uber, Sony, Viacom, RuneKeeper, Phillips, Samsung, Sprint, BandPage, Coca-Cola, Facebook and Shazam, among others. Spotify's partnership with Sony was to bring it to PlayStation users in over 41 countries, while its partnerships with Coca-Cola and Facebook would increase users through other brands (Etherington, 2014).

Spotify expanded into Brazil and Canada in 2014 (Washenko, 2015). Brazil is the 10th largest world economy and houses over 200 million people, of which 69% are 29 or younger (Hill, 2015). Spotify acquired Echo Nest in 2014. Echo Nest worked on the same principles Pandora's Music Genome did. Its big data analytics would provide Spotify with clear look into its users, further driving customization and convenience and further adding value to Spotify customers (Etherington, 2014).

In January 2015, Spotify hired Goldman Sachs to raise some funds. It was not known yet how Spotify intended to use the over $500 million raised in seven rounds from 17 investors, which included Coca-Cola Company, Goldman Sachs, Kleiner Perkins, and Founders Fund (Kosoff, 2015).

Apple. Currently, the music app market is full of competitors that industry leaders seem to be eating up. In 2014, Apple acquired Beats Music in order to enter the streaming and subscription market (Flanagan, 2014). The Beats/iTunes release was set for June 2015, but a beta version was out and its release notes indicated that the new design would simplify music collection and organization, making playlist personalization easier (Houghton, 2015). In 2015, Apple also acquired a London-based music analytics service, Semetrics's Musicmetric. Musicmetrics allowed artists to track their streams and sales on a dashboard, but Apple had yet to comment on whether or not the service would be a part of Beats or solely used for iTunes artists (Schneider, 2015).

Expectations were that Apple would announce new music services that will put it in serious competition with Spotify, Pandora, and even traditional radio. It was believed that while Apple would offer unlimited on-demand streaming for a price comparable to Spotify's $10 a month, it "won't let listeners stream its entire music catalog on demand free of charge. [However] it plans to augment its free, ad-supported Internet radio service with channels programmed and hosted by human DJs" (Smith & Wakabayashi, 2015).

Other competitors. Google Play Music acquired Songza in 2014 to enhance its music offerings, specifically curating music. Other acquisitions and partnerships included Spotify's use of the BandPage to allow artists to promote themselves and Deezer's partnership with Lyricfind to allow users to find lyrics to the songs they love.

Although Sony had a large catalogue and music licenses to spare, its Sony Music Unlimited app lacked playlist, sharing, search and other capabilities (Wilson, 2014).

Music app companies also were utilizing creative partnerships for distributing and promoting their own products. Examples included Deezer's partnership with Sonos and Boss, which enabled Deezer to distribute the app to thousands of U.S Sonos and Boss users. This also gave Deezer the chance to narrow its focus on one specific target market. Spotify was hoping to achieve the same results with partnerships with Phillips and Samsung Hi-def in home systems. Pandora, Spotify and Beats also were utilizing partnerships in the automobile and airlines industries. Pandora currently was enabled in all Ford cars, reaching millions of consumers. Spotify was hoping to reach the same consumers through its partnerships with UBER, while Beats hoped to achieve the same with the help of Southwest Airlines.

The creative partnerships didn't end there. In order to expand internationally, Spotify and Deezer joined forces with one or more communication/wireless service corporations. In 2014, Spotify teamed up with Vodaphone Australia to give complimentary Spotify accounts to all Australian Vodaphone RED users. That same year, Deezer teamed up with Samsung in Europe, Cable& Wireless Communications in Latin America, and Vodacom in South Africa.

There were sure to be more creative partnerships for distribution and promotion in the future. One could consider partnerships with music talent (consider how Dr. Dre drove the Beats brand); with a music video streaming company such as VEVO; with an app about upcoming artists' performances such as Songkick Concerts; with the Listener app, a gesture based music app; or with the Magic Piano app, where users could learn how to play their favorite songs on the piano (Widder, 2014). Other unique partnerships could include music apps that focused on customization of interfaces, customization of playlists and playback features, utilization of an in-house DJ to create beats users could download into their playlists, music discovery features based on location, moods or social features, and lastly, utilization of music creation apps in order to feature music creation and/or music alteration features. Currently, most music entertainment apps focused on a user's ability to listen to music, not to create music. One music creation app, SMULE, was expecting $40 million in revenues in 2014, double its 2013 revenues (App Annie, 2014).

ENVIRONMENTAL TREND ANALYSIS

Smartphones

Several factors were helping drive the music streaming industry around the world. One of the biggest factors was the "introduction of low-cost smartphones in many emerging markets," giving more access to affordable music to users worldwide, especially in China, Malaysia, India and Nigeria (PwC, 2015). Nielsen reported that as of October 2014, 76% of U.S. mobile subscribers were using smartphones; over half (51.9%) of these smartphones had Android operating systems, and 42.9% had Apple's iOS (Nielsen, A, 2014). iOS users spent up to four times more than Android users on apps (Edwards, A, 2014). Most industry professionals felt that "Android users don't pay for apps, they don't have data plans, you can't monetize them easily, and designers are all iPhone users and don't really understand Android users" (Edwards, B, 2014).

Political and Regulatory Trends

The music industry was complicated and the revenue scheme, including payment for licenses and royalties, was not simple and had undergone many changes as consumers found new ways to listen to and stream music. Songwriters were paid differently than artists who performed the music and this payment also differed depending on where the songs were played (AM/FM radio or digital music services) and where they were sold (online or physical brick and mortar stores). The following sections provide a quick look at the music streaming licensing landscape.

Licenses for streaming music. The permissions and licenses needed depend on how music is used. This also determines whom to pay. Any business involved in digital media (including smartphones) that uses music requires some sort of license to make the use legal. What follows is a quick overview of the licenses needed to stream music (Oxenford & Driscoll, 2011).

Rights to musical composition. The Copyright Act gives the owner of copyrighted musical composition exclusive rights to control his/her public performance. This includes rights to any distribution of that performance to the public through various means (website, radio, phones). In order to digitally play a music performance to the public, a company must obtain a public performance license from the songwriter or publisher. In order to play multiple songs from various artists, companies usually obtain a "blanket license" from a performing rights organization (PRO)[115].

---

[115] The three main PROs are: American Society of Composers, Authors and Publishers (ASCAP), Broadcast Music, Inc. (BMI) and The Society of European Stage Authors and Composers (SESAC) (PrometheusRadioProject)

Rights to sound recordings. There are some differences in licenses for sound recordings. Due to the digital public performance right in sound recordings, companies streaming music digitally must obtain a license to "digitally transmit those recordings to their listeners." For digital media companies, there is a "statutory license" that can be received through SoundExchange on behalf of the record labels. The statutory license, however, depends on the "interactive" service features the company is offering when playing music. For example, a non-interactive service would be one in which a "certain degree of user influence is permitted" and would be allowed a statutory license given certain restrictions (must limit the number of songs played from the same album or by the same artists, must show information about the song being played and other such rules). An interactive service, on the other hand, is one that allows on-demand streams, shows what music is coming up or allows the selection of songs or artists to be played. For an interactive service, companies must obtain "public performance licenses in the sound recordings directly from the copyright holders." Typically this means the record company releasing the record. In sum, a company streaming music online must obtain several licenses, one to three licenses from the PROs, and one from SoundExchange (Oxenford & Driscoll, 2011).

Royalties. At the end of 2015, the Copyright Royalty Board (CRB) was to set future royalties to be paid by webcasters to SoundExchange for the release and distribution of public performance of sound recordings. The CRB was currently considering information and expert testimony from all interested parties. SoundExchange believed that the industry was healthy and growing and that royalties should increase from $.0023 per performance, the current price (per song per listener), to $.0025 in 2016 and $.0029 in 2020. The music services (i.e., Pandora and others) argued that streaming wasn't profitable even at the current rates and they proposed a decrease in rates. Broadcasters and others also argued for a decrease in rates (Oxenford, 2014).

Although the U.S. Copyright Office had no authority to change the current system, it could advise Congress on how to rewrite laws. In February of 2015 it released a report detailing recommendations on how current copyright laws on music licensing could be updated, to fit the changing music listening landscape. Some of its recommendations included:

- Government licensing processes should aspire to treat like uses of music alike
- Require AM/FM radio stations to pay performance fees to recording artists like satellite and Internet radio stations
- Close a loophole that allows digital streaming services to avoid paying royalties on songs recorded before 1972
- Consolidate all rate-setting activities within the Copyright Royalty Board, instead of having some rates set by federal district courts (thanks to decades-old industry consent decrees with the Justice Department)

The report has had mixed reviews. Currently, the ASCAP, Recording Industry of America and even Pandora have said the report is necessary, while The Association of Broadcasters released a statement stating that the Copyright Office has a biased view of the industry and is only looking out for the best interest of copyright owners (Schatz, 2015).

Social Trends

Capture Culture. As more and more music apps come onto the market, users are finding new ways to enjoy their music. Today, users are shifting from collecting music on their hard drives and cds cases to accessing music wherever it's available. Today, users find music in all sorts of environments and thus want to capture the music they like best. This capture trend has led to the growth of apps like Shazam and SoundHound, apps that let users capture a song in any environment and store it for later use.

The capture trend also provides added immersive features for users. Once a user is able to "capture"/ identify a song, she/he can then also use the capture to learn about artists, find lyrics, buy merchandise and concert tickets, discover new but similar music, and much more depending on the app they use. It seems users don't just want to capture a song for listening purposes, but also want to learn more about the song and/or artist. The identification of a song "empowers fans to turn any passive listening session into an active one," thus fully immersing users into the music world they love. Capture and interactive features combined in a music app can only increase the time spent in those music apps (Bylin, 2011).

The capture trend is only beginning. There are few music apps that have such features, but more and more companies are jumping on the capture train. Spotify, for example, has formed partnerships with Shazam so that once users capture the song they like on Shazam, users can then press "Play now in Spotify." This allows users to listen to the song in Spotify and/or add it to their Spotify playlist (Shazam, 2014). Rdio has also formed a partnership with Shazam so that its consumers could do the same thing. Now, when users utilize Shazam, they can connect their Spotify or Rdio accounts, and any time they use Shazam they can then listen to those tracks in their other streaming accounts (Elliott, 2015). Research by Edison Research and Triton Digital (2014) suggests that there is room for growth. Their 2014 study found 39% of respondents were aware of Shazam and 15% were aware of SoundHound (p. 37).

Usage Trends. A reported 93% of the country's population listens to music and spends 25 hours or more a week listening to their tunes. Users prefer to listen to music in their cars the most, listening while working (at home or in the office) second, while doing chores third, while doing other activities fourth and exercising last (Nielsen, C, 2014). Nielsen also reports that while out of the car, users are listening to music on smartphones rather than listening to music on their iPods.

Technological Trends

Digital trends. In 2014, for the first time ever, total digital recorded music revenue surpassed physical recorded revenue at 10.18 billion compared to 10.16 billion (Orchard, 2014). Over the last two years, 2013 and 2014, pay-per download sales have slowly declined while the demand and supply for streaming services, especially in North America, have seen a vast growth. It is expected that by 2021 the mobile music market will grow to 21.3 billion compared to the 12.8 billion in 2014 (PR Newswire, 2015). In 2014, music subscriptions counted for $1.1 billion of the $5.9 billion global digital trade revenue (Peoples, 2014).

Companies and artists need to figure out how to make money in the ever-changing music listening landscape. More companies are turning to the "freemium" business model.[116] In 2014, Rdio changed to a freemium music model, while Spotify introduced the Family plan. Deezer, in 2015, released tiers of freemium plans.

New formats for listening. Industry leaders in the music streaming app services are helping drive the fourth phase of digital music. Spotify's acquisition of the Echo Nest in 2014 will give Spotify an enhanced music intelligence (a more enhanced algorithm), and thus, allow them to provide better curated music experiences to their customers (AppAnnie, 2014). Google's acquisition of Songza, which utilizes human curation by music experts (DJ's and Rolling Stone writers), will give Google a unique selling point to customers when offering this feature as part of its streaming service. Furthermore, Songza also utilizes geosocial features, such as acquiring "data around what people like to listen to based on the time of day, the weather, location, and activity." (Crook, 2014)

Gender Trends. When it comes to gender differences, most reports indicate that millennial males are the biggest consumer group for music apps. In September 2010, Pew Internet and Nielsen released a report, *The Rise of Apps Culture*, in which it was stated that "app users are disproportionately male, young, educated and affluent" (p.12). In the Pew Research, 57% out of 460 app users were male (p.12). The Pew research went on to show that it was also younger, more educated males that were more likely to download apps when compared with the full U.S adult population[117] (Purcell, et. al 2010). According to Nielsen reports, millennial males (aged 18-34) are racially diverse, live in digital worlds and love to shop for electronics *(see Figure 4)* (Nielsen, E, 2014).

---

[116] The freemium business model: where products are provided free of charge at the basic level, but are paid for by subscription at higher levels with richer functionality (Seave, 2014).
[117] Both the Pew Survey and Nielsen survey were on adults 18+

Figure 4. Millennial Male Profile

Adapted from "The Men, The Myths, The Legends: Why Millennial 'Dudes' Might Be More Receptive To Marketing Than We Thought" by Nielsen 2014. Copyright 2014 by The Nielsen Company.

Ethnicity Trends. As Nielsen indicates, the American consumer is the multicultural consumer. Since the 1990s more and more people are identifying themselves as African-American, Asian-American or Hispanic. More importantly, these multicultural consumers are said to "represent the vanguard of musical trends in the U.S." These consumers drive new tastes and new ways of consuming music, and in essence, "pioneer pathways of taste and adoption."(Nielsen, F, 2014)

Nielsen reported that in 2014, 53% of the Multicultural population was under the age of 35. These millennials were also more "racially and ethnically diverse than any previous generations", with 40% of millennials identifying as African-American, Asian-American or Hispanic. Furthermore, this millennial multicultural population is 24% of the country's overall population. Currently, 19% of the millennial population are Hispanic, 14% are African-American and 5% are Asian. A clear majority (71%) of millennials "appreciate the influence of other culture on the American way of life" (Cohen, 2014).

The multicultural consumer spends an average $7 more on music than the white consumer and accounts for 31% of the total spending on music. These consumers are also more likely to attend and spend on concerts and music festivals, more likely to customize a playlist on streaming services, more likely to share posts from musical artists and bands, and finally, overall are more socially engaged (Nielsen, G, 2014).

Although there are a multitude of differences among Hispanics, the one thing that binds them together "is a passion for music." In 2014, Hispanics spent $30 dollars more per year (spending on average $135) than the average consumer. Most was spent on live music ($72), followed by physical CDs ($14), digital albums ($13), and satellite radio ($8). (Nielsen, H, 2014).

Millennials. Millennials are the largest forecasted population and are most likely to use and consume music in large amounts. As Nielsen reports indicate, in 2014 there were more than 77 million millennials living in the U.S., making up about 24% of the total population. By the end of 2015, Millennial spending power would equal $2.45 trillion worldwide. By 2020, millennials would account for one third of the population.

A 2013 report by Eventbrite, "Millennials Fueling the Experience," noted that 8 out of 10 (83%) millennials attended or participated in a live experience event, which included concerts, festivals, shows, etc. (pg.2) More recent research by Nielsen backs these findings. In 2014, Nielsen reported that on average, consumers spend $109 annually on music activity, with live music events accounting for over half of the total music activity spending. The report also stated that more than 32 million people would attend a festival at least once a year (Loynes, 2015).

Millennials don't just love music, they also love brands that sponsor music. Nielsen reports that a quarter of millennials would try a brand or product that sponsors a music event for an artist or group they like. Furthermore, sponsoring a concert increases purchase rate more than 25% among millennials. Lastly, artist endorsement increases brand market share by up to 2.4 points among fans. This trend, however, changes as age increases. Nielsen revealed teens are the most likely consumers who will try a product if the product sponsors an event for an artist they like, but as age increases this number gets significantly smaller.

Millennials have more access to technology (cell phones and Internet) and are more connected to technology than any other age group (White House Council of Economic Advisors, p. 7). Most important however, in 2015 millennials surpassed all other age groups to become the largest living generation (The Pew Research Center). By 2020, millennials were projected to account for one third of the total adult population (Searcey, 2014).

The *US Mobile App Report* (comScore 2014) indicates these age segments, 18-24 and 25-34, spend the most time on "leisure oriented apps," with the most time spent on social networking apps followed by entertainments apps.

According to Salesforce's *2014 Mobile Behavior Report*, 90% of mobile respondents aged 18-24 said, "mobile devices are a central part of their everyday lives" (p.6). This age group spent the most time on smartphones overall, with an average of 5.2 hours spent per day (p.11).

A 2013 Flurry study found that males age 25-34 were heavy users of music, media and entertainment (Khalaf, 2013). See Figure 4 for a Nielsen profile of the Millennial male consumer.

Music Streaming Demographics

Music streaming appears to be a young consumer's game. Figure 5 shows the use of three important music streaming services by the following age categories: 12-24, 25-54, and 55+. As features are added to a service, the older consumers dropped out of the market. This might suggest that older users simply do not have the time, the knowledge or the desire to use such features (McCarthy, 2014).

Figure 5. Age and Music App Usage

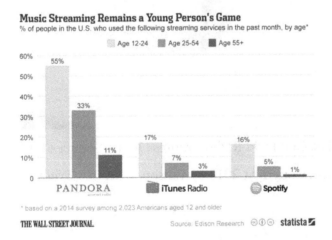

Age and music app usage in the US. Adapted from "Music Streaming Remains a Young Person's Game" by Niall McCarthy, 2014. Copyright 2014 by Edison Research, Statista.

Consumer Behaviors, Attitudes and Values

U.S music consumers across all age categories use the same tools to discover music. In an Edison Research and Triton Digital report, 35% of consumers aged 12+ said they use AM/FM radio when it comes to discovering music and staying up-to-date with music trends (see Fig. 6). 21% of those consumers said they also rely on friends or family. Another report, *2014 Nielsen Music U.S. Report*, also highlighted this pattern. It noted that 51% of consumers use radio to discover music, while 59% of consumers use a combination of both on air and online radio streams for discovering music (Loynes, 2015).

Figure 6. How American Use Various Music Sources to Discover Music

The Good Old Radio Trumps Online Services for Music Discovery
% of Americans aged 12+ who use the following sources most to stay up-to-date with music

- Others 10%
- Apple iTunes 3%
- SiriusXM 4%
- Music TV Channels 4%
- Facebook 4%
- Pandora 9%
- YouTube 10%
- 35% AM/FM Radio
- 21% Friends/Family

Base: ~950 Americans aged 12+ saying it's "very important" or "somewhat important" to stay up-to-date with music

@StatistaCharts   Source: Edison Research, Triton Digital

statista

Adapted from "The Good Old Radio Trumps Online Services for Music Discovery" by Statista 2014. Copyright 2014 by Edison Research, Triton Digital, Statista.

The White House Council of Economic Advisors' report on millennials provides some input as to what makes them so distinctive:

1) Millennials are now the largest, most diverse generation in the U.S
2) Millennials have been shaped by technology
3) Millennials value community, family and creativity in their work

4) More Millennials have a college degree than any other generation of young adults; they also have more loans

5) Millennials tend to get married later

6) College-educated millennials move into urban areas faster than less educated peers

Nielsen has several similar highlights:

1) Millennials are diverse, expressive and optimistic

2) Millennials are connected and want personal touch and authenticity from companies

3) Given their small income and love of technology, millennials are savvy deal shoppers

4) Millennials are driving and fueling urban revolution, wanting creative, energetic cities

Finally, Nielsen statistics solidify the millennials' values:

1) 75% of Millennials have made a financial donation to a not-for-profit organization.

2) 71% of Millennials have raised money for a not-for-profit organization

3) 57% of Millennials have volunteered for a not-for-profit organization

4) Over 60% of Millennials will pay more for a product where the company is environmentally friendly.

5) 70% of Millennials say that a firm's commitment to the community is a factor in their employment decisions.

According to CEB's report, *Inside the Millennial Mind*, millennials value happiness, passion, diversity, sharing and discovery, more than the boomer generation's justice, integrity, family, practicality and duty. Millennials want to be involved and feel like a part of the community, the workplace, the environment, and even, like part of the brand. Millennials are smart but don't have money to spend. They are also do-gooders. With all these similarities, however, millennials are still very diverse in terms of gender, ethnicity, class, etc.

Consumer Segments

The music aficionado segment is the "heartbeat of recorded music revenues." Aficionados spend $17.57 every three months on music, listen to 15 hours of music a week, and although they are only 17% of all music consumers, they represent 60% subscribers. But there are other segments to consider. Currently, the industry defines these segments as the Forgotten Fans, Passive Majority and Collectors. And each has a unique position when it comes to buying and listening behaviors. The Passive Majority comprises 47% of the total music segment and will spend some money and some time on music. The Forgotten Fans, on the other hand, comprise 30% of the market and will spend more time but less money on music (See Figure 7) (MIDiA, 2014).

Figure 7. Music Consumer Segmentation by MIDiA

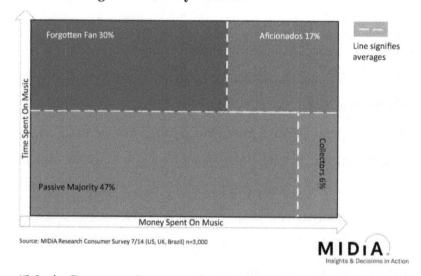

Adapted from "Music Consumer Segmentation" by MIDiA 2014. Copyright 2014 by MIDiA. Source: Mulligan and Severin (2014)

A TRIO IN TROUBLE?

Velson, Hanneman, and Hendrick were working hard to make Song.com work. They had investment capital, they had coding and networking capability, and most importantly they had passion. The research they had compiled on the music streaming industry and the application product market had been thorough. What they realized they needed was a marketing strategy that would help to operationalize their vision. They planned to interview marketing consultants to see if they could help.

Issues to Consider

Before launching a music streaming app to the main public, Song.com still had much to contemplate. The biggest challenges facing the company were how to generate revenues, how to appropriately allocate resources, which customer segments to market, and most importantly, what to offer ideal customer segments. This last challenge was more problematic when considering the heavily saturated industry. As more millennials "digitized" their music habits, start-up companies everywhere were emerging to support those habits. An even bigger threat was posed by industry leaders that were constantly reinvesting into fine-tuning their products and marketing mixes.

References

App Annie Index for Music September 2014 - App Annie Blog. (2014, October 29). Retrieved from http://blog.appannie.com/app-annie-index-music-september-2014/

Bylin, K. (2011, September 12). The Rise of Capture Culture: How Apps Are Revolutionizing Music Collecting. Retrieved from http://bit.ly/1DaFIa1

CEB. (2014). Infographic: Inside the Millennial Mind. Retrieved from http://bit.ly/1vgCXBa

Chandler, N. (2011, October 3). How Spotify Works. HowStuffWorks.com. Retrieved January 25, 2015, from http://bit.ly/1Banv99

Cohen, H. (2014, February 21). 30 Millennial Demographics You Need [Charts] - Heidi Cohen. Retrieved from http://heidicohen.com/30-Millennial-demographics-chart/

comScore. (2014, August 21). *The US Mobile app report*, 5-14, Reston, VA:
    comScore, Inc. Retrieved from http://bit.ly/1pURyzL

Crook, J. (2014, April 29). Sprint Announces Spotify Partnership, Unveils HTC One M8
    Harman/Kardon Edition Smartphone. Retrieved from http://tcrn.ch/1D4dfjy

Dickey, M. (2014, March 20). The 39 most valuable startups in the world. Retrieved
    January 25, 2015, from http://read.bi/1ySE2l4

Edison Research and Triton Digital. (2014, March 04). *The Infinite Dial 2014*. Retrieved
    from http://bit.ly/1GjIXgl

Edwards, J. A (2014, January 02). Google's Dirty Secret: Android Phones Are Basically
    Used As Dumbphones. Retrieved from http://read.bi/1EGTAZw

Edwards, J. B (2014, April 03).These Maps Show That Android Is For People With Less
Money. Retrieved from http://www.businessinsider.com/android-is-for-poor-people-maps-
2014-4

Elliott, M. (2015, February 18). Get a Spotify or Rdio playlist of your Shazams - CNET.
Retrieved from http://cnet.co/1w1GN4r

Etherington, D. (2014, March 6). Spotify Acquires The Echo Nest, Gaining Control Of The
Music DNA Company That Powers Its Rivals. Retrieved from
http://techcrunch.com/2014/03/06/spotify-acquires-the-echo-nest/

Eventbrite. (2014, January). *Millennials: Fueling the experience economy*, 2-5, Boston:
Eventbrite. Retrieved from http://bit.ly/1rbDSMX

Flanagan, A. (2014, November 19). Apple's Beats Music Relaunch Reportedly Coming in
March. Retrieved from http://bit.ly/1wgRS1u

GuruFocus Premium Membership. (2014, September 25). Pandora Media: This Internet Radio Service Provider is Primed for Better Times. Retrieved From http://bit.ly/1zaYt8v

Heine, C. (2012, October 5). Why Pandora Ads Target Hispanics and Spotify's Don't. Retrieved from http://bit.ly/1A1oQOg

Hill, B. (2015, January 30). Spotify seeks $500M new funding; Jason Calacanis predicts Facebook takeover. Retrieved from http://bit.ly/17Oi0F7

Hotch, D. (2014, September 16). Time in app increases by 21% across all apps. Retrieved January 25, 2015, from http://bit.ly/1ybHzvU

Houghton, B. (2015, April 14). Apple Releases New Beats Inspired Music Player in Beta. Retrieved May 31, 2015, from http://www.hypebot.com/hypebot/2015/04/apple-releases-new-beats-inspired-music-player-in-beta-video-walkthrough.html

Hurd, M. (2013, October 31). How Much Does it Cost to Develop an App? - Fueled. Retrieved January 25, 2015, from http://bit.ly/KmBTIN

Khalaf, S. (2013, June 13). Flurry Insights. A Day in the Life of a Mobile Consumer. Retrieved from http://flurrymobile.tumblr.com/post/115189471585/a-day-in-the-life-of-a-mobile-consumer.

Khalaf, S. (2015, January 6). Flurry Insights. Shopping, Productivity and Messaging Give Mobile Another Stunning Growth Year. Retrieved from http://flurrymobile.tumblr.com/post/115194992530/shopping-productivity-and-messaging-give-mobile.

Kolodny, L. (2014, July 10). Bop.fm Raises $2 Million to Become the 'Switzerland' of

Streaming Music. Retrieved January 25, 2015, from http://on.wsj.com/1L8W7QO

Kosoff, M. (2015, January 29). Spotify Is Looking To Raise $500 Million In New Funding. Retrieved from http://read.bi/1AovFy6

Loynes, A. (2015, January 7.). Nielsen Music U.S. Report. *2014 Nielsen Music U.S. Report*. Retrieved January 7, 2015, from http://bit.ly/1CGi4Vc

McCarthy, N. (2014, March 13). Infographic: Music Streaming Remains a Young Person's Game. Retrieved from http://www.statista.com/chart/1998/music-streaming-in-the-us/

Mulligan, M. and K. Severin. (2014, December 5). MIDiA Research.com Blog. Music Consumer Segmentation: From Lagging Indicators to Leading Indicators. Retrieved from http://www.midiaresearch.com/blog/view/music-consumer-segmentation-from-lagging-indicators-to-leading-indicators.html

Nielsen. A. (2014, December 18). Tops of 2014: Digital. Retrieved from http://bit.ly/16H92cT

Nielsen. C. (2014, October 2). Music 360: Americans Make Music Their Top Entertainment Choice. Retrieved from http://www.nielsen.com/us/en/insights/news/2014/music-360-americans-make-music-their-top-entertainment-choice.html.

Nielsen. D (2015, January 22). Newswire . Retrieved from http://bit.ly/1wAV8hG

Nielsen. E. (2014, December 10). Newswire . Retrieved from http://bit.ly/1vQZi4n

Nielsen. F. (2014, August 25). Newswire . Retrieved from http://bit.ly/1vraFXn

Nielsen. G. (2014, August 25). Newswire . Retrieved from http://bit.ly/1pd2p9e

Nielsen. H. (2014, August 11). Listen Up: Hispanic Consumers and Music. Retrieved from http://bit.ly/1lAxOlc

Orchard, P. (2014). Music. Retrieved from http://pwc.to/1whDjpA

Oxenford, D. (2014, October 19). Webcasting Rate Proposals for 2016-2020 Now Public – What Will the Copyright Royalty Board Be Considering in Setting Royalty Rates for Internet Radio? | Broadcast Law Blog. Retrieved from http://bit.ly/1zoHyW4

Oxenford, D. D., & Driscoll, R. J. (2011, February 22). The Basics of Music Licensing in Digital   Media: 2011 Update. Retrieved from http://bit.ly/1EGUO6S

Pandora. (2014, July 22). Press Release: Pandora Hires Lars Murray as Vice President of Industry Relations. Retrieved from http://investor.pandora.com/phoenix.zhtml?c=227956&p=irol-newsArticle&id=1949715

Pandora. (2014, October 22). Press Release: Pandora AMP Opens up Large Scale Artist Analytics. Retrieved from http://investor.pandora.com/phoenix.zhtml?c=227956&p=irol-newsArticle&ID=1980273.

Peoples, G. (2014, September 10). Deezer Finally Coming to America on Sept. 15. Retrieved from http://www.billboard.com/articles/business/6244190/deezer-expanding-united-states

Polovets, L. (2014, January 24). How Do Investors Value Pre-Revenue Companies? Retrieved January 25, 2015, from http://onforb.es/1ca93p0

PR Newswire. (2015, February 3). Streaming Behind the $21Bn Mobile Music Market in 2021. Retrieved from http://prn.to/1vr9Spl

PrometheusRadio. (n.d.). Music Licensing for Noncommercial Broadcasters and Webcasters. Retrieved from http://www.prometheusradio.org/musiclicensing

Purcell, K, R. Entner and N. Henderson. (2010, September 15). The Rise of Apps Culture. The complete report PDF was retrieved from http://www.pewInternet.org/2010/09/14/the-rise-of-apps-culture/

PwC. "Music." *PwC*. PwC, n.d. Web. 18 Feb. 2015. Retrieved from http://pwc.to/1whDjpA

PwC. (2015) "Global entertainment and media outlook: music." Retrieved from http://www.pwc.com/us/en/industry/entertainment-media/publications/outlook/music.jhtml

Salesforce Marketing Cloud. (2014, February 25*). 2014 Mobile Behavior report*, 33, Salesforce. Retrieved from http://bit.ly/1hvCOCf

Schatz, A. (2015, February 05). Copyright Office Has Thoughts on What Streaming Music Services Should Pay for Music. Retrieved from http://on.recode.net/1EM7Hjn

Schneider, M. (2015, January 21). Apple Reportedly Buys Analytics Company Semetric Ahead of Beats Music Relaunch. Retrieved from http://bit.ly/1z9K1O7

Searcey, D. (2014, August 21). Marketers Are Sizing Up the Millennials. Retrieved January 25, 2015, from http://nyti.ms/1vqlxQK

Seave, A. (2014, August 27). New Research Helps Find the Perfect Strategy for 'Freemium' Business Models. Retrieved from http://onforb.es/1AlgVAc

Shazam. (2014, December 10). Shazam Unveils New Music Content, Discovery, and In-App Listening Experience. Retrieved from http://bit.ly/1BxIrIU

Smith, E. & D. Wakabayashi (2015, June 1). Apple to Take On Spotify With New Streaming Services. Retrieved from http://www.wsj.com/articles/apple-to-announce-new-music-services-1433183201?mod=LS1

Smith, M. (2014, January 17). 15 of the Best Music Streaming Platforms Online Today. Retrieved from http://tnw.co/18gcKeH

Washenko, A. (2015, February 2). Spotify reportedly drops plans for Russian launch. Retrieved from http://bit.ly/1weIImq

White House Council of Economic Advisors. (2014). *15 Economic Facts about millennials*, 7-, NASPA. Retrieved from http://bit.ly/1GUq8Es

Widder, B. (2014, May 05). Best music apps for your smartphone (iPhone, Android, or Windows). Retrieved from http://www.digitaltrends.com/mobile/best-music-apps/

Wilson, J. L. (2014, October 20). Sony Music Unlimited (for Android). Retrieved from http://www.pcmag.com/article2/0,2817,2421119,00.asp

USS Midway Museum:
Building a Sustainable Future for All Generations

By

Blodwen Tarter, Golden Gate University

Imagine standing on the upper deck of a ship that is more than three football fields long, 258 feet wide, and extends over four acres. That deck is more than 55 feet above the water line and is one of the ten decks in total, the equivalent of a 20-story building. Four propellers, weighing about 40 tons, move the ship in the water. More than 4000 men served aboard this aircraft carrier so that 200 aviators could fly its aircraft. This crew consumed 10 tons of food per day, including 3000 pounds of potatoes and one thousand loaves of bread daily. Two million pounds of laundry were washed each year.

Ladies and gentlemen, welcome to the aircraft carrier USS Midway, a maritime museum located in beautiful San Diego, California and open to the public since 2004.

The world's largest ship until 1955, the USS Midway has become a major attraction for San Diego tourists and residents alike. As the foremost museum on a ship in the United States, this living history museum is not your typical destination. But after 10 years serving more than one million guests annually, it is time to step back. What will be the USS Midway's vision for the next 10 years? How can marketing help build a sustainable future for this unusual venue, appealing to multiple generations?

The Ship's History

The USS Midway was the longest-serving US Navy aircraft carrier of the 20th century. It began its service in 1945 just one week after the hostilities of World War II ceased. It sailed the Atlantic, patrolling European seas for the North Atlantic Treaty Organization (NATO) for

10 years of peacetime duty. During the Vietnamese conflict in the 1960s, the USS Midway served as a floating base for air strikes against North Vietnam. When Saigon fell in April 1975, helicopters used the USS Midway to help evacuate more than 3000 men, women, and children. Later, the USS Midway deployed to the Arabian Gulf where it acted as the flagship for naval air forces during Operation Desert Storm, the response to the Iraqi seizure of Kuwait. During its final mission in 1991, USS Midway aircraft evacuated civilian personnel from Clark Air Force Base when Mount Pinatubo erupted in the Philippines. In 1992, the ship was decommissioned from the active Navy of the United States. In its heyday, more than 120 airplanes and helicopters were housed aboard the ship. [118]

The Creation of the Museum

When the Navy's plan to decommission the ship was announced, civic leaders in the city of San Diego began to explore turning this enormous ship into a floating museum. After 12 years of fundraising, due diligence, environmental abatement work, 35 permits, and a 3,300-page application to the Navy, the USS Midway Museum opened its doors (or should we say gangways?) in 2004. As a consequence, the USS Midway Museum became the first ship museum established in the US since 1972. It required an initial $8 million investment, all privately raised funds.

The original vision for the museum was that it would be open seven days per week, serve as a venue for major events such as civic fundraisers and corporate parties, provide a robust education program for children, and act as a community resource. San Diego was a perfect location. The city is the birthplace of naval aviation with a sizable naval base and many active duty naval personnel, as well as a large number of Navy retirees.

A major tourist destination in Southern California, San Diego itself draws more than 20 million overnight visitors annually. In addition, three million residents actively explore the many attractions of San Diego. However, many venues compete for the tourist dollar in

---

[118] http://www.midway.org/files/USS-Midway-Historical-Overview.pdf

sunny San Diego. It is the home of Sea World, a renowned zoo, a major league baseball team, outdoor sports such as windsurfing and sailing, attractive beaches, several superb art museums, and major universities such as University of California. There are many things for the out-of-town visitor to enjoy.

The museum founders wanted the USS Midway Museum to become a badge of civic pride as well as a community resource for children and adults. From the beginning, the business model called for visitors to tour a wide cross-section of the ship, interacting with live docents and recorded audio tours. Stories from those who served on the ship provide authentic voices to help visitors learn what it was like to live and work on board a 1,001-foot long ship. Today, audio tours are available in English, Spanish, Japanese, French, German, and Mandarin. Ninety-five percent of the visitors are on the ship for the first time, stopping at over 60 locations on the self-guided audio tour. The tour begins on the hangar deck where aircraft were originally stored and where you can now try out a flight simulator. The tour ends on the flight deck in the open air, where planes took off and landed, high above the water. There, you can see 29 retired planes and helicopters, climb into the cockpit of a fighter jet, or enter the open doors of helicopters to sit in the pilot's seat. By the time the tour is finished, visitors have learned what life was like on this floating city.

Original Strategies for the Museum

The initial strategies for USS Midway Museum were fivefold.[119]

1. *Leverage those who have a stake in our success.* The museum focused on working with the people and organizations devoted to bringing visitors to San Diego for pleasure work. These included the public relations and promotions staff of the San Diego Convention and Visitors Bureau (also known as the San Diego Tourism Authority), responsible for attracting out-of-town visitors. Concierges from hotels throughout the city were targeted for outreach so that they would recommend a visit to the USS Midway Museum to their guests. More than 100

---

[119] Scott McGaugh, Marketing Director, USS Midway Museum, October 2014

conventions take place at the San Diego Convention Center and attract more than 867,000 attendees[120] yearly, so the staff of the Convention Center were important collaborators. San Diego residents would be visitors as well as the source of volunteers to maintain and staff the museum. And for the education program for children in the community, the USS Midway Museum involves teachers, principals, and other educators.

2. *Own the patriotic holidays*. Major events on the ship celebrate or commemorate Memorial Day (the last Monday in May), Independence Day (July 4), Veterans Day (November 11), and Pearl Harbor day (December 7). This is a logical tie-in to the USS Midway's military heritage.

3. "*Hunt where the ducks are*." Capture the tourists in San Diego by reaching them with ticket reseller programs, hotel concierges and anyone else who touched the tourists in the city. Take advantage of the strong Navy presence for volunteers, reunions, and word-of-mouth marketing.

4. *Become a community resource*. By identifying youth, business, nonprofit, and civic organizations with which to work, the USS Midway Museum has become a location for meetings and events. Girl Scouts, the American Red Cross, Toys for Tots holiday gift-giving program, the Wounded Warrior Project, and the U.S. Navy were only a few of the organizations taking advantage of this stellar location.

5. *Become a national resource*. Not only was the USS Midway Museum a great place for live local events, it has become a venue for well-known broadcast events. American Idol, Wheel of Fortune, the Antiques Roadshow, Extreme Makeover, The Bachelor, and Fox network news (live) have all used the USS Midway Museum. It has ample space and an unusual setting to make a broadcast from the ship interesting and different.

---

[120] 2015 estimates, http://www.utsandiego.com/news/2015/jan/08/convention-center-attendance-steady-growth/

A Successful First Decade

By 2014, 10 years after its opening, the USS Midway was able to report impressive results. Visitors numbered 1.2 million annually while one in four visitors were under the age of 17 years – the museum was a definite family destination. It was listed as San Diego's most-popular attraction and the seventh most popular museum of any type in America on TripAdvisor.

Seven hundred events are held annually on the ship with reservations limited to three years in advance. Each year, more than 400 military events (such as re-enlistments, retirements, changes of command, and memorials) are conducted on board. During museum hours, the public is invited to observe these ceremonies, furthering strengthening the patriotic symbolism of the ship.

Approximately 50,000 students are served in educational activities on board or in their own classrooms. More than 700 volunteers donate 250,000 hours each year while 14,000 members of the Museum provide financial support in exchange for modest benefits.

With consistent use of targeted advertising and feature stories in San Diego tourist-oriented publications, a presence on tourist-oriented websites for San Diego (such as sandiego.org), public relations, and community outreach and development efforts, the USS Midway Museum had become a well-established and well-known fixture in San Diego. Though a non-profit organization, it was also financially stable-- not an easy task in a very competitive environment. The USS Midway Museum was profitable in its first month of operation in 2004 and was debt-free in 18 months. Now, its Foundation had a capital fund of more than $20 million.

The museum receives no funding from the Navy or the US government. It is a self-sustaining non-profit organization. Income comes from a variety of activities: ticket sales for touring the ship, membership dues, fees for hosting public and private events (see Appendix Five), food and beverage revenue from the Fantail Café on board, the gift shop sales of books and memorabilia, fees for educational events, and donations. Memberships cost from $50-$2500 per person per year (see Appendix Two). In 2012, membership fees were $765,682. The bulk of the earned revenue came from program services with $16,772,675 reported. Ticket sales are the single largest contributor to income (> $11 million) so maintaining and increasing attendance has been the highest priority. Event fees are another important component of program services revenue but substantially less significant (>$2.4 million).[121] A modest budget of about $78,000 for postage, $190,000 for printing and publications, and $108,000 for promotions were the direct expenses for marketing program services.[122] Marketing staff salaries were budgeted separately.

The Museum is required to maintain a substantial reserve, primarily for maintenance. A ship, docked at a pier in salt water with constant exposure to the elements, deteriorates quickly if regular maintenance is not performed. A recent major focus was on underwater hull preservation—needed to keep the museum from sinking! Specifically, this almost $4 million project[123] "involved cleaning and sealing of the vents located below the waterline of the ship. This process will protect the hull and should be able to take the place of dry-docking of the ship in future years."[124] This leads to an interesting problem:

> "The biggest challenge we face is the public perception that because the Midway is so successful as a museum, and the gate receipts large, the ship has an abundance of wealth. Many do not recognize the Museum's extensive multi-million dollar project to preserve the hull and ensure that the Museum remains afloat in later years without an expensive dry-docking (and down time as a community attraction). In addition, the Museum often donates its spaces for community events

---

[121] "Detail Financial" section, http://bettergivingsd.guidestar.org/NonprofitProfile.aspx?OrgId=40308

[122] Based on Form 990 for 2011, Part IX, Line 24E, Other Expenses

[123] Audited Financial Report 2011, http://bettergivingsd.guidestar.org/NonprofitProfile.aspx?OrgId=40308

[124] Audited Financial Report 2012, http://bettergivingsd.guidestar.org/NonprofitProfile.aspx?OrgId=40308

and sponsors free educational programs for many San Diego children which are only possible through donations specifically for that purpose."[125]

The Next 10 Years: Building a Sustainable Future

At the 10-year mark, the board of directors and staff realized that it was time to take another look at the goals, objectives and strategy for the USS Midway Museum. They recognized that they were currently "missing" more than one million visitors to its website annually. Social media efforts include Facebook, Twitter, Instagram, Twitter, and Flickr. But how useful are they? Are they reaching the intended audience and helping achieve the Museum's objectives? The heavily-visited website, midway.org, may need a refresh.

The target audience for visitors is evolving. Military personnel now account for less than 1% of the total US population. Nevertheless, that is 1.31 million service members on active military duty with an additional group of more than 500,000 people in the National Guard and Reserve forces.[126] Veterans, who are former members of the military, are estimated at almost 22 million.[127] Regular guests from the older generations may remember the USS Midway in service or might have served on the ship itself. But the younger generations, both Gen X and Gen Y adults, are now the parents the Museum needs to attract. And the youngest generation, just being named (Gen Z/Digital Natives/Centennials) includes the children and young adults who must fill the pipeline of visitors to build a sustainable future for the Museum over the long term.

Marketing for the Future

---

[125] "Organization Comments" section,
http://bettergivingsd.guidestar.org/NonprofitProfile.aspx?OrgId=40308
[126] http://www.military.com/daily-news/2014/02/24/hagel-budgets-for-smallest-army-since-world-war-ii.html and http://www.military.com/daily-news/2014/12/16/air-force-secretary-vows-no-more-layoffs-in-2015.html
[127] http://www1.va.gov/vetdata/docs/Quickfacts/Stats_at_a_glance_12_31_14.pdf, 22 million estimated as of Sept 2014

After a Fall 2014 board retreat, the organization emerged with a new vision. The goal was to "become America's living symbol of freedom."

How can the USS Midway Museum continue to be the world's foremost aircraft carrier museum, with the express mission to "Preserve the historic USS Midway and the legacy of those who serve, inspire and educate future generations, and entertain our museum guests"?[128]

This is the challenge facing the USS Midway Museum today. Its five-person marketing staff must develop both a short-term tactical plan and a long-term strategic marketing plan for the next 10 years. All the while, the staff must keep in mind that the Museum is a non-profit organization with a relatively modest budget for marketing communications.

Given the specific objectives listed below, what can the Museum do to attract more visitors, both from the US and abroad? How can the marketing staff expand the appeal of the ship to all generations? What might they do to increase the number and size of events held on the ship to generate event revenue and increase visibility? What role do the educational programs play in revenue generation? Or are educational programs more appropriately considered community service, even though some income is derived from educational programs? How does it all fit together for the long-term viability of the USS Midway Museum as a premier destination and a tribute to the ship's legacy of service to the nation?

The objectives:

1. Diversify and increase attendance on the ship.
2. Increase attendance for on-board student events.
3. Generate revenue in the form of museum ticket sales, membership dues, and fees for on-board corporate and private events.

---

[128] "About Us" http://www.midway.org/about-uss-midway-museum

4. Remain relevant and engaging to future generations in the context of an authentic historic artifact.

Generational (age) cohorts:

- The Greatest Generation (born 1901-1927, experienced World War II, rapidly declining numbers)
- The Silent Generation (born 1928-1945)
- Baby Boomers (born 1946-1964, very large number of people)
- Gen X (born 1965-1980)
- Gen Y/ Millennials (born 1981-1996, next largest age cohort after Baby Boomers)
- Gen Z/ Centennials/ Digital Natives (born 1997 to present)

APPENDIX ONE

Ticket prices for museum admission[129]

March 2015

General Admission

$20 Adults (18+)

$17 Seniors (62+)

$15 Students (13-17 or w/ college ID)

$10 Retired Military (with valid ID)

$10 Youth (ages 6-12)

Children under 5 are free

Online Price

$18 Adults

$15 Seniors (62+)

---

[129] USS Midway Museum website March 2015

$13 Students (13-17 or with college ID)

$8 Retired Military (with valid ID)

$8 Youth (ages 6-12)

Children under 5 are free

Members are FREE!

(See Appendix Two for details about membership benefits)

Complimentary Admission

Children 5 years old or younger

Active-duty military personnel (including Reservists) with valid ID (daytime admission only)

Group discounts for groups of 25 or more

$13 adults

$7 youth (7-12)

$10 seniors (62+)

APPENDIX TWO

Membership
Dues and Benefits

	Individual $60	Individual Senior $50	Individual Hero $50	Family $90	Family Senior $75	Family Hero $60	Crew $125	Chief $175	Commander $250	TOPGUN $500	Captain $1,000	Admiral $2,500
							CIRCLE LEVELS					
Daily admission for cardholder and one guest	⚓	⚓	⚓									
Daily admission for four*				⚓	⚓	⚓	⚓	⚓	⚓	⚓	⚓	⚓
Subscription to *Currents* magazine	⚓	⚓	⚓	⚓	⚓	⚓	⚓	⚓	⚓	⚓	⚓	⚓
$2 OFF Additional Tickets	⚓	⚓	⚓	⚓	⚓	⚓	⚓	⚓	⚓	⚓	⚓	⚓
20% OFF at Fantail Café	⚓	⚓	⚓	⚓	⚓	⚓	⚓	⚓	⚓	⚓	⚓	⚓
10% OFF at The Jet Shop	⚓	⚓	⚓	⚓	⚓	⚓	⚓	⚓	⚓	⚓	⚓	⚓
HNSA Individual Member Admission Exchange**	⚓	⚓	⚓	⚓	⚓	⚓	⚓	⚓	⚓	⚓	⚓	⚓
Guest Passes							4	8	10	12	14	20
Circle Level Discounts to Membership Events							⚓	⚓	⚓	⚓	⚓	⚓
Invites to Behind-the-Scenes Tours							⚓	⚓	⚓	⚓	⚓	⚓
Flight Simulator Passes								1	1	1	2	3
Midway Polo Shirt									⚓	⚓	⚓	⚓
Tickets to Parade of Lights										2	2	4
One-Time Private Event (Restrictions Apply)											⚓	⚓

* Identification required with Membership card for admission. Cardholder must be present and counted in admission. Family and Circle Memberships receive one card with up to two names of adults residing at the same household address. **Hero (Active and Retired Military, Police Officers, and Fire Fighters) and Senior (age 62+) Memberships require cardholder(s) to have appropriate ID.**

** Free admission for cardholder to participating Historic Naval Ships Association museums. www.hnsa.org/memberexchange.htm

Source: http://www.midway.org/files/members/membership-comparisons-20140620.pdf

APPENDIX THREE

Recent Financials

USS MIDWAY MUSEUM

STATEMENT OF ACTIVITIES
Year Ended December 31, 2012

(With Summarized Financial Information for the Year Ended December 31, 2011)

	Unrestricted						
	Operations	Depreciation	Total Unrestricted	Temporarily Restricted	Permanently Restricted	2012 Total	2011 (Note 14)
OPERATING SUPPORT AND REVENUE							
Admissions	$ 11,755,327	$ -	$ 11,755,327	$ -	$ -	$ 11,755,327	$ 10,335,680
Concessions	2,542,193	-	2,542,193	-	-	2,542,193	2,257,946
Group events and programs	2,475,155	-	2,475,155	-	-	2,475,155	2,012,291
Contributions	579,194	-	579,194	1,024,666	46,925	1,650,785	783,475
Memberships	765,682	-	765,682	-	-	765,682	765,682
Education	726,238	-	726,238	-	-	726,238	691,586
Other	142,861	-	142,861	-	-	142,861	87,082
Interest income	6,830	-	6,830	-	-	6,830	26,068
Net assets released from restrictions:							
Satisfaction of program restrictions	545,406	-	545,406	(545,406)	-	-	-
Total support and revenue	19,538,886	-	19,538,886	479,260	46,925	20,065,071	16,959,810
EXPENSES							
Program services							
Exhibits, curatorial, and aircraft restoration	2,695,778	589,595	3,285,373	-	-	3,285,373	3,874,167
Public programs	1,990,288	76,208	2,066,496	-	-	2,066,496	1,838,207
Education/volunteers/docents	1,705,083	76,208	1,781,291	-	-	1,781,291	1,535,326
Guest services	1,729,265	5,081	1,734,346	-	-	1,734,346	1,539,079
Hull preservation expenses	1,724,853	-	1,724,853	-	-	1,724,853	2,023,875
Navy pier plan development	757,599	-	757,599	-	-	757,599	269,886
Membership	544,936	1,130	546,066	-	-	546,066	545,325
Safety and security	192,297	2,540	194,837	-	-	194,837	185,809
Save the kiss	164,380	-	164,380	-	-	164,380	-
Total program service expense	11,504,479	750,762	12,255,241	-	-	12,255,241	11,811,674
Supporting services							
Fundraising	966,986	1,677	968,663	-	-	968,663	968,025
Sales and marketing	1,145,255	572	1,145,827	-	-	1,145,827	1,114,559
Management and general	1,139,853	2,539	1,142,392	-	-	1,142,392	1,010,337
Total supporting services	3,252,094	4,788	3,256,882	-	-	3,256,882	3,092,921
Total expenses	14,756,573	755,550	15,512,123	-	-	15,512,123	14,904,595
Change in net assets from operations	4,782,313	(735,550)	4,026,763	479,260	46,925	4,552,948	2,055,215

APPENDIX FOUR

Historical photos of the

USS Midway on active duty

APPENDIX FIVE

USS Midway Museum Today

USS Midway aerial view, courtesy of USS Midway Museum

Preparing for an event on the flight deck, October 2014, courtesy of the author

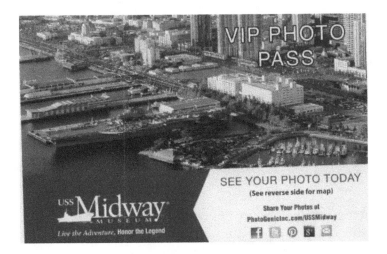

Pictures are taken of guests as soon as they enter the ship. They can purchase the commemorative photos near the Visitor Information desk and are encouraged to share the photos via social media.

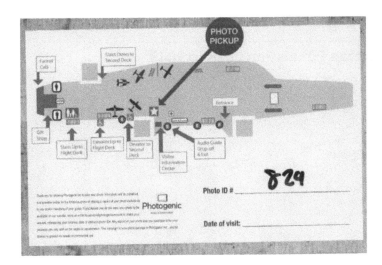

APPENDIX SIX

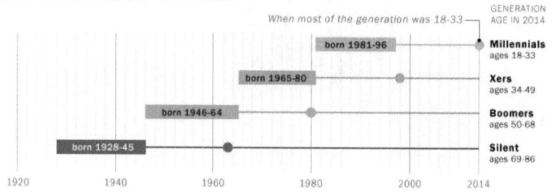

http://www.pewresearch.org/fact-tank/2015/03/19/how-millennials-compare-with-their-grandparents/

APPENDIX SEVEN

US Veteran Statistics[130]

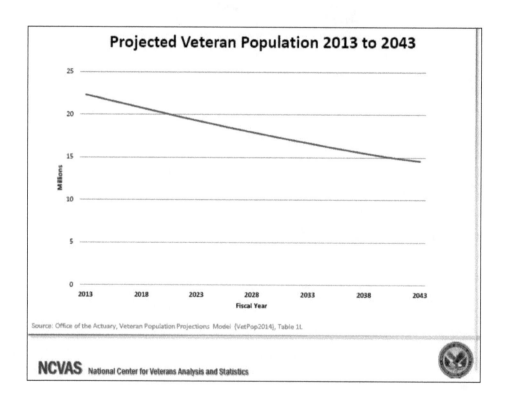

---

[130] http://www.va.gov/vetdata/docs/QuickFacts/Population_slideshow.pdf

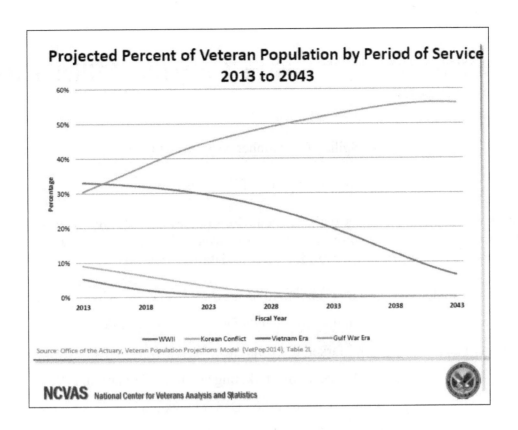

Williamsburg Tourism Targeting Millennials

By

Lisa D. Spiller, Christopher Newport University

Carol Scovotti, University of Wisconsin-Whitewater

Although the case is based on a real-life scenario, some of the case details have been created and some of the case data have been disguised. The authors would like to thank Corrina Ferguson and Dan Dipiazzo for their assistance with this case.

Corrina Ferguson left the early morning board meeting with an extra skip in her step. She had just heard a fantastic presentation, *Make Way for the Millennials,* delivered by one of the Williamsburg Area Destination Marketing Committee (WADMC) Advisory Group chairmen, Dan Dipiazzo, Vice-President of Marketing at Busch Gardens and Water Country USA® in Williamsburg, Virginia. Corrina asked Dan if he would share his presentation slides with her so she could present them to her marketing staff and he graciously agreed. Marketing to Millennial family travelers was the new focus for Williamsburg tourism and recently Corrina had been charged with creating a campaign for doing so. That was fine with Corrina as she thrived on taking on new challenges, and this one was going to demand every bit of the marketing knowledge, experience and solid intuition that she could muster. Tackling new challenges was not just part of her job, but it was part of her nature as her experience in tourism marketing ran deep.

Corrina Ferguson was the Director of Destination Marketing for the Williamsburg Area Destination Marketing Campaign, overseeing all aspects of the Visit Williamsburg marketing campaign. Prior to arriving in Williamsburg two years ago, she had been the Vice President of Destination Marketing, New Media & Strategy for VisitNewEngland.com, a New England tourism online travel guide.

As the former general manager and director of marketing for 12 years at The Dinosaur Place in Connecticut, Ferguson developed and created educational curriculum, special events, community outreach initiatives, and marketing and public relations programs. Extremely involved in regional tourism marketing efforts, she had served on the board of directors and co-chaired the marketing committees for the regional tourism marketing groups including

Exhibit 1: Corrina Ferguson, Director of Destination Marketing for the Williamsburg Area Destination Marketing Campaign

Mystic Coast and Country TIA (2003-2009) and the Greater Mystic Visitor's Bureau (2011-2012). Corrina had founded and fostered several cross-discipline marketing partnerships resulting in significant savings and increased visitation to the partners. Corrina's position was always a bit challenging as she was responsible for marketing the entire Williamsburg destination, as opposed to a single attraction or entity.

DESTINATION MARKETING ORGANIZATION (DMO)

Founded in 2004, the Williamsburg Area Destination Marketing Committee (WADMC) was created by the state of Virginia to represent and promote the Historic Triangle area (which includes all of the City of Williamsburg, James City County and York County), as an overnight tourism destination. Funding for this advertising campaign was received from revenues collected via an additional $2.00 per night room tax on destination transient lodging stays as well as partner funding. WADMC, an 11-person board made up of various industry representatives, oversees the use of these funds to market the Greater Williamsburg area as an overnight travel and tourism destination.

One of America's favorite family destinations, the Greater Williamsburg region (See Exhibit 2) includes Jamestown, Williamsburg and Yorktown, offering a unique juxtaposition of contemporary and historical experiences for all ages. Visitors can choose from hands-on

Exhibit 2: Map of the Historic Triangle area

interactive attractions, scenic outdoor adventures and sophisticated arts and culture experiences, making Greater Williamsburg a top choice among travelers.

<u>Major Attractions:</u>

- *Busch Gardens®:* is an action-packed, European-themed adventure park with 17th-century charm and 21st-century technology, boasting more than 100 acres of fun-filled exploration.

- *College of William & Mary:* The second oldest university in the United States, and a cutting edge research university, the College of William & Mary is situated on 1,200 acres in historic downtown Williamsburg.

- *Colonial Williamsburg:* Colonial Williamsburg interprets Virginia's 18th-century capital of Williamsburg, Va., as a 21st-century center for history and citizenship with more than 400 restored or reconstructed original buildings, museums and educational programs.

- *Historic Jamestowne:* Site of America's first permanent English settlement, Historic Jamestowne continues to make history as an active archeological dig site, offering a tour with the archaeologist or behind-the-scenes tours in the lab with the curator.

- *Jamestown Settlement*: Traces America's colonial beginnings through expansive gallery exhibits and film, and historical interpretation at outdoor re-creations of three ships that sailed to Virginia in 1607, the colonial fort and a Powhatan Indian village.

- *Water Country USA:* Virginia's largest water park offering water rides, slide, pools and play areas with a retro surf theme.

- *Yorktown Battlefield:* The National Park Service welcomes visitors to explore interpreted trails and sites from the last major battle of the American Revolution.

Exhibit 3: Williamsburg Images

- *Yorktown Victory Center:* The American Revolution is chronicled through exhibits, films and re-created military encampment and Revolution-era farm. The site will become the American Revolution Museum at Yorktown in late 2016, with new exhibition galleries and expanded outdoor living-history areas.

CURRENT SITUATION

The Williamsburg area offered a variety of activities for visitors in a safe, convenient, family-friendly destination. However, one of the destination's greatest strengths – its strong association with the history of America's founding – was also one of its major challenges, as young families showed less interest in historical attractions. Since young Millennial families encompassed the new target market for Williamsburg tourism that meant it was "outside-the-box" thinking time for Corrina and her staff. She was about to get down to work as her staff gathered in the conference room, eager to get started.

"Good Monday morning all," Corrina said with an enthusiastic voice. "As some of you already know based on my recent comments, our board has approved the creation of a new marketing campaign targeting Millennial family travelers. That's the good news. The bad news is that we've got a mere two weeks to put our campaign plan together before I present it to the board for approval. Earlier this morning at the board meeting I heard an enlightening presentation on Millennials and I'm going to share some of the slides with you. Then, I'll present the results of the recent visitation research that we've conducted. Any questions before I begin? Since nobody has any questions, let's begin with the slideshow." Corrina began presenting the following slides one-by-one shown in Exhibit 5, as her staff took notes.

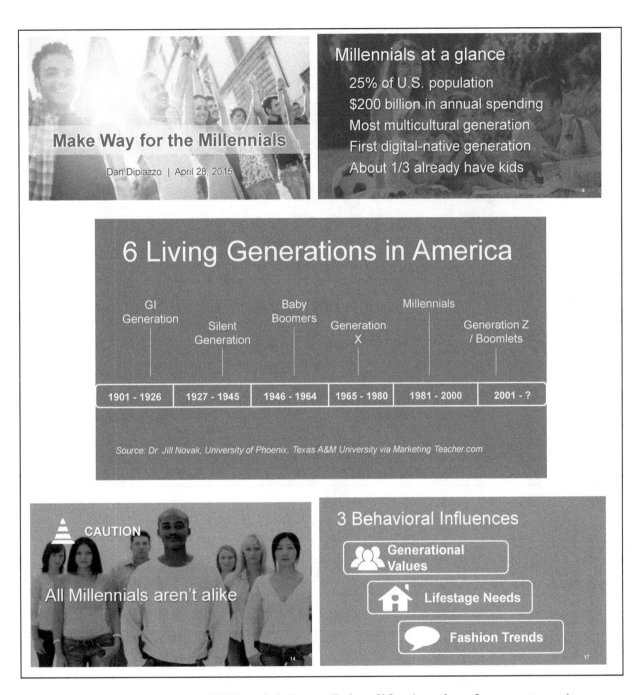

Exhibit 5: Make Way for the Millennials PowerPoint slides (continued on next page)

Six Millennial Values

- Authenticity
- Self-Awareness
- Enrichment
- Connection
- Community
- Immediacy

They are more ethnically diverse than their predecessors

	Millennial	Generation X	Baby Boomer
Hispanic	21%	18%	10%
Non-Hispanic White	57%	62%	72%
African-American	14%	13%	11%
Asian	6%	6%	4%
Other	3%	3%	2%

Source: 2012 American Community Survey

Millennial Beliefs Change with Parenthood		
Millennial Beliefs	**Before**	**After**
Identify as conservative evangelical Christians	10%	33%
Belong to environmental group	10%	0.2%
Likely to buy environmentally friendly products	60%	37%
Buy same products celebrities use	21%	6%
Want to hear about new products via email	17%	32%
Use internet less because of privacy concerns	10%	29%
Source: *Barkley, SMG & BCG, 2014*		

As Corrina finished presenting Dan's final slide, she explained, "While this presentation provides a broad overview of Millennials, we need to dig deeper and really understand this target market. That's where you all come in. I'd like each of you to conduct additional secondary research on Millennials and be prepared to present your findings in another staff meeting this Thursday morning at 10:00 a.m. I'll divide the research topics so that you are not duplicating each other's content. Does anyone have questions?" Suzanne inquired: "How do you plan on dividing up the topics?" Corrina answered: "Suzanne, you investigate Millennial population statistics and demographic characteristics; Chad, you research their social and psychological influences; Jack, you explore their media preferences; and Olivia, you focus on Millennial consumer behavior, especially as related to travel and tourism."

PRIMARY & SECONDARY RESEARCH FINDINGS

Corrina continued, "Are there any other questions before I present our destination visitation research findings?" Since nobody had any other questions, Corrina said, "I'll begin with the research methodology, followed by an overview of the results. Keep in mind that the study we conducted this past year was an online survey with 1,500 completed interviews in our key geographic markets. The first slide shows the geographical distribution." **Exhibit 6 below.**

Market	Completed interviews
New York City	241
Philadelphia	186
Baltimore	226
Washington, DC	235
Raleigh-Durham	183
200-mile Williamsburg Radius	82
Other Virginia	348

Corrina continued presenting the research findings to her staff. "As shown in the next slide, our destination research reveals that a majority of potential visitors who have decided against a trip to Williamsburg cite either a lack of interest in what the area offers (24%) or a belief that one visit is enough – been there, done that mentality (27%). (See Exhibit 7).

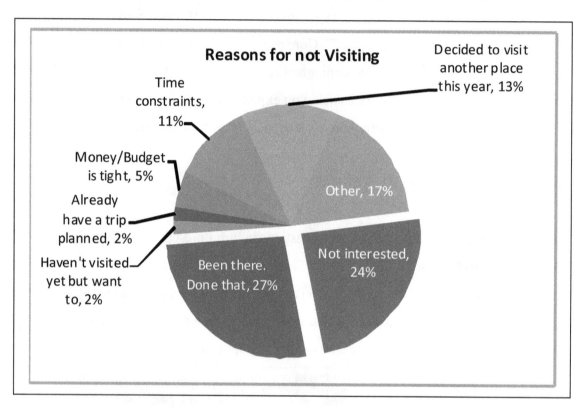

Exhibit 7: Reasons for not visiting Williamsburg

"Additionally, research on several attributes associated with vacations shows that Williamsburg has strong association with characteristics such as *history* and *learning*, which are not deemed very important, while suffering from lower association with highly-valued characteristics such as *fun*, *relaxation* and *affordable*." See Exhibits 8 -10 for graphs of these market research findings.

What are the first words or phrases that come to mind when thinking about Williamsburg, Virginia?

(Shown: Coded open end responses 5%+)

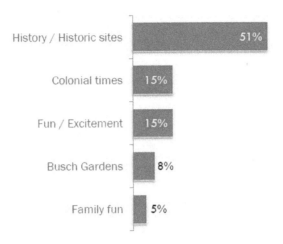

History / Historic sites	51%
Colonial times	15%
Fun / Excitement	15%
Busch Gardens	8%
Family fun	5%

Exhibit 8: Tourist perceptions of Williamsburg

Exhibit 9: Words associated with Williamsburg

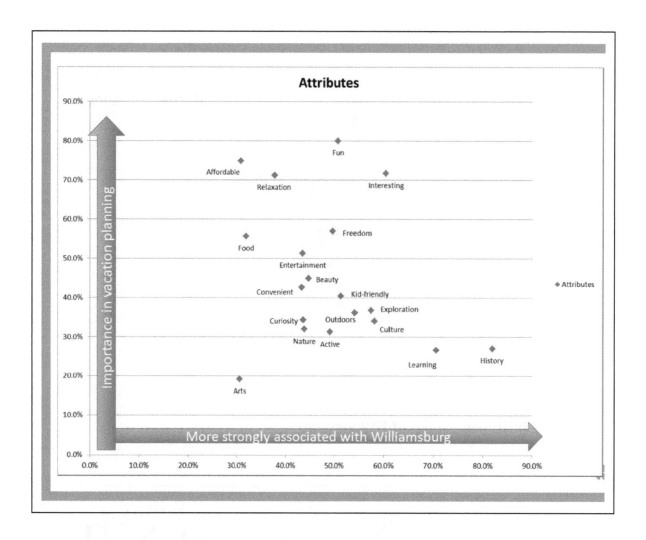

Exhibit 10: Importance of attributes when planning a vacation getaway

"Finally," as Corrina concluded, "research regarding the other vacation destinations that Williamsburg tourists have visited in the past three years and which locations they plan to visit in the next three years show that our top competitors continue to be Orlando, New York City, Washington, D.C., Baltimore, and Virginia Beach." (See Exhibit 11.)

Other Destination	% Visitors in the past 3 years	% Visitors Planning to Return in the next 3 years
Orlando	55.2%	59.5%
New York City	51.1%	54.7%
Washington, DC	50.5%	48.6%
Baltimore, MD	43.8%	41.6%
Virginia Beach, VA	37.8%	42.9%

Exhibit 11: Top destinations visited by Williamsburg visitors

Corrina concluded her presentation and before adjourning the meeting, she reminded her staff about their research assignments and also explained that at Thursday's meeting she would be presenting additional research findings from the positioning and language options study that the destination also conducted last year. And so the week went by uneventfully and now Thursday morning was upon them.

"Good Thursday morning everyone," Corrina said in a cheerful manner. "Who wants to begin presenting their research findings?" "I do," exclaimed Suzanne as she quickly jumped up and eagerly walked to the podium. A summary of Suzanne's research findings on Millennial population statistics and demographic characteristics are shown in Exhibit 12.

- Millennials currently represent 25% of the U.S. population, or approximately 84 million people. (U.S. Census Bureau, 2013)
- Millennials are now the largest living US generation, surpassing baby boomers by 3 million people. (BCG, 2012)
- The Millennial generation should be further segmented by age - teen, college-aged, and young adult - as behavior varies by stage of life. (Cone, 2006)
- Young adult Millennials have mastered the art of prolonged adolescence as more have moved back in with parents after graduating from college or entering the workforce. (Cone, 2006)
- About 40% of Millennial mothers are either the sole or primary income source for the family. (Pew Research Center, 2013)
- One-third of children with Millennial parents live in non-traditional arrangements. The number of children with same sex Millennial parents increased 11% over the past decade. (Mintel, 2014)
- Millennials will have more spending power than any other generation by 2018. (Oracle Financial Services, 2010)
- By 2020, U.S. Millennial spending power will total more than $1.4 trillion. (eMarketer, 2014)
- By 2020, 50% of the workforce in the U.S. will be Millennials. (Pew Research Center, 2010)
- By 2025, Millennials will make up 75% of the global workforce. (Schawbel, 2013)

Exhibit 12: Secondary research findings on Millennial population statistics and demographic characteristics.

"Great job, Suzanne, who's next?" Corrina asked her staff. "I will be," replies Chad. A summary of Chad's research findings on Millennial social and psychological influences are shown in Exhibit 13.

- About 76% of Millennials have friendships based solely on social media; and 32% feel close to people they have only met online. (Millennial Central, 2014)
- Adult Millennials view their parents as friends and involve them in decision-making. (Feldman & Berberich, 2014)
- While 70% have purchased products that support a cause, Millennials are less likely to make a direct monetary contribution to a cause. (Cone, 2006; Fromm & Lindell, 2012)
- Few 'green' products make it into a Millennial's shopping cart due to higher prices and mistrust about actual benefits. (Faw, 2014)
- Millennials are willing to compromise on a preferred brand for a lower price. (Fromm & Lindell, 2012)
- Millennials rely on more visual signs to demonstrate their social consciousness, such as bringing their own bags to shop. (Faw, 2014)
- Millennials respond positively when content is tailored to their age (54%), location (55%), and cultural interests (63%). (NewsCred, 2014)
- Millennials will interact and share content that is inspiring, educating, or entertaining. Content should be smart and humorous. (NewsCred, 2014)
- More than 60% of Millennials rate products and services online to share their experiences about a company or brand. (Fromm & Lindell, 2012)
- Millennials respond to sales promotions that offer something tangible such as gas benefits, free products or percentage discounts. They don't clip coupons and they don't care for loyalty programs that base rewards on accumulated points. (Faw, 2014)
- Millennials value experiences over things and 64% said they would like to experience everything from rock climbing to opera once. (Magid, 2015)
- Millennials hate advertising. Authenticity is vital. They will ignore anything that sounds like it came from an ad agency. (Feldman & Berberich, 2014)

Exhibit 13: Secondary research findings on Millennial social and psychological influences.

"Wow, impressive research, Chad. Thank you, now who's next?" Corrina asked her staff. "I'll go next," replied Olivia. A summary of Olivia's research findings on Millennial media preferences is shown in Exhibit 14.

- Millennials receive more than 5,000 marketing messages per day. They have become experts at ignoring advertising. (NewsCred, 2014)
- Millennials use multiple sources to engage with a brand including company website (52%), social media (49%), email newsletters (31%), brand specific apps (29%), and articles (25%). (NewsCred, 2014)
- Despite their high-tech media preferences, Millennials enjoy receiving offers through direct mail for its 'old school' novelty. (NewsCred, 2014)

- Millennials are the first generation to make smartphone usage their norm. (eMarketer, 2015)
- Millennials think a brand is more modern when advertised on a mobile device. (IPG Media Lab, 2015)
- Nearly 94% of Millennials use social media platforms, but over 50% find advertising on social media sites annoying. (Fromm & Lindell, 2012)
- Despite the annoyance, 31% of Millennials are likely to check out brands advertised on social media sites. (Feldman & Berberich, 2014)
- Facebook is the top social media platform among Millennials to search and share content. (NewsCred, 2014)
- About 72% of Millennials check Facebook at least once a day, while 59% get their news from nontraditional sources like social feeds. (Meagher, 2014)
- By fall 2013, Instagram usage among Millennials was equal to that of Facebook. (eMarketer, 2014)
- Millennials watch an average of 15 hours of television per week, compared to 22 hours for those older than 35 years of age. (Feldman & Berberich, 2014)
- Millennials view substantially more video content through YouTube and other streaming video sources than do older generations. (Friedman, 2014)
- Streaming video activity has doubled since 2011. (ANA, 2014)
- Nearly 94% of Millennials multitask while watching videos. As a consequence, ad recall rates are generally 2 to 12% lower than those of older generations. (ANA, 2014)

Exhibit 14: Secondary research findings on Millennial media preferences

"Well done, Olivia. Thanks. That leaves you, Jack" declared Corrina as Jack made his way toward the podium. A summary of Jack's research findings on Millennial travel and tourism behavior are shown in Exhibit 15.

- Only 34% of Millennials plan to take a vacation away from home lasting longer than a week, compared to Gen X (37%), baby boomers (35%), and seniors (46%). (Harris Interactive, 2014)
- About 58% of Millennials enjoy traveling with friends. 78% want to learn something new when they travel; 79% would like to visit all 50 states in their lifetime. (BCG, 2012)
- Millennials take, on average, 75 days to plan a vacation. Older generations plan for 93 days. (PCAV Destinations, 2013)
- Adult Millennials with children consider taking outdoor trips to be their most favorite family activity. Watching TV with their children is second. (AFE, 2014)
- Fun is the most important verb in regards to vacation. Not interested in history but rather beaches, amusement parks, and spectator sports. (Kesterson, 2013)
- Expect to be rewarded for their hard work and expect vacations where everyone wins and gets what they want. ("Millennial Travelers Loom Large, Take Charge", 2014)

Exhibit 15: Secondary research findings on Millennial travel and tourism behavior.

"Outstanding work, Jack! Thank you all for the detailed insight on Millennials. Now it's my turn to present the positioning and language options research findings from the study we conducted last year," Corrina proclaimed. "Once again, this was an online survey of 1,000 total respondents, 200 vacation decision makers in each of our five target geographical markets (Washington, DC, Baltimore, MD, Raleigh-Durham, NC, Philadelphia, PA and New York, NY.) In order to qualify for the survey, participants must have spent a total of 10 or more days on an overnight leisure travel in the last three years. In addition, each participant had to self-identify as the sole or primary vacation destination maker for his/her family. The results represent a 50/50 split between families with children and those without. The first slide shows the respondent demographics," explained Corrina. (See Exhibit 16.)

- *73% female*

- *78% 30+ years old, ~30% 60+ years old*

- *55% had bachelor's degree or better*

- *85% with $50K+ HHI, 30% with $100K+ HHI*

- *50/50 mix of families with children at home and those with children at home*

- *75% had 10+ leisure nights over the last three years, 25% had 7 to 9 leisure nights*

Exhibit 16: Respondent demographics

Corrina continued presenting the research findings to her staff. "As shown in the next slide, respondents were asked to state how interested they would be in a vacation that focused on four different options of what Williamsburg has to offer." (See Exhibit 17.)

•*Option A* –	*A real focus on history and the existing perception*
•*Option B* –	*Focus is on relaxation and recharging (no history)*
•*Option C* -	*Focus is on an active vacation*
•*Option D* -	*Focus is on curiosity and learning*

Exhibit 17: Language option research

"The findings reveal that more respondents are interested in a vacation that allows them to either *chill (relax)*, followed by *be active*," stated Corrina. (See Exhibit 18.)

How interested are you in this type of vacation/getaway destination?

LANGUAGE OPTION A: HISTORY		LANGUAGE OPTION B: CHILL	
Interested	66%	Interested	88%
Uninterested	34%	Uninterested	12%

LANGUAGE OPTION C: ACTIVE		LANGUAGE OPTION D: CURIOUS	
Interested	80%	Interested	74%
Uninterested	20%	Uninterested	26%

Exhibit 18: Language option research findings

Corrina continued, "The survey went on to ask respondents to pick up to three destinations which are most closely aligned with each of the four options—history, chill, active and curious. Let me now show you the research findings for each option. The first language option is not surprising and confirms the findings of the other online study. However, the other slides offer great promise and align well with our future positioning." (See Exhibits 19–22).

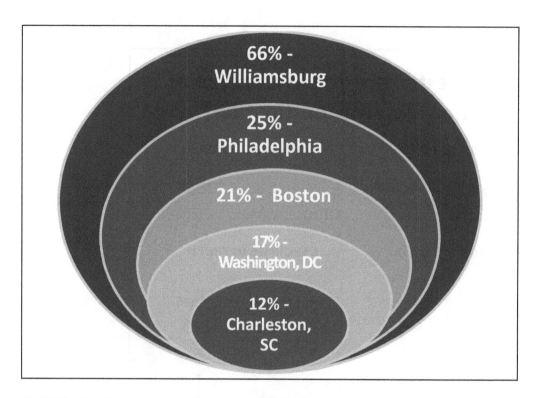

Exhibit 19: Language option research findings – "History"

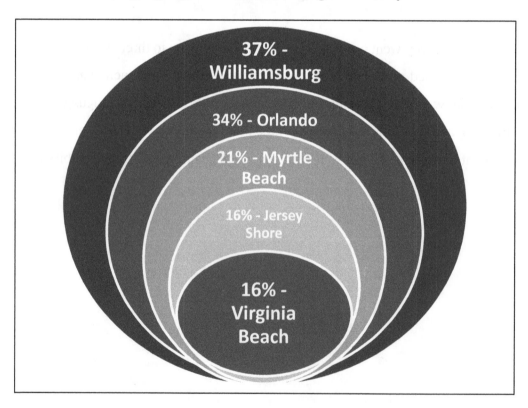

Exhibit 20: Language option research findings – "Chill"

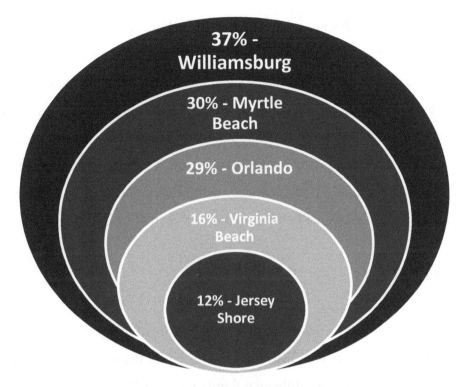

Exhibit 21: Language option research findings – "Active"

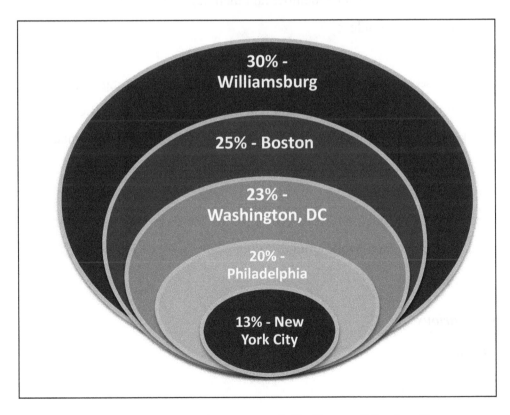

Exhibit 22: Language option research findings – "Curious"

"As I mentioned earlier, the research shows that while Williamsburg has been described as being most strongly associated with *history*, it can also hold its own with relax, fun and curious messaging. These details, along with the fact that the destination's competitive set changes when the focus of the messaging changes, will be important for us to address as we develop our new marketing campaign targeting Millennial family travelers. On that point, I'll conclude my research presentation," Corrina asserted. "Now it's time for us to begin processing all of the research findings—both secondary and primary—that we've gathered and critically analyze the data to strategically develop our new marketing campaign plan."

STRATEGIC CHALLENGE

"Before we begin our research analysis, let me remind you, by way of this packet of materials, of the important criteria that WADMC has established for the new Williamsburg destination marketing campaign targeting Millennial family travelers," Corrina stated. She distributed an information packet to each staff member and then begins to review each of the items with her staff. Those criteria included:

First - Williamsburg seeks to drive family summer vacations, encouraging longer stays that generate more hotel room nights and visitation to more attractions. Specifically, the destination would like to reshape its image to be more appealing to Millennial parents, whose young families are vital to the long-term growth of the destination,"

Second - Based on research and analysis of visitor trends and consumer perceptions, WADMC has created a new brand framework around *Williamsburg's Three Freedoms*:

Freedom to Have Fun

Freedom to Be Curious

Freedom to Relax

"These three themes are captured in the positioning statement shown in the handout that I've just distributed to each of you," Corrina asserts as she shuffles the papers. (See Exhibit 23). "The destination's new advertising campaign must be centered on promoting these three themes," she adds.

Find your freedom in Williamsburg

Ready for a vacation that gives you the freedom to have fun, the freedom to satisfy your curiosity and the freedom to relax?

Then come to Williamsburg where you'll find more vacation freedom than any destination in America.

Ready for some excitement? Then feel free to start your vacation with a trip to the world's most beautiful theme park. Next find your thrill at one of our two top-10 water parks. Challenge yourself at one of our championship golf courses or visit any of our many other adrenaline-pumping attractions.

Want the freedom to satisfy your curiosity? History repeats itself daily in our world-class living history museums. Still not satisfied? Then a trip to America's second-oldest college would be a stroke of genius.

Want the freedom to relax? You've come to the right place. You can get back to nature exploring our thousands of acres of beautiful woodlands and wetlands, then enjoy an amazing array of culinary choices, including one of the top wineries in the country. Prefer a soothing hot stone massage? Your table awaits at one of our luxury spas.

So when you're ready to indulge your mind, body and spirit,

We invite you to come find your freedom in Williamsburg.

Exhibit 23: Williamsburg Tourism Positioning Statement

Third - WADMC has traditionally utilized a variety of paid and earned media opportunities to drive overnight visitation to the region. Past media has included television, radio, magazine, digital, and paid search. The advertising is to be concentrated on the domestic leisure traveler, located a sufficient distance so as to require an overnight stay of at least one night.

Fourth – Our strategic challenge is to create a compelling appeal for Millennial travelers to visit the Williamsburg area, overcoming perceptions that the destination is boring, not repeatable and focused solely on history.

Fifth – Our geographical target markets are the Northeast and Mid-Atlantic region, notably the New York, Philadelphia, Baltimore, Washington DC and Raleigh-Durham DMAs.

Sixth – WADMC has allocated a budget of $1,500,000 for this new campaign targeting Millennial family travelers.

Seventh – While this campaign is aimed at changing perceptions and the brand image of the Williamsburg destination among Millennial travelers, return on advertising investment (ROAI) calculations must be based on conversion metrics. Each consumer action has a corresponding value that must be used when calculating the return. (See Exhibit 24.)

Action	Value
Purchase of destination vacation package, including lodging and attraction tickets, via VisitWilliamsburg.com. *(Based on weighted average selling price, 3-night stay and party size of 4.)*	**$800**
Purchase of attraction combo tickets for two or more attractions, via VisitWilliamsburg.com. *(Based on weighted average selling price, per person.)*	**$105**
Registration for destination email communication at VisitWilliamsburg.com. *(Based on calculated average value of email prospects who convert to a sale.)*	**$25**
Social media connection ("like", "follow", etc.) on official Visit Williamsburg pages on Facebook, Twitter, You Tube and Instagram. *(Based on calculated average value of social followers who convert to a sale.)*	**$10**
Download a digital copy of the destination Visitor Guide (or) request a hard copy.	**$20**

Exhibit 24: Conversion Metrics

CAMPAIGN COMPONENTS & STRATEGIC QUESTIONS

Corrina requested, "Now please turn to pages 5-9 of your information packet where you will see the key strategic decision areas that we'll need to determine when developing the new marketing campaign. For each component I've listed several questions that we'll need to address." As the staff members turned to pages 5-9, they began to peruse the following bullet point list.

A. **Customer strategies** – Based on the target market (Millennial family travelers) and the background research, address the following questions:
   A. What consumer segments should be targeted?
   B. Are there any differences in the benefits that each market segment desires?
   C. Which Millennial segments offer the greatest market potential?

B. **List strategies** – List research must be conducted and appropriate lists must be recommended.
   A. Which customer lists should be used to most effectively target Millennial family travelers?
   B. What list selects should be used for each list?

C. **Offer strategies** - Based on the target market (Millennial family travelers) and the background research, address the following questions:
   A. What specific offer(s) are most appropriate for the target market in general?
   B. Are any unique offers needed for specific sub-segments of the target market?
   C. What incentives should be promoted to entice Millennials to like, follow and visit Williamsburg on social media?

D. **Creative strategies** – The entire campaign must be centered on a consistent branded theme or "big idea" which must incorporate *Williamsburg's Three Freedoms.* A couple of the creative executions that have been used in the past for *Visit Williamsburg* are shown in Exhibits 25-26. The newer creative executions that have already been created with the new "Freedom" positioning focus are shown in Exhibits 27-31.

Exhibit 25: Visit Williamsburg Space Advertisement - A

Exhibit 26: Visit Williamsburg Space advertisement – B

Exhibit 27: Outbound Email – Summer Freedom

Exhibit 27: Print Ad – Freedom to Set Your Own Course

Exhibit 29: Banner advertisement – Relax

Exhibit 30: Banner advertisement – Curiosity

Exhibit 31: Banner advertisement – Fun

Next Page: Exhibit 32: Exhibit 31: Visuals from Williamsburg Promotions

1. Given all of the secondary research on Millennials that was detailed in this case, what additional information would you desire in order to create a compelling marketing campaign to connect and engage with this target market?

2. Given all of the survey research findings on Williamsburg as a tourist destination that were presented in this case, what additional survey and/or other primary data collection research would you desire in order to be able to confidently promote Williamsburg to the Millennial family traveler market?

3. If you were one of Corrina's staff members and you were tasked with analyzing all of the primary and secondary research findings and developing strategic recommendations for the new marketing campaign targeting Millennials, how would you approach this challenge?

4. Using the conversion metrics provided in Exhibit 24, what response rates would you need on your marketing campaign to break even on the allocation of the $1.5 million campaign budget?

5. Address the strategic questions provided for each of the marketing campaign components as if you were a member of Corrina's staff and this was your task to complete by the stated deadline.

REFERENCES

AFE - Alliance for Family Entertainment. (2014). "Millennials: A deep dive: Programming and habits & practices studies." Association of National Advertisers. http://www.ana.net/miccontent/show/id/rr-afe-media-habits-practices-millennial

ANA – Association of National Advertisers. (2014). "Capturing Millennials' attention." *ANA Spotlight Magazine*. Feb. 1. http://www.ana.net/miccontent/show/id/sl-2014-feb-capturing-millennials

Boston Consulting Group (2012). "The millennial consumer: Debunking stereotypes." Apr. 16.

https://www.bcgperspectives.com/content/articles/consumer_insight_marketing_millennial_c
onsumer/

Cone, Inc. (2006). "Millennial cause study: Pro-social and empowered to change the world."
http://www.greenbook.org/Content/AMP/Cause_AMPlified.pdf

eMarketer. (2014) "Adult Millennials as consumers: Sifting through the contradictions in
their shopping behavior." http://www.slideshare.net/hoovazqtank/e-marketer-
millennialsroundup

eMarketer. (2014). "Sizing up the selfie generation." Feb. 11.
http://www.emarketer.com/Article/Teens-Really-Unfriending-Facebook/1010598

eMarketer. (2015). Millennials and their smartphones: How many have them and what do
they do with them. http://www.emarketer.com/newsroom/index.php/category/press-releases/

Faw, L. (2014) "Getting Millennials to buy CPGs: Bring on the BOGOs." Association of
National Advertisers. Nov. 15. http://www.ana.net/miccontent/show/id/kp-mediapost-
getting-millennials-to-buy-cpgs-bring-on-the-bogos

Feldman, J. & Berberich, M. (2014). "ANA insight brief: Millennial marketing." Association
of National Advertisers. http://www.ana.net/mkc

Friedman, W. (2014). "Millennial TV viewing differs via ethnicity, gender." Association of
National Advertisers. Dec. 11. http://www.ana.net/miccontent/show/id/kp-mediapost-
millennial-tv-viewing-differs-via-ethnicity-gender

Fromm, J. & Lindell, C. (2012). "American Millennials: Deciphering the enigma
generation." Association of National Advertisers. http://www.ana.net/insightbriefs

Harris Interactive. (2014). "The Harris Poll" press release, July 2.
http://www.harrisinteractive.com/NewsRoom/HarrisPolls/tabid/447/ctl/ReadCustom%20Def
ault/mid/1508/ArticleId/1460/Default.aspx

IPG Media Lab. (2015). "Millennial report: Video viewing discoveries." YuMe.
http://www.YuMe.com/millennials

Kesterson, K. (2013). The Relationships Between 'push' and 'pull' Factors of Millennial
Generation Tourists to Heritage Tourism Destinations: Antebellum and Civil War Sites in the

State of Arkansas (Order No. 1549257). Available from ProQuest Dissertations & Theses Global. (1490739276). Retrieved from http://0-

Magid. (2015). "Navigating the on-demand world of millennial shoppers." Frank N. Magid Associates, Inc. Jan. 29. http://www.ana.net/miccontent/show/id/er-moc-jan15w-magid

Meagher, M. (2014). "Do Millennials exist?" *Internationalist Magazine,* May 7. http://www.redpeakyouth.com/millennials-exist/

Millennial Central. (2014). "Intrepid millennial explorers: Changing the face of modern consumerism." June. http://www.millennialcentral.com/#!research/cf87

Millennial Travelers Loom Large, Take Charge. (2014). *Travel Agent*, 344(8), 6.

Mintel. (2014). "Marketing to kids and tweens - US" May. http://store.mintel.com/marketing-to-kids-and-tweens-us-may-2014

NewsCred. (2014) "The millennial mind: How content drives brand loyalty." http://newscred.com/theacademy/learn/millennial-mind

Oracle Financial Services. (2010). "Are banks ready for the next generation customer?" Sept. http://www.oracle.com/us/industries/financial-services/gen-y-survey-report-165297.pdf

PCAV Destinations. (2013) "The new destination visitor: Travel motivations in the post recession era." *Destinationology, 10*(2), May. http://content.yudu.com/A2rset/DestinationVisitor/resources/index.htm?referrerUrl=http%3A%2F%2Fwww.pgavdestinations.com%2Finsights%2Fresearch

Pew Research Center. (2010). "Millennials: Confident. Connected. Open to change." Feb. 24. http://www.pewsocialtrends.org/2010/02/24/millennials-confident-connected-open-to-change/

Pew Research Center. (2013). Breadwinner moms. May 29. http://www.pewsocialtrends.org/2013/05/29/breadwinner-moms/

Schnabel, D. (2013). "Why you can't ignore Millennials." *Forbes*. Sep. 4. http://www.forbes.com/sites/danschawbel/2013/09/04/why-you-cant-ignore-millennials/

U.S. Census Bureau. (2013). "Population by age and sex: 2012." https://www.census.gov/population/age/data/2012comp.html

XTRM Performance Network

By

Matthew Sauber – Eastern Michigan University

Chelsea Lockwood-White, ForeSee

Introduction

XTRM Performance Network (www.xtrm.com) is an online enterprise that helps companies manage sponsorships, reward athletes, and connect with channel partners and event organizers. XTRM provides online communities for companies and individuals to connect and communicate with athletes, enthusiasts, sponsors, and promoters of action sports such as Motocross, BMX, skating, surfing, biking, and snowboarding. To increase the growth of the XTRM Performance Network, the CEO and President, Richard Grogan-Crane[131], is looking into a number of strategies to increase awareness of XTRM among its multiple target audiences, i.e., sponsors, event promoters, and athletes. He wants to increase the number of members who sign up to use XTRM's cloud-based software and to increase revenue streams.

Sponsors are the primary audience XTRM wants to target, due to the high potential revenue associated with the group. A secondary target audience is the large group of sports organizers and promoters who arrange, publicize, and promote the various action sports events. Finally, XTRM would like to improve its awareness among actual extreme sports athletes and fans. However, the CEO maintains that athletes will become aware of XTRM as a side effect of sponsors and promoters being connected with the performance network.

---

[131] *Grogan-Crane, Richard.* (n.d.): http://www.linkedin.com/in/rgcrane

Company Background

Richard Grogan-Crane, an ex-VP of Strategic Business and Market Development at Oracle and an ex-Director of Marketing and Business Development at IBM/LOTUS, founded and launched XTRM.com (originally known as XBUX, before a lawsuit with Microsoft over the name's similarity to the XBOX gaming system), a venture-backed, virtual startup, in January 2004.[132] As an online performance management network, XTRM had connected athletes, sponsors, and promoters of action sports, providing platforms for marketing, event promotion, incentive processing management, sponsorship management, and data integration. Since its inception in 2004, XTRM highlights included:

- Managed over $20 Million in funds paid out in cash and promotions
- Over 750,000 transactions flow through its performance management system yearly
- Over 400 companies using its system to build communities, to sponsor, and to pay out
- Over 50,000 event registrations
- Over 200,000 people (athletes) sponsored via the XTRM platform
- More than 400 companies participating in the XTRM platform (paying, sponsoring, managing communities)
- Global 100/500 corporate customers including Adroll, Honda, Intel, BMW, Sony, Nvidia, and others.[133]

XTRM had become an innovator in changing the way companies, associated with extreme and action sporting events, rewarded their employees, channel partners, and performance athletes. Because of its knowledge of the industry, advanced technology, and process automation, XTRM was able to provide a significant ROI to all parties involved in the performance network – athletes, sponsors (including Global 100/500 companies), and promoters

---

[132]Kaplan, D. (2007, August 22). *Microsoft demands XBUX change its name.* Retrieved March 11, 2013, from VentureBeat: http://venturebeat.com/2007/08/22/microsoft-brings-back-the-bully-routine/

[133] XTRM Performance Network Company Profile, 2015, http://xtrm.freshdesk.com/support/solutions/articles/4000008068-customers-on-xtrm

Table 1.   XTRM Milestones

2004	Richard Grogan Crane founds XBUX
2005	XTRM raises enough venture capital to launch its internet platform V1.0
2006	XTRM launches its online cash and e-coupon contingency and performance payout services
2007	KTM North America joins XTRM, as the first big OEM customer XBUX changes its name to XTRM (Kaplan, D. 2007)
2008	Over $2M in performance payout, sponsorship, promotion XTRM hosts over 100 brands, including Global 500 company Michelin
2009	XTRM hosts to over 200 brands globally, hosting more than 300 events and series; BMW's Husqvarna was signed as first Global 100 customer
2010	XTRM reaches over $6M in payouts
2011	Honda becomes XTRM brand member American Motorcycle Association joins the XTRM Platform
2012	Fastrak program released
2013	XTRM Introduces advanced reporting and Paypal Mass Payments Integration
2014	Invidia, Marketsar, and HP become XTRM new members
2015	XTRM launches Global Virtual Visa as a new payment method

Performance Management Network

XTRM Performance Network allowed companies of any size to participate in event sponsorships, promotions, and payments for performance. XTRM's use of cloud computing allowed targeting sponsored athletes, employees, and various channel members with incentives, awards, and promotions such as SPIF (Sales Performance Incentive Fund), Rebate, MDF (Marketing Development Fund), Contingency and Gaming to increase sales and maximize brand awareness, visibility, and loyalty. The company used social integration to build brand value for sponsors, event organizers, and athletes. Utilizing channel sales and performance data, XTRM's performance network system electronically prepared payments of cash and Ecash rewards and sped up payment using multiple payment methods such as credit and Debit Cards or Paypal to reward recipients promptly and globally.

The following are brief descriptions of the various proprietary platforms that XTRM Performance Network used to communicate and meet the needs of all its target audiences: sponsors, promoters, athletes, and fans.

Automated Sponsorship

XTRM's automated sponsorship system was designed to streamline the sponsorship processes, saving companies time and money while allowing the flexibility to use the company's own branded coupons, awards, and products. The system was completely automated, saving corporate clients the hassle of sorting through piles of resumes and paperwork. It worked with a unique ranking system for sponsors and allowed the careful targeting of athletes in multi-tier sponsorship programs. It fully included dealer networks and their incentive programs. The XTRM's cloud-based computing system secured athlete data from the issuance of payouts to redemption. The automated system reduced the need for extra administration, reduced fraudulent claims, and lowered the cost of sponsorships for companies. In addition, the XTRM system allowed for easy tracking and comparison of data such as patterns, demographics, results, and athlete data.

Performance Payout System

XTRM's payout system was automated to save clients time, money, and hassle. Cash performance payout was a powerful method of providing awards and incentives to athletes and channel members while promoting clients' brands, products, and services. The payout system directed performance awards and marketing money to top performers who drove brand recognition and sales. The system was fast, payouts occurred within hours of events, and transaction data were subject to real-time authentication and available online 24x7. Payouts were in cash paid directly to a VISA-backed stored value, cash debit card, or Paypal Account, available in 193 countries worldwide. Payouts also were made to company accounts or branded eCash coupons, redeemable online over phone or on location. The system offered the convenience of web-based, on-demand access to information and eliminated the need for extra paperwork. Like the sponsorship system, all information was secured and authenticated. Comparable to performance measures, payout data could be shared with channel partner sales and marketing teams. They could track and manage performance rewards as follows:

- Personalized online company accounts to track channel sales people
- Review performance payments to channel sales personnel
- Access detailed information on payments, products sold and amounts
- Track statistics of best performers
- Export data for further analysis and dissemination into any other system

The system also reduced costs to sponsors and athletes through reduction of fraudulent claims and a lesser need for administration costs. Brand promise was supported among athletes because of the receipt of payouts soon after events. Finally, similar to the sponsorship system, the payout system gave access to data including spending patterns, demographics, redemptions, event data, and athlete data, allowing for easy tracking, comparison, and analysis.

Marketing and Event Management

XTRM offered marketing services to businesses of all sizes (small retailers, manufacturers, and Global 100/500 companies) to help promote brands, products, and services to athletes, fans, and consumers. Marketing services offered included eCoupon marketing, email marketing, and event/athlete sponsorship and management. Brief overviews of these services are detailed below.

eCoupon marketing. Companies could use XTRM Performance Network to direct electronic coupons to highly targeted customers. The system allowed companies to issue and track thousands of coupons using targeted audiences with self-identified interests who opted in to receive promotions. Based on the interests of the target audiences, XTRM offered coupons and included discounts on company products, services, and currencies, redeemable through manufacturers and dealers. Coupons each were identified with their own number, so they were traceable for effective tracking in marketing campaigns. XTRM's proficiency as a social network also came into play with the transferability of coupons; XTRM members could search and exchange coupons through social networks.[134]

Email marketing. Manufacturers could use email marketing within the XTRM Performance Network system to target audiences who opted in to receive promotions (XTRM Coupon Marketing). Manufacturers also could use their own email lists with selected demographics, sports interests and behavior. XTRM's email marketing campaign was customizable and could be scheduled for certain date / time slots with traceable results.

Event/Athlete Sponsorship. XTRM helped athletes and event organizers to find sponsors for their sports, using XTRM's automated sponsorship system. The system allowed automated search for matching sponsors by geography and industry sector and contact to

---

[134] Gwinner, K., & Bennett, G. (2008). The Impact of Brand Cohesiveness and Sport Identification on Brand Fit in a Sponsorship Context. *Journal of Sports Management* (22), 410-426.

potential sponsoring companies.   In addition, XTRM worked in event management by helping extreme sports events through publishing events details and sponsorship offerings and fees as well as linking offerings directly to an event's website and tracking responses and feedback. XTRM offered a complete end-to-end online event promotion and management system that included event registration, membership and results management, and promotional email and eCoupon campaigns for extreme sporting events. Early event registration was available online. It was integrated at multiple promoter membership levels to accommodate multi-class price discounts and waivers. Advanced registration also was integrated at event and scoring levels, and insured that there were no time conflicts for athletes. Finally, advanced registration provided accurate data for event planners.[135]

In addition to a strong email marketing system, the XTRM online community and social network allowed users, who had opted-in, to receive information, promotions, and awards from sponsors.   Sponsors and event marketers could segment the audience into groups using various promotional incentives (cash, merchandise, coupons). Because this information was available from XTRM Performance Network (users who had opted-in) segmentation was simple and cost effective. Since coupons were all traceable to users, data tracking was easily done, allowing for tracking of trends and comparison of data.

Community Building

Building and organizing communities was a major feature of XTRM Performance Network. Member communities presented manufacturers and corporate sponsors with unique opportunities to market their brands to selected target audiences who shared common values, interests, lifestyles, purchasing patterns, and perspectives in action sports.

Community members used www.xtrm.com to register for events, receive awards, and exchange information with sponsors, promoters, athletes, sports fans, and others.

---

[135] http://xtrm.freshdesk.com/support/solutions/articles/108460-how-to-setup-online-event-registration

Manufacturers used the XTRM Network's features to keep dealers focused on products, promotional events, and messages. Athletes and their fans also used the community to connect with dealers, suppliers, and retailers to redeem coupons and awards.

Security and safety of information left behind by community members were very important to XTRM Performance Network. The company provided a highly secure and customizable database to house member-generated and transactional data. Email addresses were never displayed or shared with individuals, sponsors, or event prompters. They were never sold to outside parties. Individual members could also opt-in to access promotional events and services. Likewise, they could opt-out of receiving future promotional communications.[136]

Live Timing and Scoring. XTRM offered free, pc-based live event timing and scoring software that promoters, athletes, and fans could use. The software (Live) was easily downloadable from the XTRM website and featured multi-round, multi-class advance event setup for high-speed scoring with audio and video broadcasting capabilities and complete integration with transponders such as AMB, Smart-Tag, and Alien.[137] XTRM also offered real-time data solution software (XTRM Sync) that synchronized online and offline registration. The software also fully integrated with XTRM's online membership, sponsors' contingency/payout systems, and various social networking sites such as Facebook and Twitter.

Results Ratification. The XTRM Fastrak™ software used XTRM Advance Registration data to automatically publish results, allowing sponsors to pay out awards to athletes in a timely fashion.

Software Automation. The XTRM software automation simplified multi-tier distribution channel CRM workflows and processes. It aggregated and integrated data from disparate

---

[136] http://xtrm.freshdesk.com/support/solutions/articles/128204-privacy-policy

[137] http://xtrm.freshdesk.com/support/solutions/articles/130510-xtrm-live-

sources to enhance visibility, streamline operations, optimize collaboration among partners, and ensure compliance. It used the SaaS (Software-as-a-Service) model to deliver XTRM's software solution to seamlessly integrate with client's existing enterprise and sales-force management systems. The XTRM platform integrated with various PRM, ERP, and CRM source data systems from vendors such as Oracle, SAP, SalesForce, Xactly, CallidusClound and others.[138]

Industry Overview

Brian Howard described extreme sports as a "high-risk/high-reward trick-based sporting genre" consisting of events such as "...skateboarding, in-line skating, BMX, motocross, snowboarding and surfing, as well as activities such as rock climbing, paintball, and kayaking...".[139] The genre was popularized in the 1990s as X-Games, sponsored by ESPN.[140]

According to Mintel, 118 million people aged 6 and older participated in at least one type of action and extreme sports in 2009 in the U.S. An estimated global participation in action sports by 150 million people was reported in 2004.[141] Retail sales of equipment and accessories for action sports rose 8.8% in 2010, reaching the total sales of $2.4 billion, according to SnowSports Industries America RetailTRAK by the Leisure Trends Group.[142]

---

[138] http://xtrm.freshdesk.com/support/solutions/articles/135150-prm-erp-crm-data-integration

[139] Howard, B. (2003, Oct). Extreme Sports. *Target Marketing, 26* (10), pp. 166-168.

[140] *Extreme Games, Commercialism Taken Too Far?* (1996, June). Retrieved March 11, 2013, from Performance Research: http://www.performanceresearch.com/espn-xgames-sponsorship.htm

[141] Solomon, B. (2008, Jan). Attracting the Next Generation. *Dealerscope, 50* (1), pp. 40-42.

[142] Mintel (2011). Action and Extreme Sports – US – March 2011. Retrieved from the Mintel Reports database

With extreme sports stars like Bam Margera having MTV shows (Viva La Bam), the once-fringe activities done by misfits gained major ground and become mainstream.[8,11] The emergence of mainstream action sports events like the ESPN X-Games or the Mountain Dew Action Sports Tour (Dew Tour) and their rapid growth over the past two decades attracted Millennial Generation (Generation Y) and impacted their lifestyle and choices of fashion, music, TV programs and movies, and branded products and services. With the 2013 announced expansion of the X-Games into Asia, Europe and South America, action sports were poised to continue in popularity. The Growing acceptance of extreme sports also was acknowledged by the fact that the International Olympic Committee (IOC) had announced the adoption of extreme sports like snowboarding and BMX in the winter and summer games.[143]

The sponsorship of these sporting events had been in existence since the first X-Games in the 1990s, and it was growing along with the industry as a whole. Red Bull, Mountain Dew and other energy drinks had grown in popularity with their sponsorship of extreme sports activities.[144,145] Red Bull had even gone so far as to sponsor the ultimate in extreme; Felix Baumgartner's skydive from 23 Miles above the earth, breaking the sound barrier wearing only his space suit.[146]

Competitive Analysis

XTRM's competition came from sports-related fields of sponsorship, media, event management, licensing, and talent representation. The list was populated by names such as IEG, ESPN, IMG, Alli Sports, Dew Tour, Sky Sports, and World of Adventure Sports. IEG

---

[143] Huffington Post (2012). The Extreme Future of Olympic Sports: http://www.huffingtonpost.com/alex-layman/olympics-extreme-sports_b_1519109.html
[144] Bennett, G., Ferreira, M., Lee, J., & Polite, F. (2009). The Role of Involvement in Sports and Sport Spectatorship in Sponsor's Brand Use: The Case of Mountain Dew and Action Sports Sponsorship. *Sport Marketing Quarterly* (18), 14-24.

[145] Helm, B. (2005, January 4). Energy Drinks Build Their Buzz. *Bloomberg BusinessWeek*.

[146] Knapp, A. (2012, October 16). The Technology Behind Red Bull's Space Jump. *Forbes*.

LLC was the global leader in sponsorship consultancy that provided analytics, measurement, research, and publications. With more than 30 years of experience, IEG's expertise extended beyond sponsorship to partnerships in branded entertainment, strategic alliances, promotional partnerships, and cobranding. It provided expert insights, evaluation, and guidance to top brands, organizations, and properties throughout the worlds of sports, arts, entertainment, associations, and causes to develop strategies, create opportunities, and maximize results.

ESPN X-Games was perhaps XTRM's closest competitor. ESPN broadcast extreme sports games and athletes in the summer and winter X-Games. It invited and aligned brands with athletes for highest marketing impact. Sponsorship opportunities included logo placement on athletes' helmet and equipment; use of athletes' image & likeness on brand / company websites, promotional materials, and television commercials; world-wide coverage on ESPN network; and event pictures and video clips, distributed through world-wide media outlets

Another of XTRM's major competitors was IMG Worldwide -- the world's largest sports talent and marketing agency, operating in over 30 countries. Through its high-impact action sports properties, IMG helped brands to reach the elusive youth market. It created meaningful brand interactions through athlete sponsorship, licensing, event management, media distribution, and talent representation.

Other competitors to XTRM in the sponsorship of action sports included sponsors of individual athletes, such as Nike and Degree antiperspirant by Unilever.[147] Mixed Martial Arts such as the Ultimate Fighting Competition was a formidable competitor for both spectatorship and sponsors, similar to the energy drink NOS.

---

[147] Smith, C. (2012, May 2). Extreme Sports Are Conquering A New Frontier: Your Living Room. *Forbes.*

Target Markets

XTRM Performance Network had different target markets for the different types of customers it attracted. XTRM was primarily a Business-to-Business (B2B) enterprise that marketed its services to corporate sponsors, promoters, and organizers of action sports. XTRM, however, acted as a traditional consumer marketing (B2C) outfit in order to attract and persuade extreme sports athletes and fans to sign up and participate. The following describes the three target audiences that XTRM tries to attract and how these audiences are related to one another.

Figure 1: XTRM's Target Markets

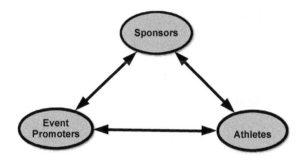

Sponsors

Brand sponsors were the primary audience that XTRM tried to attract. Of course, not every brand became a potential sponsor of action sports events. It was important to understand why a corporation might want to sponsor an extreme sports event, and what brands were likely to be successful as XTRM sponsors. A brand would want to sponsor an action sports event as a means to attract the core demographic audience making up the action sports top market, namely the Millennials.[148] Solomon suggested that sponsorship of risk-taking events was a way to reach the millennial consumers, based on the generation's affinity for TV

---

[148] Holman, K. (2008, September 1). Sk8er Buy: Investors, in Touch with Generation Y, May Look More Closely at the Extreme Sports Segment. *Mergers & Acquisitions: The Dealmaker's Journal* .

programs that display risk-taking in sports such as skateboarding, and shows like The Deadliest Catch.[11] Although the target audience for action sports had a male majority (70%), the number of millennial females following the field was increasing.[9]

Simply sponsoring popular extreme and action sporting events did not automatically lead to a favorable consumer response to a brand. An extensive review of psychological and communication theories by Cornwell et al.[149] suggests that brand sponsorship is most effective when there is a logical match between the sponsoring brand and the sporting event that the target audience can relate to.[150] Similarly, Gwinner and Bennett[3] found that higher levels of brand cohesiveness and brand identification with a sport result in a higher perceived fit between the sporting event and the sponsoring brand, a better overall perception of the sponsoring company, more positive attitude toward the brand, and higher purchase intention. Bennett et al.[13] emphasize the importance of actual spectatorship of the brand at sponsored events. To increase exposure and spectatorship, they recommend heavy advertising during the event, product placement within video games and television programs, contests, promotions, and strategically placed signage at the sponsored events.

Event Promoters

XTRM's marketing to event promoters (organizers) should go hand-in-hand with its strategy to attract sponsors since the company's goal was to pair sponsors with action sporting events and organizers. XTRM helped promoters to connect with the right sponsoring brands by searching and matching sponsors, large and small, per geographical area and industry sector using XTRM's automated matching platform. Event promoters would be attracted to XTRM services not only for booking and finding sponsors, but also for other automated services such as publishing event details, sponsorship offerings and fees, and linking offerings to event websites.

---

[149] Cornwell, T. B., Weeks, C. S., & Roy, D. P. (2005). Sponsorship-linked marketing: Opening the blackbox. Journal of Advertising, 34, 21-42
[150] Weeks, C.S., Cornwell, T.B., Drennan, J.C. (2008). Leveraging sponsorships on the internet: Activation, congruence, and articulation. Psychology and Marketing, 25, 637-54.

XTRM's online event registration helped promoters to streamline and automate the process of registering event participants with advanced features of multiclass / group fees, discounts, refunds, and social network integration and promotion. The process completely eliminated time-consuming and error-prone manual registration.

XTRM also could attract event organizers / promoters through its payout (contingency) programs where an event's athletes and attendees were rewarded by receiving electronic coupons and eCash from sponsoring brands. Event organizers / promoters could improve attendance by marketing payout programs to potential participants and publicizing attendees' winnings on social networks.

Athletes

XTRM's cloud-based platform guaranteed fast payouts to athletes, fans, and event attendees where they could get paid in cash using the XTRM Visa debit card or Paypal, earn discounts from top brands, receive e-coupons from favorite brands, and exchange awards with, or request and grab awards from, other XTRM members. By entering www.xtrm.com and simply logging on to the Participant Home Page, action and extreme sports athletes and fans could access XTRM's fully automated system, be greeted by appropriate information and exchange opportunities and become engaged and persuaded. As shown in Figure 2, the XTRM website had the ability to attract and retain action sports athletes and fans and build relationships.[151] It was a destination site with an assortment of content and jumping-off points, intended to serve as a portal for action and extreme sports enthusiasts. The website promoted participant interactivity and individuality. It was designed to facilitate relationships among action and extreme sports sponsors, promoters, athletes, and fans. The site was informational, communal and transactional. It allowed customization per user

[151] XTRM Performance Network Live Overview. (n.d.). Retrieved March 11, 2015, from XTRM Performance Network Corporate Website: http://www.xtrm.com/web/XTRMExternal/Common/Documents/XTRM%20Live%20Overview.pdf

objectives and status. And it encouraged fan-athlete-promoter-sponsor communications to build favorable brand relationships.

Figure 2. XTRM Website

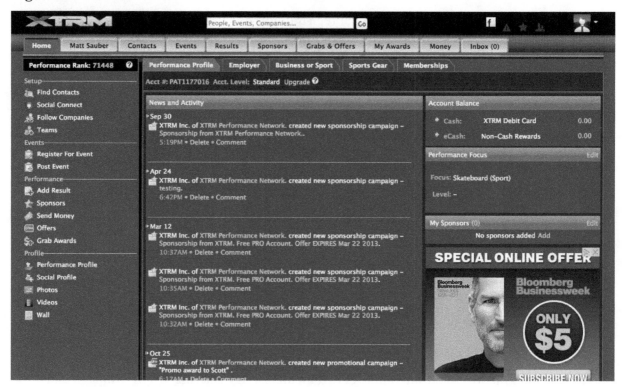

Opportunities

The action sports industry had been a growing segment of sports among the Millennial Generation in the past decade, attracting corporate sponsors and brand endorsements. It provided great expansion opportunities for performance management companies such as XTRM. Much of the growth was attributed to the Millennials, their purchasing power, and lifestyle spending.

Market Potential

There were about 80 million Millennials (born in 1980-1999) in the United States. They viewed their sports radically differently than other generations. They multitasked and consumed sports on multiple platforms. The Millennials' purchasing power estimates were $200 billion of direct purchasing and $500 billion of indirect spending attributed to the spending of their baby boomer and Gen X parents, whom they influenced.[152]

In the bigger picture of sponsorship marketing, spending was projected to grow by 4%, to $21.4 billion, in North America for 2015. Sports commanded 70% share of this market according to the IEG's 2014 annual forecasts (Figure 3). Worldwide, sponsorship spending was expected to grow to $57.5 billion in 2015, an increase of 4.1% over 2014 spending (Figure 4). Excluding the North American market, the spending for the rest of the world was expected to reach $36.1 billion in 2015 per IEG's estimates.[153]

---

[152] Barkley, SMG, Boston Consulting Group (September 2011) American Millennials: Deciphering the Enigma Generation. http://blog-barkleyus-com.s3.amazonaws.com/ wp-content/uploads/2011/09/BarkleyMillennial-ResearchExecSummary.pdf

[153] IEG Sponsorship Report (January 7, 2015). Where the Dollars Are Going and the Trend for 2015. http://www.sponsorship.com/IEG/files/4e/4e525456-b2b1-4049-bd51-03d9c35ac507.pdf.

Figure 3. 2015 Shares of North American Sponsorship Market (projected)

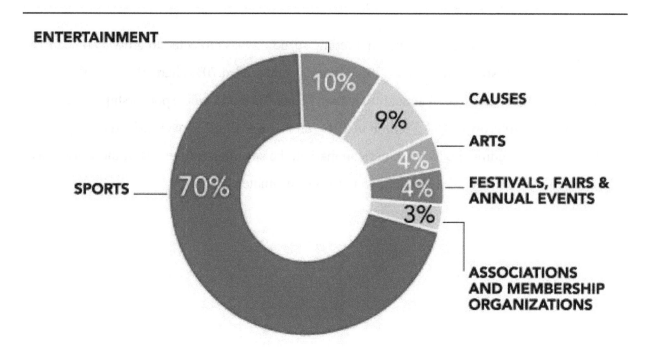

ENTERTAINMENT
10%
CAUSES
9%
ARTS
4%
FESTIVALS, FAIRS & ANNUAL EVENTS
4%
SPORTS 70%
3%
ASSOCIATIONS AND MEMBERSHIP ORGANIZATIONS

Figure 4. Global Sponsorship Spending (2011-2015)

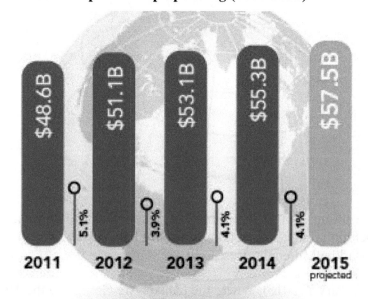

$48.6B $51.1B $53.1B $55.3B $57.5B

5.1%   3.9%   4.1%   4.1%

2011   2012   2013   2014   2015 projected

Digital Media Usage and Engagement

Because of their affinity for digital technology, Millennials could be an attractive target audience to XTRM. They were heavy users of mobile devices; 2.5 times more likely to be early adopters of technology; and more likely to use digital communication to convey thoughts and contribute content.[154] Millennials also were heavy users of social media. The majority (over 75%) had a profile on social media networks where they spent hours daily.[155]

Media engagement was generally higher among Millennials. They became even more engaged when they chose content on digital media.[156] Millennials sought buying information and recommendations from friends and peers using online sources including social media. They became excited about buying choices when approved by their peers.[157]

The majority of Millennials used social media to connect with brands and as such they were the darlings of action sports sponsors.[19] Millennials' ability to carry 24/7 dialogues with brands and brand users and followers was sought-after by sponsors. Because they could network and voice their opinions, marketers valued Millennials' word of mouth. More importantly, they were willing to share their brand choices online, making them a top identifier.[21]

---

[154] comScore (January 2012) Next Generation Strategies for Advertising to Millennials. http://www.comscore.com/Press_Events/Press_Releases/2012/1/comScore_Releases_ Report_Next_Generation_Strategies_for_Advertising_to_Millennials

[155] Ott, Adrian (November 2010) How Social Media Has Changed the Workplace (Study), Fast Company. http://www.fastcompany.com/1701850/how-social-media-has-changedthe-workplace-study

[156] Galloway, Scott (December 2010) Gen Y Affluent Media Survey, L2 Thank Tank. http://www.l2thinktank.com/genyafflents/GenYAfflents.pdf

[157] Innerscope Research, Time Inc. (April 2012) A Biometric Day in the Life. http://www.timeinc.com/pressroom/detail.php?id=releases/time_inc_study_digital_natives.p hp

Challenges

Marketing to Millennials

XTRM's opportunities notwithstanding, the firm faced several external and internal challenges. Targeting and engaging Millennials was a multi-faceted marketing endeavor that went beyond digitally appealing to these individuals. Millennials' needs for connecting personally and emotionally to others and sharing and following experiences influenced their lifestyle that combined music, art, fashion, food, movies, video games, youth gatherings, and role models as well as sports. The emergence of mainstream action sports events like the ESPN X-Games or the Mountain Dew Action Sports Tour, and their rapid growth over the past two decades, was a direct by-product of a lifestyle that had attracted millions of participants and fans to action sports. The subculture combined music, art, fashion, and movies into a lifestyle, receptive to interactive branding (on line as well as on site), which could be acknowledged and actively used when marketing to Millennials. XTRM's sports-dominated only approach to the millennial audience fell short of fully embracing and engaging these individuals and their lifestyle.

Declining Participation in Action Sports

Although action sports primarily remained the domain of 12- to-17 year olds and were more popular than NASCAR, the NHL, and Major League Soccer across every demographic of sports fans, its popularity seemed to be leveling off. Research showed that the number of participants in the 12-17 age group considering themselves avid fans of action sports had declined in the past decade. Average ratings for the X Games and Dew Tour also had decreased slightly in recent years according to Sports Business Journal.[158] The Sporting Goods Manufacturers Association reported a 31 percent decline in skateboarding and a 26 percent decline in BMX participation in the first decade of the 21st century.[25]

---

[158] Mickle, Tripp (January 23, 2012), "Balancing Act", SportsBusiness Journal. http://www.sportsbusinessdaily.com/Journal/Issues/2012/01/23/In-Depth/Main.aspx

Entrenched Competition

Competition was another challenge before XTRM. Sponsorship/event marketing was a multiplatform, omni-channel enterprise that extended beyond digital channels and embraced the entire marketing ecosystem, according to eMarketer: "Online Sponsorship: Defining, Tracking and Measuring an Amorphous Channel."[159] Major competitors such as IEG LLC and IMG Worldwide, and ESPN, offered corporate sponsors and brands multiplatform channels in sports, fashion, music, arts, and entertainment towards customized marketing solutions. These competitors enjoyed global visibility with top brands and events worldwide. They offered brand engagement to resonate with Millennials' cultural and social identity.

XTRM's Limited Marketing

Faced with *three* distinct audiences: corporate sponsors, event organizers, and athletes, XTRM was challenged to target each segment effectively given its limited marketing resources. Compared to competition, XTRM was a small niche-player primarily focusing on action sports, process automation, and advanced cloud-based technology to connect with sponsors, organizers, athletes, and fans. The company's strength was its online processing capabilities in incentive management, performance payout, virtual tracking of electronic coupons, and connectivity / interactions of brands and fans through social media. XTRM's process automation extended to event management including event promotion, registration, membership, performance measurement (timing and scoring), and posting.

As a small company, XTRM could afford limited marketing to get its name out. It enjoys very little brand awareness and recognition beyond its online domain. The company's digital-oriented strategy was appealing to Millennials and action sports enthusiasts. It had enhanced limited fan engagement with online features such as performance payout and registration. XTRM's strategy however lacked pervasiveness to determine and monitor how brands

---

[159] Sponsorship May Be Hard to Define, but Marketers Still Invest (July 16, 2013). http://www.emarketer.com/Article/Sponsorship-May-Hard-Define-Marketers-Still-Invest/1010046#sthash.JoM2Ikhi.dpuf

approached and engaged action sports fans and followers beyond the Internet. Brand online visibility alone might not be enough to elicit the same level of awareness as on-site (on-ground) exposure. Sports fans who were exposed to sponsors' marketing communications, both online and onsite, displayed higher recalls than those who were exposed only to one type or the other.[160]

Perhaps, the biggest challenge facing XTRM was determining how to engage Millennials in a way that was relevant to their demographic and lifestyle. Millennials' brand consciousness was fragmented; they were not as receptive to traditional marketing communications as their predecessors. To attract sponsors and event organizers, XTRM needed to provide a seamless experience in places where Millennials gathered, frequented, and sought value regardless of channel or device. Millennials could engage with brands in a physical store or a sporting event; an art gallery or a music festival; on the company website or mobile apps; and through cable TV, catalogs, or social media. Using multi-platform, omni-channel communications, XTRM should recognize and acknowledge Millennials' lifestyle in action sports, music, art, and fashion -- receptive to interactive branding.

The CEO Seeks Your Marketing Advice

To grow and be profitable, the CEO, Richard Grogan-Crane, believes that XTRM Performance Network needs effective marketing strategies to sign up more athletes and fans and add more corporate sponsors and event promoters. He has hired you as a consultant and wants your advice to achieve the following marketing objectives:

1. Increase brand awareness and develop XTRM's customer base among its three key target audiences, i.e., corporate sponsors, event organizers / promoters, and athletes and fans of action sports. Richard believes that The XTRM's brand awareness resides

---

[160] Humphrey, W. (2012). A comparison Study of Sponsorship Effectiveness Between On-Site and Web-Based Sponsorship Activities. Retrieved August 14th, 2013 from http://www.sportmarketingassociation.com

predominately with action sports athletes and fans. This brand awareness is realized from performance payouts and online registrations for events.

2. Evoke change in adoption of technology in the action sports industry. Richard maintains that the members of the industry, particularly event promoters, are very slow in adopting cloud-based process automation and communication technologies. Their resistance tends to retard the realization of benefits from fully integrated platforms for managing events, sponsorship, and interactive communications. He would like to see XTRM to be a change agent to promote new technologies across the action sports industry.

3. Increase customer base and the number of members who sign-up to use XTRM's cloud-based services and ultimately result in an increase in revenue streams.

Use a Systematic Approach to Analyze the Case

Start with SWOT analysis. Assess XTRM Performance Network's Strengths, Weaknesses, Opportunities, and Threats. Use information provided in the case and search sources of information relevant to action sports, sponsorship, and athletes and fans. Monitor the environments surrounding XTRM, its industry, and its various markets.

Do market opportunity analysis. Analyze and highlight opportunities that are favorable to XTRM's market development and expansion. Can XTRM convincingly articulate and offer value to its defined target markets? Can XTRM locate, reach, and communicate with its target markets effectively and efficiently? Does the company possess or have access to capabilities and resources to deliver unique customer value to its target markets? Can XTRM deliver customer value and benefits better than its competitors, actual or potential? Can XTRM deliver customer value and benefits profitably to meet or exceed its required return on investment?

Analyze threats and challenges. Use the information provided in the case and searchable sources to identify and assess current and foreseeable threats and / or challenges that XTRM is likely to face in pursuing its market opportunities. These are the challenges of the target markets and external environmental forces such as demographics, socioeconomics, and lifestyle trends with unfavorable potential on XTRM's future development and growth. There are also threats of industry competitors, present and potential, that XTRM has to assess. Competitive advantages of main industry rivals typically pose a challenge for new entrants in particular markets. These advantages include the ability to innovate, and become omnipresent at different industry, market, and channel levels. Entrenched competitors typically have a higher market share, pronounced market power, connection, and presence, not to mention a deep pocketbook and industry recognition as well as powerful competitive strategy.

Formulate marketing strategies. In response to the marketing objectives stated by the CEO, Richard Grogan-Crane, and the conclusion of the SWOT analysis, formulate actionable marketing strategies to achieve the CEO's requirements for growth and profitability:

➢ Increase XTRM's awareness among its target audiences, i.e., sponsors, promoters, and athletes and fans.

➢ Evoke the adoption of digital communication technology among the target audiences.

➢ Increase the number of members who sign-up to use XTRM's online network and to increase revenue streams.

You Brew: Crafting a Winning Marketing Strategy

By

Carol Scovotti, University of Wisconsin-Whitewater

Lisa D. Spiller, Christopher Newport University

He shoots! He scores! Jamie Benn of the Dallas Stars just scored his third goal for the game —a hat trick— and it was only the second period. Chad Abbott, Will Blanton and Brandon Cokey were thrilled as they reminisced about their own college hockey days while cheering for their local NHL team. Now "grown up" business professionals, the trio were partners in a startup craft beer business. While they enjoyed the game they also discussed a few of the new flavors of beer their competitors had recently introduced, including "Smashed Blueberry" and "Agave Nectar Ale" produced by Shipyard Brewing Co. and "Harvest Pumpkin Ale" made by Fullsteam Brewery.

When the game came ended, the trio visited one of their favorite local brewpubs where they continued their informal business conversation and socialized with the locals. If there was one thing these young entrepreneurs had learned about craft beer during their short business experience, it was the importance of "local" in everything a craft brewer does. Socialize with local people, understand local taste preferences, and support local nonprofit groups. When it came to the craft beer industry everything *local* was crucial.

From Class Project to Profitable Business

In early 2014, Abbott, Blanton and Cokey were 24 years old. Their friendship began when they met as freshmen at tryouts for their university hockey team in Colorado. Later they became fraternity brothers. Chad Abbott was from Cedar Rapids, Iowa. At age 10, he badgered his father to take him to a local brewpub after hearing about a beer named "Hanging Chad Ale." The beer name, which received national media coverage, was a spoof on the 2000 Presidential election controversy in Florida. Abbott recalled his father buying a growler so he could taste the beer when they returned home.

That growler shaped Abbott's destiny. He became fascinated with beer and the brewing process. He got to know the brew master, who ultimately became a private tutor after his father bought him a beer making kit. Abbott was too young go behind the scenes at the brewery so the brew master helped him craft beer in the basement of his parent's home. When he wasn't playing hockey, he was inventing beer formulas. His interest in brewing influenced his course of study: engineering major with a marketing minor. While in college, he worked at a nearby microbrewery as an assistant to the brew master.

Will Blanton was Colorado born and bred. A natural leader both on and off the ice, he was captain of his college hockey team and possessed a real knack for problem solving. Blanton studied business analytics and strategy in college.

Brandon Cokey grew up in Texas. He was a daredevil who thrived on taking risks. Cokey chose to go to school in Colorado so he could snowboard, play hockey, and drink great beer. He studied marketing.

In their senior year, Abbott, Blanton and Cokey took an Entrepreneurial Marketing course together. The term assignment required them to launch a business. Given Abbott's brewing experience, they formed "PuckPub", a craft brewery inspired by their hockey buddies, fraternity brothers and fans. They created a website where teammates, fans, and frat brothers could submit recipe ideas (known as formulas in the industry), then vote on the one that PuckPub would ultimately brew and sell. The trio intended to work with respondents to refine formulas each thought had the best chance for success. They labeled the formula options "A" for Abbott, "B" for Blanton, and "C" for Cokey.

The trio worked together on every aspect of the business, but each accepted primary responsibility for the areas that best suited his talents and experience. Abbott took responsibility for operations and brewing. Blanton handled business management and logistics. Cokey was the "front man" responsible for marketing and sales.

A project requirement was to integrate social media into the communications program. Cokey used Facebook and Twitter to promote the launch. Response to the prelaunch campaign went viral. Thousands of people beyond teammates, frat brothers and friends *liked* PuckPub's Facebook site. Hundreds more either "favorited" or retweeted the Twitter posts. By the time the business was actually launched, "friends" from across the country were sharing beer formulas. It was as if the floodgates had opened.

And then the unthinkable happened. The university shut down the site within 24 hours of its launch because of the "possibility of promoting underage drinking" and "concern over violating alcohol distribution laws." Despite PuckPub's immediate shut down, Abbott, Blanton and Cokey were not discouraged. They set up a website not affiliated with the university and re-launched the business.

However, within weeks they discovered their business model had four major flaws. First, initial buzz wasn't sustainable and the quality of responses was lacking. The website drew lots of lookers but ultimately few who submitted beer formulas. Of those who submitted a recipe, most were not feasible (e.g. bratwurst, pretzel, chocolate chip cookie, etc.) Something had to be done, as Abbott said, "...to eliminate the crazies."

Second, distribution across state lines was more complicated than anticipated. They knew they had to deal with the regulatory environment, but alcohol distribution laws were, as Blanton said, "Neanderthal." They couldn't sell to people who submitted formulas from out of state. Third, the local niche was ultimately too saturated to sustain the business model. With so many options available locally (Colorado is ranked third in number of microbreweries), crowdsourced formulas didn't garner sufficient interest among craft brew fans. They had to get out of their college mindset and start thinking beyond hockey fans and frat brothers if this business was to be successful. Finally, they realized more capital was needed if they were to make the venture more than a class project.

You Brew Company History

Cokey's uncle, Ross Stevens, was a wealthy Texas businessman who adored his nephew and followed the PuckPub situation. He offered the trio $20,000 of seed money to help start a new brewery business, but only if they established it where there wasn't so much competition.

Abbott and Cokey had already chosen to pursue their MBA degrees at a university in Dallas, so they decided to establish the business there. Uncle Ross was thrilled. However, Texas presented its challenges. By law, brewpubs are required to sell food and may not showcase their beer at festivals. Breweries may sell at festivals but not on premises. In 2013, just as Abbott and Cokey had finished their graduate degrees, the trio overcame these challenges by finding a brewing incubator where they could lease professional equipment within an adjoining restaurant. Through this arrangement, they could sell their small batch beers to restaurant customers, and also self-distribute in 22 oz. "bombers" and half-gallon "growlers" to locals who frequented the restaurant as well as their web-based niche in Texas.

When they moved to Texas, they renamed the business *You Brew* to separate themselves from the college hockey crowd. The name also highlighted the crowdsourcing aspect of the formulas, an advantage they thought would help them build community among those serious about craft brewing. Their college experience proved that there were people who liked the idea of influencing the specialty flavors of beer. Given that they were members of the millennial generation, they understood how important it was to give young customers an opportunity to express their opinions, insights and preferences.

Since its first batch in 2013, You Brew had sold most, and in some cases, all of its production. Unlike other craft breweries, You Brew has never made the same beer twice. This was unique in this highly competitive industry.

The Beer Industry

After several slow growth/no growth years following the 2008 recession, beer sales had recently started to foam up. The Brewers Association estimated 2013 U.S. beer sales at $100 billion, a 1.9 percent decrease from the previous year (www.brewersassociation.org). As shown in Exhibit 1, beer supplier gross revenue has increased each year for the past three years (www.discus.org).

Exhibit 1

Exhibit 1 - Beer Supplier Gross Revenue in U.S.		
Year	$ Amount (in billions)	% Percent change from previous year
2003	24.87	2.9
2004	25.62	3.2
2005	25.62	No change
2006	26.34	2.7
2007	27.59	4.6
2008	28.56	3.6
2009	28.82	1.1
2010	28.64	(-0.7)
2011	29.24	2.2
2012	30.32	3.7
2013	31.96	5.4
Source: *Restaurant, Food & Beverage Market Research Handbook 2014-2015, p. 428.*		

There are seven distinct product categories in the beer industry. Exhibit 2 indicates that craft beer is the fourth largest category based on size, and is the only one with double-digit annual growth. Flavored malt beverage is the only other segment with positive growth rates (Dowling, 2013). In 2012 craft beer sales represented 7.3 percent of all U.S. beer sales. In 2013 its share jumped to an estimated 17.2 percent. (www.brewersassociation.org).

Exhibit 2

Exhibit 2 – Beer Market by Category in U.S.		
Product Category	**Market Share Percentage %**	**% Percent change from previous year**
Light	51.7	(-0.2)
Premium & Super Premium	12.3	(-3.1)
Popular	7.7	(-1.2)
Craft	**7.3**	**14.6**
Ice	3.6	(-1.2)
Malt Liquor	2.3	(-3.0)
Flavored Malt Beverages	1.7	7.8
Source: *Restaurant, Food & Beverage Market Research Handbook 2014-2015, p. 429.*		

According to the Brewers Association, domestic beer accounts for 86.7 percent of U.S. beer consumption. There are more than 3,500 brands of beer produced by over 2,000 brewers and importers. In 2013 more than 2,500 breweries operated in the U.S., an increase from 2,196 breweries in 2012. As Exhibit 3 reveals, microbreweries represent the largest brewery type in the U.S. with 1,221. Brewpubs represent the second largest type of beer operation with 1,165 (www.brewersassociation.org).

Exhibit 3

Exhibit 3 – Type of Brewery Operation in U.S.	
Brewery Type	**Number**
Large breweries	24
Regional non-craft breweries	31
Regional craft breweries	97
Microbreweries	1,221
Brewpubs	1,165
Source: *Restaurant, Food & Beverage Market Research Handbook 2014-2015, p. 429.*	

The can is the most popular beer package, with one-way (no refill/disposal) bottles a close second (www.beerinstitute.org). Exhibit 4 presents the package mix of beer sold in the U.S.

Exhibit 4

Exhibit 4 – Type of Beer Package	
Package Type	**Market Share Percentage %**
Cans	48
One-way Bottles	42
Draught	9
Refills/Plastic/Other	1
Source: *Restaurant, Food & Beverage Market Research Handbook 2014-2015, p. 429.*	

The U.S. beer market landscape is changing. High-end products, which includes imported and craft beers, are gaining favor with consumers over premium domestic and sub-premium brands. The U.S. beer industry is extremely diverse and industry growth continues to come from craft and imported beers, flavored malt beverages, and cider.

The Craft Beer Industry

Craft beers are described as those made by small, independent breweries. They typically have a distinct flavor as well as a unique brand name and label. To be considered small, a brewery must have annual production of no more than six million barrels. Independent means that the brewery has no more than 25 percent ownership by an alcoholic beverage alcohol company that produces anything other than craft beers. The traditional aspect of the production assumes that the majority of the brewer's total beverage alcohol volume is in beers made from traditional brewing ingredients, such as water, starch, hops, and yeast (www.brewersassociation.org).

The craft beer industry is further defined by four distinct segments: brewpubs, microbreweries, regional craft breweries, and contract brewing companies. A brewpub is a combined restaurant and brewery that sells at least 25 percent of its beer production on site. In 2013, there were more than 1,200 brewpubs in the US. A microbrewery produces less than 15,000 barrels of beer a year with at least 75 percent of sales taking place off site. There were a total of 1,412 US. based microbreweries in 2013. A regional craft brewery is an independent, regional brewery that has 50 percent or more of its production devoted to malt beer. In 2013 there were 119 domestic breweries in this category. A contract brewing company is a business that hires another brewery to produce its product but handles its own marketing, sales, and distribution in-house (www.brewersassociation.org). In 2012, the craft brewing industry contributed $33.9 billion to the US. economy. This represents more than 360,000 jobs (www.brewersassociation.org).

The growth of small craft breweries in the U.S. began in 1979 when federal legislation repealed restrictions on home-brewing beer in small quantities. In 1979 there were only 42 breweries in the US. However, as of June 2013 there were 2,483, according to the Brewers Association. The Brewers Association claims that retail sales of craft beer in 2012 were $10.2 billion, with 13.24 million barrels sold. (www.brewersassociation.org). According to Beverage Marketing Corporation and *Beverage World,* the leading craft brewer in 2012 was Boston Beer Co., maker of Samuel Adams beer brand. Exhibit 5 lists the top 10 craft brewers in the U.S.

Exhibit 5

Exhibit 5 – Top Ten Craft Brewers in U.S.		
Brewery	**Location**	**Amount (000 in cases)**
Boston Beer Co.	Boston, MA	2,700
Sierra Nevada Brewing Co.	Chico, CA	970
New Belgium Brewing Co.	Fort Collins, CO	764
The Gambrinus Co.	San Antonio, TX	594
Deschutes Brewery	Bend, OR	252
Lagunitas Brewing Co.	Petalurna, CA	235
Bell's Brewery	Galesburg, MI	216
Matt Brewing Co.	Utica, NY	202
Harpoon Brewery	Boston, MA	192
Stone Brewing	Escondido, CA	177
Source: *Restaurant, Food & Beverage Market Research Handbook 2014-2015, p. 431-432.*		

One of the drivers of the craft beer craze is consumers' increasing preference for foods and beverages that are locally sourced. Restaurants also are embracing the craft beer movement by hosting tastings and staffing peer sommeliers to help diners select the right match for their meals. More consumers are ordering craft beer in restaurants than ever before. Exhibit 6 lists the top selling craft beer brands in bars and restaurants, ranked by market share.

Exhibit 6

Exhibit 6 – Top Selling Craft Beer Brands				
Brand	Dollar Sales (000)	% Change vs. prior year	Case Sales (000)	% Change vs. prior year
Samuel Adams	$329,422	12.2	10,453	11.4
Sierra Nevada	$190,116	11.0	5,799	10.4
New Belgium	$137,241	9.8	4,200	10.1
Shiner	$116,656	13.4	3,820	10.7
Lagunitas	$56,247	84.9	1,433	84.6
Deschutes	$53,422	13.4	1,727	13.7
Redhook	$40,981	9.0	1,434	10.6
Widmer	$39,498	(-5.2)	1,286	(-5.3)
Kona	$34,706	29.2	1,114	27.8
Stone	$34,467	39.5	641	39.4
Source: Information Resources Inc., Chicago; *Beverage Industry, 2014 (Report by Jessica Jacobsen) p. 24.*				

Craft beer brewing is not a recent phenomenon. It first gained popularity in the U.S. in the late 1800s as European immigrants who owned bars often brewed their own beers. These operations quickly ended when prohibition was enacted in 1920. After the repeal of prohibition, stringent distribution regulations made it difficult for independent brewers to produce beer that could compete in value with large corporate brewing producers. It was not until the 1970s that micro brewing began to gain popularity among brewers and consumers. In 1976, Jack McAuliffe opened New Albion Brewing in Sonoma, California. He is credited with being America's first craft brewer. McAuliffe formulated the first modern American pale ale, and also produced a porter, stout, and draft ale. He sold out quickly, but he was a better brewer than a businessman. He spent all of the brewery's cash on an expansion plan only to discover that no investor back then would finance a microbrewery. In 1982, New Albion filed for bankruptcy and McAuliffe quit the beer business. Many aspiring craft brewers learned from McAuliffe's mistakes, opting to keep operations small and local.

In the 1980s, craft brewing was considered a radical notion. Today the craft beer industry is the most crowded it has been since before prohibition. Many breweries are started by entrepreneurial home-brewers, just as McAuliffe did three decades ago. However, since then, there have been a growing number of consumers willing to pay more for beer with more taste and alcohol content. The market has evolved.

Craft beers feature traditional ingredients, such as malted barley and hops, as well as nontraditional ingredients, such as chocolate, raspberries, blueberries and pumpkin. Craft beer formulas also rely on natural flavors and colors. Many craft breweries capitalize on seasonal tastes, such as pumpkin in the fall, blueberry in the spring, citrus in the summer. Fullsteam Brewery, in Durham, North Carolina, is known for its offbeat flavors, including "First Frost" winter persimmon ale, "Paw Belgian-style Golden Ale" made with paw tree fruit, and "Fruitcake Beer," a bourbon barrel-aged old ale brewed with roasted local chestnuts and grilled figs.

With over 300 varieties, honey is an extremely versatile ingredient for craft beers. Different floral sources, including alfalfa, wildflower, buckwheat and tupelo, create distinct flavors in beer (Landi, 2014). The growth of innovative and sometimes wacky flavors of beer supports the concept that most craft brewers are creative entrepreneurs who will formulate any recipe to please customers. Some craft brewers also are diversifying their brands with non-beer products. Hard cider is especially popular.

Craft Beer Customers

It's a misnomer to think that economic influencers favor traditional, mass-marketed beer brands. Price appears to have minimal impact on the purchasing habits of the craft beer enthusiast. Younger consumers are driving the craft beer craze. Approximately 50 percent of the millennial generation above the age of 25 drinks craft beer. According to the Pew Research Center, the number of Americans in their 20s hit 77 million in 2013—about equal to the size of the massive baby boomers generation (Voight, 2013). However, it's not only the size of the craft beer market, but also the composition of the crowd that matters.

The surge in the number of microbreweries and demand for craft beer is due, in part, to a generation of consumers between 25 and 39 years old who are more affluent than traditional beer drinkers and are not afraid to experiment. This consumer group demands a greater variety of beer styles than those offered by traditional industrial breweries. Many young enthusiasts have traveled freely and tried microbrews that emerged in the Western U.S. in the 1990s (Maier, 2013, p. 140). Mintel Research reports that craft beer's *sweet spot* is with 25-34 year old consumers. The research also found that 43 percent of Millennials and Generation X say that craft beer tastes better than domestic beer. In contrast, only 32 percent of Baby Boomers prefer its taste (Riell, 2014).

Three consumer trends behind the craft beer craze have been identified – premiumization, individualization and feminization (Saporito, 2012).

- **Premiumization** is a focus on fewer but better. More consumers are purchasing two bottles of craft beer over four bottles of domestic premium beer. The social status associated with drinking craft beers often justifies the higher prices paid for these beverages. With most bars and pubs offering a wide selection of craft beer brands, consumers are getting what they want.

- **Individualization** is all about the Millennial Generation (those born between 1980 and 2001). They represent an intriguing and demanding breed of consumers who possess great—often outlandish—expectations. These young people want to have as many different experiences as possible, including the chance to sample authentic brands of craft beer.

- **Feminization** refers to marketing to women. Most traditional beer brands have not done this well. Women have changed their drinking patterns and now are as likely to drink a beer or shots as they are a Cosmopolitan or white wine. Women enjoy the variety of tastes represented in craft beers, flavored malt beverages, and hard ciders.

Overall, beer drinking consumers have become much more adventurous in their craft beers, cocktails and flavored malt beverage consumption. This phenomenon also has triggered the craft beer movement. Consumers perceive craft beer as unique, high-quality, and locally focused. It may cost more, but the experience is worth it. A Mintel research report found that 50 percent of craft beer consumers were interested in locally made beer, while 25 percent were interested in purchasing craft beer only on site where it is brewed (Voight, 2013). This suggests that consumers see consumption of the product as a means to support a local business, which in turn, makes them feel better about themselves while enjoying a higher quality product. Whether this sentiment is true doesn't really matter. That's the beauty (or the challenge) of consumer perception.

Craft Beer Market Competition

You Brew considered its primary competitors to be craft breweries based in Texas. In 2012, the year before the company opened, there were 97 craft breweries in the state, an increase of 36 from 2011. Exhibit 7 shows the breakdown of breweries in Texas by type. Overall, these businesses produced 848,259 barrels of beer and had a $2,316.2 million impact on the state's economy (www.brewersassociation.org).

Exhibit 7

Exhibit 7 – Type of Brewery Operation in Texas	
Brewery Type	**Number**
Large breweries	2
Regional non-craft breweries	4
Brewpubs	41
Microbreweries	56
Source: Brewers Association - http://www.brewersassociation.org/statistics/national/ (accessed 6/23/14)	

Anheuser-Busch, Inc. (Houston) and MillerCoors Brewing Co. (Fort Worth) were the two largest breweries in the state. The 97 craft breweries, 41 brewpubs, and 56 microbreweries were scattered across the state as shown in Exhibit 8. Abbott, Blanton and Cokey considered this when making the decision to launch in Dallas.

Exhibit 8

Exhibit 8 – Distribution of Craft Breweries in Texas		
City	# Brewpubs	# Microbreweries
Abilene	1	--
Alpine	--	1
Amarillo	1	--
Arlington	1	--
Austin	7	12
Bastrop	1	--
Beaumont	--	1
Brenham	--	1
Boerne	1	--
Buna	--	1
Canyon Lake	--	1
Cibolo	--	1
College Station	1	1
Conroe	--	1
Corpus Christi	1	--
Dallas	4	4
Dripping Springs	2	1
Dickinson	--	2
Eola	1	--
Fort Worth	1	1
Fredericksburg	1	1
Galveston	--	1
Garland	--	1
Granbury	--	1
Grapevine	1	1
Houston	1	3
Irving	1	--

City	# Brewpubs	# Microbreweries
Johnson City	1	-
Justin	--	1
Katy	--	1
Krum	--	1
Lubbock	1	--
Magnolia	--	1
Marble Falls	1	--
McKinney	--	1
Missouri City	--	1
Montgomery	--	1
New Braunfels	3	1
Pasadena	--	1
Pflugerville	--	1
Plano	1	--
Port Aransas	1	--
Richmond	--	1
Round Rock	1	--
Rowena	--	1
Rowlett	--	1
San Antonio	3	3
San Marcos	1	--
Seven Points	--	1
Sherman	--	1
Spicewood	--	1
South Padre Island	1	--
Wimberley	2	--
Wolfforth	--	1
Total	**41**	**56**

Source: Brewers Association - http://www.brewersassociation.org/statistics/national/ (accessed 6/23/14)

In addition to Texas-based craft breweries, the partners considered secondary competitors to be imported beer brands. Imported beer sales in the U.S. increased 0.4 percent in 2013, with the most growth coming from the Mexican brands. According to The Brewers Association, overall U.S. domestic beer volume decreased 1.9 percent in the same timeframe. (Strenk, 2014). Exhibit 9 lists the top 10 imported brands.

Exhibit 9

Exhibit 9 – Leading Imported Beer Brands (in million cases)				
Brand	**Brewer**	**2012**	**2013p**	**% Change**
Corona Extra	Crown Imports	100,660	102,870	2.2
Heineken	Heineken USA	55,460	53,240	(-4.0)
Modelo Especial	Crown Imports	42,440	50,080	18.0
Dos Equis	Heineken USA	19650	23,190	18.0
Stella Artois	AB InBev	17,510	20,310	16.0
Tecate	Heineken USA	15,880	15,050	(-5.2)
Corona Light	Crown Imports	13,460	13,860	3.0
Guinness Stout	Diageo-Guinness	12,900	12,590	(-2.4)
Labatt Blue	N.A. Breweries	9,520	8,880	(-6.7)
Labatt Blue Light	N.A. Breweries	6,920	6,710	(-3.0)

(p) Preliminary

Source: Beverage Information Group Handbook Advance, *Beverage Dynamics, "International Affairs" by Thomas Henry Strenk, May/June, 2014, p. 28.*

In the past, craft brewers could easily distinguish themselves from industry giants. However, larger breweries had begun to introduce new "craft" brands. This meant yet another set of competitors was emerging. And these competitors had deep pockets! Coupled with the impact of imported brands, it was becoming increasingly difficult for new craft breweries to gain a sustainable foothold in the marketplace.

You Brew Operations & Pricing

Unlike what they experienced during their Colorado college days, Abbott, Blanton and Cokey discovered Texans were extremely receptive to the crowdsourced formula concept. Enthusiasts took great pride in their recipe submissions, which reduced the quantity of overly outrageous ideas. Quality formula submissions enabled the trio to implement the plan to have each partner pick an ultimate recipe for the month - A for Abbott's choice, B for Blanton, and C for Cokey.

It takes You Brew 10 to 12 weeks to create a batch of beer. This is about 50 percent longer than most craft breweries due to the extra time needed for crowdsourcing and voting. Exhibit 10 shows the typical cycle of events to complete a batch of beer.

Exhibit 10

Exhibit 10 – You Brew Brewing Cycle

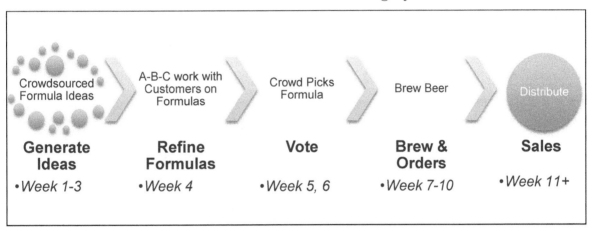

Source: Company Business Plan

The partners planned to introduce one new flavor each month, growing production from 200 gallons initially to 400 gallons by the sixth month of operation. One barrel of beer is approximately 31 gallons, which can be packaged into two kegs, or 62 half-gallon growlers, or 180 22-ounce bombers. The shared brewing facility they found had one 200-gallon and two 400-gallon brewing stations available. The monthly rent for the 200-gallon brewing and bottling facility was $1000 while the larger tanks and facilities were $1250 each. To ensure the availability of the larger tanks when they were needed, You Brew chose to lease the larger tanks before they were ready to produce at that capacity.

Other expenses included an average ingredient cost of $1.50 per gallon, $1.10 for each bomber bottle with cap, and $4.78 for each (refillable) growler and cap. Quantity discounts were available, but not at the amounts You Brew needed. With a monthly manufacturing cost of $3500, ingredient cost per gallon of $1.50, and each partner taking only $1000 a month for living expenses, Uncle Ross's $20,000 seed money would be spent in only three months … about the time the first batch was ready for distribution.

Prices of exclusive craft beers vary by container size. The retail price of a keg (15.5 gallons) is typically $160, while bombers range between $8 and $11. Growlers sell for $15 to $20 each. The trio set its prices at $9 for a bomber and $16 for a growler. To offset the cost of the growler bottle, they also charged a bottle deposit of $5. If an empty growler was returned for a refill, no additional deposit would be charged. If it was just returned, the deposit would be refunded. After accumulating seven months of sales data, Blanton had yet to determine a pattern for returns and refills.

The rental agreement for the facility required a tenant to supply a minimum of one keg for every 100 gallons of beer brewed at a wholesale price of $80 each. This reduced salable production by 15.5 percent. To compensate formula creators, You Brew provided the winning recipe submitter with a free growler and 4-pack of bombers at the time the batch was tapped. Between this, the brewpub's kegs and a few gallons allocated to testing and waste, 164 gallons of a 200-gallon batch would ultimately be available for sale to the public. Those gallons were split equally between growlers and bombers.

To the partners' surprise, the first batch sold out within a week after its release—just as Uncle Ross' seed money ran out. Cokey's uncle agreed to front You Brew the revenue on its receivables with a guarantee he would be the first to be paid back. While sales varied in subsequent months, after nine months in business the company had net gain before taxes of almost $24,000. A financial summary of You Brew performance from July 2013 through March 2014 is shown in Exhibit 11.

Exhibit 11

Exhibit 11 – You Brew Financial Summary

	2013						2014			
	Jul	Aug	Sep	Oct	Nov	Dec	Jan	Feb	Mar	Total YTD
Seed Money	$20,000	- -	- -	- -	- -	- -	- -	- -	- -	$20,000
Beer Revenue	- -	- -	7,077	6,868	10,423	12,580	12,757	12,461	12,848	75,014
Growler Deposits	- -	- -	840	450	500	700	440	620	770	4,320
Total Revenue	$20,000	- -	$7,917	$7,318	$10,923	$13,280	$13,197	$13,081	$13,618	$99,334
Variable Expenses										
Ingredients	- -	350	350	450	600	600	600	600	600	4,150
Bottle Supplies	- -	2,000	700	1,000	1,200	1,200	1,100	1,350	1,200	9,750
Growler Returns	- -	- -	- -	200	320	345	400	375	350	1,990
Total Variable Expenses	- -	$2,350	$1,050	$1,650	$2,120	$2,145	$2,100	$2,325	$2,150	$15,890
Fixed Expenses										
Personnel	3,000	3,000	3,000	3,000	3,000	3,000	3,000	3,000	3,000	27,000
Facility	- -	3,500	3,500	3,500	3,500	3,500	3,500	3,500	3,500	28,000
Marketing	500	500	500	500	500	500	500	500	500	4,500
Total Fixed Expenses	$3,500	$7,000	$7,000	$7,000	$7,000	$7,000	$7,000	$7,000	$7,000	$59,500
Net Gain/ Loss	$16,500	$(9,350)	$(133)	$(1,332)	$1803	$4,468	$4,097	$3,756	$4,135	$23,944
Production in Gallons	- -	- -	200	200	300	400	400	400	400	2,300
#Kegs Sold (wholesale)	- -	- -	2	2	3	4	5	5	6	27
#Growlers Sold	- -	- -	168	165	250	305	297	310	305	1,800
#Bombers Sold	- -	- -	488	452	687	832	845	789	820	4,913
Source: Company Supplied Data										

Branding You Brew

Given the highly competitive marketplace, creative branding was vital if You Brew was to succeed. Blanton crafted a cowboy with lasso logo to symbolize the Texan roots of the business. It also served as the label for the first batch of growlers and bombers. Subsequent batches used different variations of its label, but the cowboy with lasso was always imbedded somewhere in the design.

You Brew had virtually no money for marketing activities, so the team had to rely extensively on social media. Its $500 per month budget was allocated to search engine marketing and label production. Cokey, the marketing partner, connected with craft beer and home-brewing enthusiasts on Facebook, Google+ and Twitter. You Brew's social media pages linked to its own website where beer recipes were submitted, voting took place, beer availability was announced, and orders were captured.

Exhibit 12 – Sample Tweets from You Brew

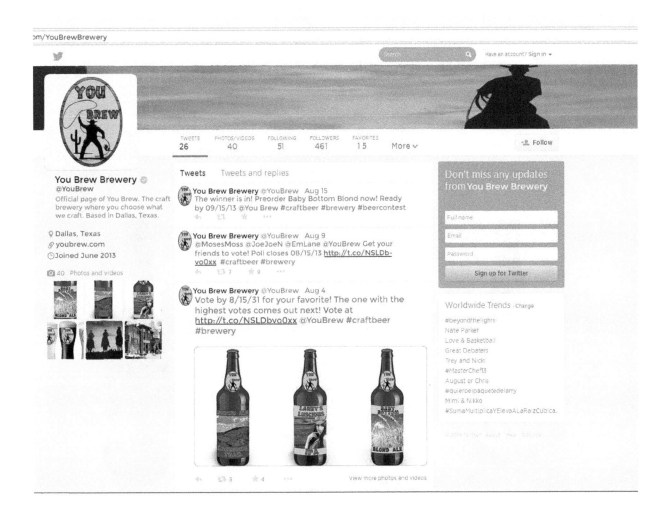

The three partners alternated weekly blogging responsibilities, with each sharing news about new formula submissions, craft brewing events in the area, and tips for better home brewing. Blanton also created a mobile version of their website so that they could stream updates to You Brew's growing list of followers and secure votes for new flavor creations.

Texas laws regulating the distribution of craft beer at special events are complicated. The partners thought beer festivals would provide great exposure, but Texas law restricted sales. To get around the problem, You Brew entered an A-beer, B-beer, and C-beer in a statewide craft brewing competition. Local media picked up the 'Vote A for Abbott, B for Blanton, C for Cokey' story. (See Exhibit 13.) By the end of the fifth month of operation, the company had more than 1,200 followers and was receiving 10 to 15 viable formulas from local clientele a month. With the number of fans and followers rapidly growing, it appeared that

313

You Brew was at the beginning of a social and mobile media triumph. It was building an army of unpaid brand ambassadors all promoting You Brew beers. It also appeared that the gamble to commit to the additional 400-gallon tanks had paid off.

Exhibit 13

VOTE A   VOTE B   VOTE C

for Abbott's Pick   for Blanton's Pick   for Cokey's Pick

Marketing Challenges

While the results were encouraging, the partners wondered how they could continue to grow. Operating at full capacity, the company's net gains were only about $4,000 per month. Local customers embraced the opportunity to try a new beer every month, but many wanted to buy more of the beer they liked. Given the same formula was never produced twice, and were brewed in small batches, repurchases were rare. After the hockey game, Abbott, Blanton and Cokey brainstormed some options as they sampled a competitor's brew.

"I think we're leaving money on the table by not creating a permanent You Brew formula," argued Abbott. "The porter we released in December was the best seller since our first batch of Baby Bottom Blond Ale. I think we should offer it again, in addition to the new brew of the month of course. We could tell customers that it's back by popular demand. If it sells well a second time, we should make it our flagship brand."

Blanton disagreed. "That goes against the company philosophy. Having a formula available for a limited time motivates our customers to act immediately. That's what makes us different. If we were to brew the same formula again, we lose our 'act now or lose out' advantage. Besides, we don't have the capacity to offer two beers simultaneously."

"I'm glad you brought up capacity," Cokey added. "We've maxed out production in our current space. This is fun, but I want to start making some money! None of us can do that selling 400 gallons a month. If we had more capacity, we could increase our distribution. Maybe we could get out of state distributors to carry our brand. If we produced more, we'd be able to decrease the cost of ingredients and bottles too."

Abbott jumped in. "Yeah, and we should also consider switching to cans. That would decrease our costs substantially."

"Funny you should mention cans," replied Blanton. "I recently read that many microbreweries are now distributing beer in cans. There are even companies out there with mobile canning units so we wouldn't have to buy equipment. Some really cool work is being done with can sizes, textures, color varieties, and labels. In addition to formulas, we could crowdsource can designs. One of our competitors, Southern Star Brewing, switched to cans a few months ago and appears to be doing well. " (Phillips, 2014).

"Can-sphan," Cokey rebutted. "Quality beer belongs in bottles. We need more distribution. Maybe it's time to think about building our own brewpub."

"None of us knows anything about food," argued Abbott. "Maybe it's time You Brew became a microbrewery. We could even take our concept to another state. Spoetzl Brewery did extremely well when it expanded into Chicago. It reached out to alumni associations from Texas colleges and universities and built an alumni database of Texas 'expatriates' living in the area. Who says we couldn't do the same in some other beer drinking state! We appeal to their Texas pride. We might be able to generate some interstate rivalries" (Mullman, 2007).

"Interesting ideas," Blanton responded. "But I think we might be getting ahead of ourselves. Setting up a small brewery would cost at least $1 million. Brandon's uncle may have given us $20,000, but I doubt he'd be so generous if we asked for a million! There has to be more we can do to strengthen our relationships with existing customers using our current capacity. Back in Colorado, New Belgium Beer generates over $50 million in sales a year from its Facebook fans. Shift Beer created a Pandora Shift station with a selection of music for its supporters. Maybe we have to rethink our social media strategy. Now that's engagement" (Schultz, 2012).

"Yeah, the online beer world is changing every day," Cokey added. "We could increase our reach by getting involved with sites like BeerAdvocate.com or BeerPulse.com. Both sites receive a lot of traffic from Facebook, Google+, Pinterest and Twitter" (Tuttle, 2014).

"Our Google Analytics indicate that over 30% of our traffic is from our mobile app," stated Blanton. "Taplister is a mobile app service for craft brewers. Over 8,000 people downloaded the iPhone app in 2013. Maybe we should consider buying an enhanced listing with them."

"Wow! That's a lot of options to consider," exclaimed Abbott. "We've had a few beers. Maybe we better sleep on these ideas and discuss this more seriously in the morning."

Blanton agreed. "Chad's right. We're all over the place with these ideas. We need to establish some priorities and realistic timeframes. Our initial plan got us to the point where we're making money. We need to figure out what Act 2 looks like. Let's meet at the brewery tomorrow morning and hash it out. Right now I want to enjoy my beer!"

References

Distilled Spirits Council of the United States (www.discus.org) accessed 6/17/14.

Dowling, Melissa, 2013. *Beverage Dynamics,* September/October, 125(5), 45-47.

Jacobsen, Jessica, 2014. The maturation of craft beer. *Beverage Industry,* March, 105(3), 24.

Landi, Heather, 2014. *Beverage World,* 133(3), 39.

Maier, T., 2013. Selected Aspect of the Microbreweries Boom. *Agris On-Line Papers in Economics &Informatics,* 5(4), 135-142.

Mullman, Jeremy (2007). Craft brews draw crowds as they expand distribution. *Advertising Age,* 78(30), 4, 32.

Phillips, Russ (2014a). Canned beer's renaissance in America. *CanTech International,* February, 21(5), 38-39.

Phillips, Russ (2014b). Canned craft beer corner. *CanTech International,* March, 21(7), 40.

Restaurant, Food and Beverage Market Research Handbook, 2014-15. Vol. 15, 428-434.

Riell, Howard, 2014. Crafting a Winning Beer Strategy. *Convenience Store Decisions,* January, 25(1), 50-52.

Saporito, Bill, 2012. Higher Spirits. *Time,* 179(2), 56.

Schultz, E.J., 2012. New Belgium toasts to its Facebook fans. *Advertising Age,* 83(7), 8.

Strenk, Thomas Henry, 2014. International Affairs. *Beverage Dynamics,* May/June, 126(3), 28-34.

Tuttle, Brad (2014). The competition for craft beer drinkers takes a bitter turn. *Time.com,* January 9, 1.

Voight, Joan, 2013. Brew Wars. *Adweek,* 54(13), 20-23.

U.S. Brewers Association (www.brewersassociation.org) accessed 6/23/14.

Some of the data provided for this case has been disguised and is not useful for research purposes. The authors would like to thank Will Blanton for his help in this project.

CPSIA information can be obtained
at www.ICGtesting.com
Printed in the USA
LVHW101559201218
601223LV00016B/457/P

9 780692 666692